ENERGISE YOUR ENTERPRISE

By the same author:

The Ascendant Organisation
The Road to Nissan
Management in the Fast Track
Lean Production and Beyond
Schlüssel zur Weltklasse Producktion (with Franz Lehner)

Energise Your Enterprise

Peter Wickens

MACMILLAN
Business

First published 1999 by
MACMILLAN PRESS LTD
Houndmills, Basingstoke, Hampshire RG21 6XS
and London
Companies and representatives
throughout the world

ISBN 0–333–74162–5 hardcover

A catalogue record for this book is available
from the British Library.

This book is printed on paper suitable for recycling and
made from fully managed and sustained forest sources.

10 9   8   7   6 5   4   3   2   1
08 07 06 05 04 03 02 01 00 99

Editing and origination by
Aardvark Editorial, Mendham, Suffolk

Printed and bound in Great Britain
by Creative Print & Design (Wales), Ebbw Vale

To Sophie
The first of the next generation

Contents

Introduction   ix

Prologue: The Business Fad Cycle   1
APPENDIX P.1: Business Fads, Sacred Cows and Transitory Techniques   18

1 **The Ascendant Organisation**   22

2 **Energising Leadership**   26

3 **The Leader as Strategist**   41

4 **The Heart of Leadership**   52

5 **Values First**   83
APPENDIX 5.1: Nissan's Philosophy Statement   96

6 **Discovering Your Values**   97

7 **A Sense of Purpose**   108

8 **Real Teamworking**   116

9 **Everyone an Innovator**   140

10 **Innovation Teams**   163

11 **Organising the Energised Enterprise**   178

12 **Energised Change**   190
APPENDIX 12.1: 20 Keys to Workplace Improvement   208

13 **A Final Word – Energising Leadership to the Energised Enterprise**   209

References   211

Index   214

List of Figures

P.1 The business fad cycle   7

1.1 The ascendant organisation   23

2.1 Energise your enterprise   27

2.2 Leadership throughout the organisation   33

4.1 Goal alignment   68

4.2 Goal alignment and MBO compared   68

8.1 Team types   117

8.2 Real teamworking   122

9.1 Japanese *kaizen* and Western radical change   143

10.1 Finding the time   175

11.1 Bonas Machine Company organisation   189

12.1 'The abyss'   191

12.2 The four levels of change   192

13.1 The route to the energised enterprise   209

Introduction

The guiding premise of *Energise Your Enterprise* is that the only elements that really count in any enterprise – be it public, private or not-for-profit; manufacturing, finance or service – are the quality of the leadership and the quality of the people. And that it is the task of the leaders to create the environment in which all people are energised to work together for the benefit both of the enterprise and themselves.

I use the word 'enterprise' because we will be discussing something which is dynamic, which seems to live in a way that 'company', 'business' or 'organisation' do not. Included in the dictionary definition of 'enterprise' are words such as 'bold', 'difficult' and 'courage' – words which are nowhere to be seen in the definitions of 'company, 'business' and 'organisation'. Exciting things happen in enterprises – but they do not just happen by themselves. They have to be made to happen. And the process of making things happen is 'energising'.

Tony O'Reilly, Chief Executive of Heinz recognised the importance of 'energising' when he said in 1994:

Nothing energises an individual or a company more than clear goals and a grand purpose. (Smith, 1994)

While correct in recognising the importance of energising, Tony O'Reilly was too simplistic in defining the means. 'Clear goals' are vital and a so-called, 'grand purpose' may be part of it, but they are not the full story. *Energise Your Enterprise* is about the full story.

Tony O'Reilly is a charismatic leader but we have to go beyond the anecdotes about so-called charismatic leaders at the very top and delve into energised leadership *at all levels* of the enterprise. A few highly publicised, charismatic leaders make great stories but they are not the norm – they are *abnormal* – and most of us who reach positions in which we can exercise leadership are not abnormal – we are normal people. And this book, while it will draw on examples from the charismatic, is about and for the vast majority of us who do not have personal biographers. It is about leadership at the top *and* throughout your enterprise. As soon as you have one person you can influence; one process over which you have some authority; one facility on which you have some control; one budget line on which you can have some impact, you can exercise leadership.

Charismatic leaders will not get very far – in fact they will fail – unless they create the climate in which leadership can exist at all levels and such leadership requires an understanding of what I call the *heart* of leadership. Being at the top is not the same as being at the heart, for being at the heart requires respect, trust, a sharing of values, a common sense of purpose and aligned goals. It requires inspiration, real teamworking and everyone to be an innovator. This book is about creating and sustaining that climate.

The leader, at whatever level, creates the environment which makes things happen. An enterprise is energised when the bolt of lightning strikes, when it is properly conducted and then generates the spark which stimulates us to achieve great things. The power of the outcomes – the continuously shining stars – is greater and brighter than the inputs. Everyone in an energised enterprise – not just those at the top – feels good. Everyone contributes, not only performing their everyday task well, but also by contributing to improvements in their own and the enterprise's performance – not just by improving productivity but because they are valued when they make their enterprise a better place in which to work. When we discuss innovation we will see that 'everyone can be an innovator' and that innovation is about both the big and the small; that it is not just about making the product, process or service 'new, better, cheaper and faster' but is also about making work 'easier, safer and more enjoyable'.

The energised enterprise recognises the power of real teamworking – and I distinguish *real* teamworking from the platitudinous, 'We're one big team in this company' so beloved by many top executives. The business book industry has performed a great disservice by seeming to regard Teams (with a capital T) as the answer to all our ills, and then by concentrating on 'that wonderful group of people from different levels and different functions who were pulled together and achieved wonderful things'.

We will see that the teams that really count in the energised enterprise are the permanent groups who work together all the time to achieve shared objectives. When such teams are in place and working effectively, the temporary, multifunctional, multi-level task forces are the icing on the cake. We will see how real teamworking can develop into innovation teams, perhaps the most powerful mechanism for enabling all people throughout the enterprise to direct their intellectual and practical energies towards innovation and growth – not just growth of the enterprise but also personal growth.

The thinking behind the energised enterprise matured slowly, beginning with my own work at Ford, Continental Can Company and Nissan. Much of this was included in my first two books *The Road to Nissan* and *The Ascendant Organisation* but there were missing ingredients. Gaining the commitment of everyone to the aims of the enterprise was always there – the combination of control of the business processes with commitment of the people was the four box formula which led me to the concept of the ascendant organisation (reprised briefly in Chapter 1).

On leaving Nissan in 1995 I had the opportunity to visit many other companies, to meet with people from all levels in many organisations both in the private and public sectors, and to work with people and companies in different countries. The more I met with others the more I came to realise that in Nissan we had created something special – an enterprise that was not only the most efficient car manufacturing plant in Europe but also regularly highly rated in lists of the best companies to work for.

But in working with these other companies I came to appreciate that Nissan was not unique, only highly publicised, that many companies were operating at the same level, that there were elements which needed to be considered in more detail and some things I had missed. There was not enough emphasis on the nature of leadership, on innovation, on shared values, on a sense of purpose and real teamworking. Some companies – the long-established as well as the new – also had that special, indefinable 'something', which if properly harnessed could teach us great things. However, it is a 'development from' not a 'substitute for' my previous work.

Visitors to Nissan often said, 'You can actually feel the energy' and as I visited other organisations, whether private, public or voluntary; manufacturing, service or financial, I came to realise what they meant – and that 'feeling' was either there or it was not. Then I found that in Japan Iwao Kobayashi, who teaches Japanese companies how to become world-class, was using the phrase 'energise the workplace' as central to his philosophy.

The pieces were falling into place. Then during a late-night discussion with Geoff Armstrong, Director General of the Institute of Personnel and Development, he suggested that 'workplace' was too narrow. 'Try "enterprise"', he said. From that spark further thinking developed, further elements were added and eventually the title became *Energise Your Enterprise*. The development of this title and its interaction with my expanding thinking are in fact an example of 'energising' in action. The spark hits something that is already there, perhaps untapped, and the subsequent reaction creates something that is bigger and more powerful than anything previously thought possible. So, thank you Iwao Kobayashi and Geoff Armstrong for your sparks at a vital time.

This title is direct – it is an imperative addressed directly to the reader. And that is the way throughout the book. I spend a lot of time on public platforms and in running in-house seminars and often discuss emerging ideas with audiences and participants, always using graphic slides to illustrate the points. The reactions and discussions help develop (or discard) those ideas, and many that survive now appear in *Energise Your Enterprise*. Developments of the slides (without the usual accompanying clipart cartoons) are scattered throughout in highlighted boxes.

Of course, a book is not a live presentation but so many people have said about previous books and articles, 'When reading you, I feel I am listening to you speak', that this book is deliberately written in presentational style – hopefully with the blemishes of the spoken word eliminated but with the flavour remaining. But in a book you can include more than on a platform so, without creating a massive tome, I have used more examples and gone into more detail. Some may not like the style and to those I apologise. Hopefully the balance is right and the message remains clear.

This issue of how much detail to include is illustrated by the Prologue, The Business Fad Cycle. Another strand of the thinking that went into *Energise Your Enterprise* was an increasing dissatisfaction with the business fad mentality that has overwhelmed us since the late 1970s. Initially as mental exercise I began building on Richard Pascale's list of 26 business fads published in his *Managing on the Edge* in 1990, added in my personal experience, discussed the experiences of others, and then began introducing a critique of business fads into what I called a 'light but not lightweight' presentation, usually given in the evenings after the heavy stuff of the day had been concluded! My thanks to all those who have contributed to the list which now exceeds 400!

It was Richard Pascale who, on hearing this presentation, encouraged its development. Eventually there emerged 'The Business Fad Cycle'. Whenever I used it – and there have been many versions before it reached the stage shown – I was inundated with requests for copies. Hopefully, by bringing it to a wider audience we can begin to spread an understanding of what we are doing to our organisations and, by appreciating that our favourite fads do go through a cycle, we can use the wisdom gained for the benefit of all.

We must progress beyond this fad mentality to arrive at (or go back to) the basics which form the heart of this book. What we require are leaders at all levels who *understand* their businesses, who can recognise that there are a number of long-term, simple, basic truths about energising leadership, energised people and the energised enterprise.

This message is the same for everyone who works – it is addressed to everyone at every level; it is addressed to the business community, to trade unionists, academics and voluntary workers, for whatever our interest we all work in enterprises. A private company, a publicly quoted company, a university, a voluntary organisation and a trade union are all enterprises. However our 'organisation' is bureaucratically categorised the message throughout is that *all of us can energise our enterprise.*

Please contact me if you think you need assistance to help you progress towards becoming an energised enterprise. If you want to comment in any way about the book and its messages I will be equally delighted to hear from you.

PETER WICKENS OBE
High View House
Ewshot Hall, Heath Lane
Ewshot, Hampshire
England GU10 5AL
Fax: 01252 851909
e-mail: profpeterdwickens@msn.com

Prologue: The Business Fad Cycle

For some reason many business executives believe that introducing something new is the sure way to motivate people!

In 1996, while visiting the engineering division of a Top 100 company, my guide, John, a headquarters-based manager, came across an old colleague, Mike, an operational engineer. Their conversation went very much as follows:

Mike: Hello, John. What are you up to now? I haven't seen you for ages.

John: Well, right now I hate to admit it but I'm leading the re-engineering programme.

Mike: Oh, that. Listen, I've been here for 42 years and I've seen all these great ideas come and go and I just can't see that this one's going to be any different. You're always telling us we need to be more competitive, take on more responsibilities and the like, but all that ever happens is that there are fewer and fewer of us around and we all have to work harder. Anyway, I'm out of it soon so it doesn't really bother me. Good luck to you, anyway. I'll send you an invitation to my retirement party.

When I repeated these comments (unattributed, of course) to a top executive of the company he responded, 'Oh yes, if it's who I think it is, thank goodness he's going – we can't afford to have people like him around any more. Unfortunately, the real problem is not his generation – they're on the way out – we've got people half his age who think the same way. We try to involve them but after a while they just back off and revert to type. And as far as I'm concerned, if they don't like it they can go too!'

This is not a dictatorial company still operating in the Dark Ages. Relationships are generally good and Mike obviously felt able to speak his mind. Its managers believe they are innovative and are always trying new ideas, and the company has survived. But interpreting Mike's perception, he believed they were suffering from initiative fatigue. The company had tried to involve the staff and gain their commitment but he had seen the number of people employed steadily falling and, while he had kept his job, thousands had not. The somewhat callous observations of the director suggests that he does not really care for the people, that he pays lip service to the new approaches and, most important of all, his actions do not match the words of the company's mission statement which appears on virtually every notice board in every unit. Maybe he is an exception, but experience in scores of other companies suggests that he is not.

The great problem is that many managers like the thrill of the new – it is certainly better than doing the same old thing day after day. We believe that activity is the same as action and that it is important to be seen to be doing something. And if that 'something' does not work and expectations are dashed there is always another 'something' to take its place. The pace of professed change is accelerating, and the sale of some $750 million of business books each year in the United States alone suggests that the search continues.

Simon Lebus, Chairman and Chief Executive of Kitchen Range Foods, a major and very successful supplier to McDonald's, reflected a growing concern, and got it spot on when he said to me:

> **All these ideas and techniques sound great. I recognise the value of teamworking, TQM, briefing groups, eliminating waste, defining our culture and so on. The trouble is that every single one is presented to us as the solution – which it is not. What we need to do is to sort out what is really relevant for us, apply it pragmatically without all the singing, dancing and consultant-speak and then leave us alone to give it a chance to work!**

In his book, *Managing on the Edge,* Richard Pascale identified 26 business fads which had come and often gone from 1950 to 1988. In a 1992 version the number had increased to 33. However, his list still did not include some of the most powerful ideas of recent years – lean production and organisations, process re-engineering, core competences, bench-marking, the psychological contract, activity-based costing, employee involvement, continuous improvement, MRP II and so on. Nor did it take account of the many minor ideas and instant success recipes that ebbed almost before they had flowed.

A great difficulty with many of the new concepts (although most are simply repackaged versions of old concepts because academics and consultants are past masters at putting old wine in new bottles with changed labels) is that, when presented, they may make you feel great, but afterwards you are left asking, 'OK, that sounds good, but what do I actually do?' The answer, of course, is often for *you* not to do very much but to hire the guru or consultant and pay them large sums of money to get *them* to do it! But how many times have you found that while the consultants were around everything seemed good and worked well but once they had departed and you were on your own it didn't take too long for everyone to revert to their old ways? By 'everyone' I mean not just people like Mike at the operational level but managers and senior executives. Still, there's always the next great idea!

The great problem is that most consultants and innovators move on before the company is equipped continuously to improve itself. Simon Lebus is right – *the search for instant success is the curse of Western business* – companies need far more time than they give themselves to understand what they are about to attempt, to bed down the practices, to achieve success and, as we shall see the most difficult of all, to sustain the gain. It is only when we learn a little more patience, when we recognise that this ability continuously to improve ourselves is central to *energising our enterprise*.

Those who indulge in this never-ending search for the 'next great idea' are surfers – similar to those who get a great thrill from riding the waves. The adrenaline flows as they ride its crest – but the thrill is temporary. The wave hits the beach and peters out, subsiding to nothing. Sometimes they wipe out or, in the surfers' language, are dumped. Either way, they paddle out again to catch the next big wave, seeking the same thrill, endlessly repeating the process until sufficiently invigorated, totally exhausted, the sun goes down or the tide turns. They always return.

The surfers of business waves are not very different. They speak of their waves with awe and are always seeking 'the big one' which, when mastered, will give *the* solution – 'We will never be the same again!' But, in business they are not 'waves' but 'fads', and those who continuously seek the next fad are 'fad surfers'. Having read the latest book or attended a conference, they want to be the person associated with introducing re-engineering or shifting the company to the balanced scorecard. They may wish to create a positive, forward-thinking image for their company or simply keep up with the Joneses. They switch between preserving the *status quo* and introducing so many initiatives that the company suffers either from lack of nourishment or initiative indigestion.

However, not everything is solely a temporary thrill. Just as with surfing the waves, regular exercise and judicious selection can increase general fitness (or can injure and kill!). There may be a genuine belief that it can bring about a beneficial, long-term change in attitudes, processes, products or service and improve business performance.

Some business fads do contain a core of value which remains long after the short-term excesses have been consigned to the waste bin, and these often develop into our sacred cows – the unchallengeable, protected species. No-one dares violate them and sacred cows become so much a part of the scenery and culture that they are barely noticed, except by strangers who see what the locals do not. But, when the practice is pointed out the locals vigorously defend their behaviour.

In business, sacred cows are practices which are just as fundamental but, also, may not be recognised as something special. They are part of the unspoken culture, policies or practices and form the defensive barrier within which the inhabitants feel comfortable. They are rarely challenged and certainly do not energise. As a result, they can become either pillars of strength or can ossify and inhibit change and flexibility. Often, a practice which initially strengthens an organisation ends up by weakening it.

The list of new ideas is seemingly endless. Building on Richard Pascale's original listing, I give more than 400 business fads, sacred cows and transitory techniques in the Appendix to this Prologue. No doubt there are many more.

Many companies have several initiatives on the go at the same time. Bain and Co. found in 1995 that around the world the average company was using 11.8 of the 25 leading techniques, with the British leading the way with 13.7! Rarely was there any degree of coordination, coherence or prioritisation.

Perhaps, to paraphrase Parkinson's law, 'The number of change programmes expands to meet the number of available consultants.' Look at these figures for the United States between 1982 and 1992, the period of greatest growth:

	1982	1992	% Increase
Consulting firms	780	1593	97
No. of consultants	30,000	81,000	170
Consulting revenue	$3.5 billion	$15.2 billion	334

Source: Nohria and Berkeley, Harvard Business Review, Jan/Feb 1994

I have not seen any later figures, but who can doubt that the growth has continued?

The great problem is that the plethora of new and repackaged ideas leads to superficiality. Often, the change agents are the proverbial 'one page ahead of the client' in the book of knowledge; lack the necessary in-depth understanding of the underlying principles and, if they have gone through the route of 'school to university to business school to consultant' in four easy stages, do not have the practical experience essential to a true understanding of the impact of change programmes on the people in the organisation.

They also fail to realise the extraordinary complexity of relationships within organisations; relationships within and between people, concepts and practices. Disturb one relationship and its impact is felt in unthought of quarters. The corollary is that to have real, long term impact a change initiative must recognise these interrelationships and address them simultaneously. When the leaders of an enterprise are unaware of these inter-relationships they should not be too surprised when single-focus initiatives do not achieve the hoped for benefits.

Often, the change agents do not have a long-term commitment to the organisation. While historical baggage can be a burden, short-term action can easily destroy that which it professes to save.

The impact of such change agents on an organisation can be likened to the impact of a diver on a shoal of fish:

The shoal is harmoniously swimming along, instinctively clear as to its purpose. The diver plunges in and the fish scatter. Some, having left the safety of the shoal, become victims. The diver passes through and the shoal reforms. Each fish may now be in a different position relative to its neighbours but the fundamental characteristics of the shoal have not changed; its purpose remains the same; its methods unaltered and it continues on its way much as before. The diver moves on, forgotten and unloved. But another will soon appear!

The fundamental mistake of many of those who seek to introduce new or repackaged, single-focus initiatives into an organisation is the failure to recognise that they usually have to be implemented by the very people who will be most affected by them. Behavioural scientist, Victor Vroom, wrote in 1964:

> **The amount of effort people put into a task depends on whether they believe the effort will produce a better performance, whether that better performance will pay off in terms of outcomes and the extent to which those outcomes are attractive.**

In short, if they think they will benefit, they will make the effort necessary for success: if not, they will not. The proponents of process re-engineering who argued that it must be a top-down imposed programme and then bemoaned the fact that the majority of such programmes have not achieved the hoped-for success should have read Victor Vroom!

Despite their bad experiences, many managers continue their fascination with business fads. It is difficult to avoid jumping on the surf board to hit what just might be 'the big one.' But in so doing, do we really energise our company or do we pile one initiative on top of another until the people suffocate? If we look at the life cycle of a business fad it will help us appreciate not only where it has come from but also where it will take us.

THE BUSINESS FAD CYCLE

Business fads seem to have a twelve-stage life cycle. While not the same for every fad, and with numerous overlaps and omissions, the generic business fad cycle is represented in Figure P.1.

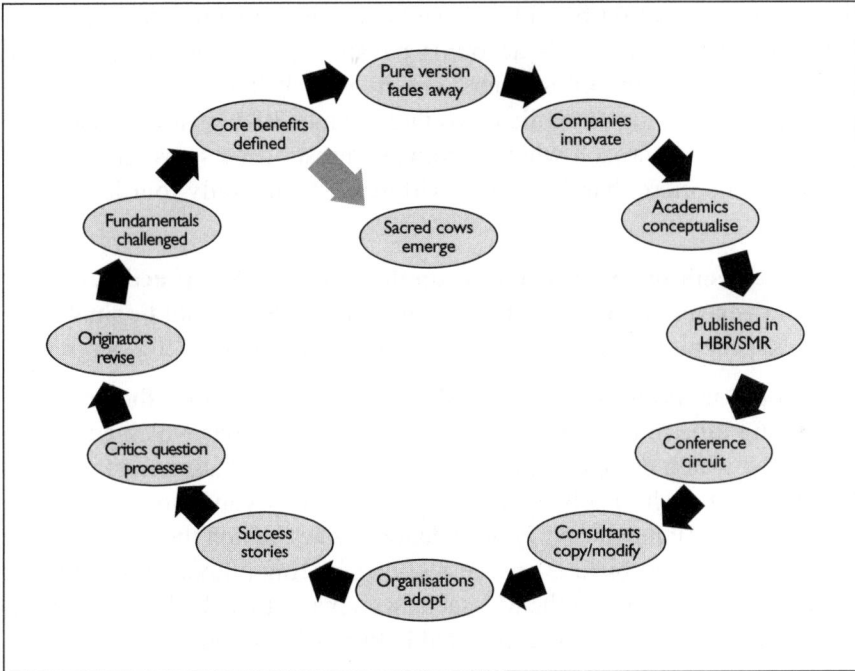

Figure P.1 The business fad cycle

In discussing Figure P.1, The business fad cycle, I use the somewhat extreme example of business process re-engineering which, within a relatively short time, has gone through all 12 stages of the cycle. We begin at one o'clock.

1. **An improved practice (only rarely is there anything that is totally new) is developed in innovative companies.**

Within these companies it may not even have a name, simply resulting from a few people doing things in a better way. The same companies keep cropping up – Ford, Wal-Mart, Motorola, Xerox, Honda, Hewlett-Packard, 3M, Proctor and Gamble, Toyota, ABB, Unilever and so on. Some fall out of favour – IBM, General Motors, Apple – in fact it can be the kiss of death to appear on a list of best-run companies. As Arnold Toynbee said:

Nothing fails like success!

Process re-engineering is said to have begun in companies such as Ford, who learned from Mazda's accounts payable group how to implement invoiceless processing of accounts; and in Mutual Benefit Life where the multi-step processing of applications taking up to 30 days was replaced by a case manager approach which eliminated most of the steps and reduced the time to no more than five days, with some taking only four hours.

2. **An academic or consultant picks up the new or revised practice, gains knowledge of practices in other organisations which could be similarly packaged, puts it into a conceptual framework and gives it a new name.**

The people in Ford, Mazda and Mutual Benefit probably thought they were doing little more than distinguishing those activities which add value from those which do not, optimising the former, eliminating the latter and then adding a dash of job enlargement and activity value analysis. Along came Michael Hammer and James Champy, who studied the practices and popularised them as business process re-engineering (although the concept was first identified during the Massachusetts Institute of Technology study, 'Management in the 1990s' conducted between 1984 and 1990).

3. **Secure publication in an eminent American business journal – preferably the *Harvard Business Review*, *Sloan Management Review* or *California Management Review*.**

Generally it is best to avoid the more esoteric academic journals, although they can be useful if the aim is to establish academic credibility. Michael Hammer's seminal article, 'Reengineering Work: Don't Automate, Obliterate', was published in the *Harvard Business Review* in July-August 1990. He argued that companies were mistakenly using technology to mechanise and speed up old ways of doing business, whereas:

> **We should obliterate them and start over. We should reengineer our businesses.**

Essentially, the message was that by shifting the focus from 'functional silos' to 'business processes', by concentrating on the customer and by using the power of modern information technology, organisations will be able to achieve dramatic improvements in their performance.

There followed in 1993 his first book, *Reengineering the Corporation – A Manifesto for Business Revolution,* written with James Champy, which has sold around two million copies worldwide. Hammer and Champy introduced their book as a seminal work aimed at replacing Adam Smith's concept that work is most effectively performed when broken down into a series of clearly defined small tasks (Smith, 1776), with the concept that these tasks should be reunified into business processes. It is about 'reversing the industrial revolution'.

At the end of his second book, *The Reengineering Revolution,* co-authored with Steven Stanton, Hammer asks the question, 'What comes after reengineering? The reply is 'A new world'. Somewhat presumptuous, I think! Adam Smith genuinely contributed to a new world. If Hammer's books are read in two centuries time he may then lay claim to having the same influence as Adam Smith!

4. **Following publication, the author, his consultancy and publisher set up seminars and conferences and meet with the top managers of major corporations.**

The word is spread and detailed implementation programmes are developed to turn the concept into a 'product' that does not require the presence of the guru at all times and can be implemented by a 'senior consultant' aided and abetted by a hoard of young MBAs. Mike Hammer and James Champy became celebrities on the business conference circuit and were able to turn their writing and lectures into lucrative consultancy contracts.

5. **It becomes obvious to other consulting firms that there is money to be made out there, and they realise that many of their existing techniques can be dusted down, reinvigorated and re-presented so that they are able to suggest that they have been working in this area for a long time.**

The original concept becomes a commodity, used by those who appreciate that intellectual property rights are difficult to defend and that it needs only minor modifications to be presented as the property of the secondary consultant. Business process re-engineering became a tool of every major consultant and, while the antecedents were obvious, there was usually enough clear water for it to be presented as somewhat different. McKinsey called its variant 'The Horizontal Organisation'; Arthur D. Little used the term 'High Performance Businesses'; Gemini used 'Business Transformation'. A. T. Kearney with its 'Transforming the Enterprise' methodology might, in the 1980s, have called it 'Implementing Concurrent Engineering'!

6. Large-scale adoption of the fad.

In June 1994, *Information Week* reported that 81 per cent of 400 US manufacturing companies had at least one so-called re-engineering project under way. A CSC Index survey of 600 senior managers in large corporations published in that same magazine in September 1994 reported that 69 per cent of North American and 75 per cent of European companies claimed at least one re-engineering project and that half of those who had not yet begun intended to do so. A 1994 survey of 96 companies in the financial services sector found that 75 per cent had started down the re-engineering road (*Quality Initiatives in the Financial Services*, Financial Services Research Centre, 1995).

7. Conferences, case studies and reports show that the concept works.

Ciba-Geigy, the Swiss chemical and drugs company, was said to have re-engineered its order filling process, increasing sales by five per cent; Rank Xerox in Britain reorganised work into cross-functional teams bringing down delivery time from 33 to six days and quoted a ten per cent improvement in personal satisfaction, twenty per cent increase in customer satisfaction and thirty per cent increase in productivity. AT&T in the United States decentralised and simplified, reducing the number of project handoffs between sale and final installation from twelve to three, the result of which was a dramatic improvement in all-round performance with 88 per cent of customers rating the project management of their installation, 'excellent'. In 1996 AT&T implemented 28,000 redundancies! GTE, the American telephone company, cited re-engineering as being the reason for its being able to reduce its customer service centres from 171 to eleven and its revenue collection centres from five to one – accompanied by $1.7 billion investment in technology and 17,000 job losses!

Britain's Lloyds Bank began a major re-engineering exercise called a 'Service quality improvement programme' in 1992. By introducing new technology and enlarging peoples' jobs it was, for example, able to give responsibility for opening a new account to just one person, replacing the previous practice in which forms were shuffled from one person to the next with each undertaking a small part of the process. It went much further than that – the number of branches was cut from 2,100 to 1,800 with associated staff losses and more than fifty per cent of the eighty area manager positions were stripped away.

8. Critics question success of the process.

Almost before the ink was dry on the first book critics began to question the success of the process. In 1993 the OTR Group in Belgium concluded that re-engineering had real value but the hype confused the picture. They even had the temerity to question the achievements at one of the flagship companies, Hallmark Cards, where they thought the main change was no more than the installation of barcode readers. Another 1993 study by McKinsey consultants Gene Hall, Jim Rosenthal and Judy Wade, 'How to Make Re-engineering *Really* Work' showed that performance improvement in eleven out of twenty cases was less than five per cent in terms of reduction in total business-unit cost. They summarised the reasons for failure as being:

◆ Lack of strong leadership at the top
◆ Projects too narrow
◆ Projects too broad and indiscriminate
◆ Assignment of average performers
◆ Measurement of the plan but not of performance
◆ Settling for the *status quo*
◆ Overlooking the need for comprehensive communication.

Michael Hammer and Steve Stanton themselves criticised the implementation process in the *Financial Times* (5 October 1994). They referred to 'Failures of intellect, where a company simply does not know what it is doing.' They said that many companies spend too much time on the initial analysis, they are too timid and, most important of all, leadership is insufficiently committed.

The most powerful criticisms came, however, from the human resources perspective and in particular from Christopher Grey and Nathalie Mitev, and from Hugh Wilmott, all writing in *Personnel Review* (1994/95). Three short quotations from Wilmott summarise their views:

It is remarkable how little attention is given by BPR to the human dimension of organising.

Implicitly, employees are assumed by BPR to be infinitely malleable.

This lack of appreciation of the human dimension perhaps accounts for the fact that the name of Hammer's consultancy, CSC Index is an abbreviation of Computer Science Corporation!

There are many more detailed critiques – but no doubt, you get the picture!

9. The original model is modified and/or developed by the originators.

Re-engineering is unusual in that Hammer and Champy split and went in different directions. Hammer joined with Steven Stanton to produce a 'handbook', *The Reengineering Revolution,* aimed at providing practical guidance on 'the nuts and bolts of reengineering', 'how to avoid mistakes' and so on.

However, part of this book is taken up with a defence of the statement that fifty to seventy per cent of re-engineering efforts were not successful.

Many people think it means that 50 to 70 per cent of all reengineering efforts *will* fail. Nothing could be further from the truth. There is no inherent success or failure rate for reengineering. The results depend entirely on the quality, intensity and intelligence of the effort... Failure is caused by people who don't know what they're doing and who don't pursue reengineering the right way. (1995: 14–15)

They also make dramatically clear the need for it to be driven from the top down and they indicate that failures, where they occur, are the result of a lack of maintained drive. Hammer's third book, *Beyond Reengineering,* is not really about life after re-engineering but a concentration on the 'processes.' It adds virtually nothing that is new and is 'a book too far'.

10. Critics, often from academia, begin to challenge the fundamentals of the concept.

The challenges to the fundamentals of process re-engineering come from various directions. Gary Hamel and C. K. Prahalad (1994) argued that:

> **Whereas downsizing and core process redesign are legitimate and important tasks, they have more to do with shoring up today's businesses than creating tomorrow's. (p. 5)**
>
> **What if all that cash and all that 'redundant' brain power had been applied to creating tomorrow's markets. (p. 12)**

Others argued that process excellence, on its own, rarely leads to sustained competitive advantage and it requires senior executives to create the break-throughs. There are those who believe that it inevitably leads to downsizing and downsizing without innovation leads only to short-term benefits.

Charles Handy has said:

The trouble with re-engineering when it is done badly – which it mostly is – is that it leaves people shattered, even the people left behind.

In December 1995, Tom Davenport, who with Hammer and Champy was one of the three original proponents of re-engineering, applied the *coup de grâce* when he wrote *Why Reengineering Failed*:

Reengineering didn't start out as a code for mindless bloodshed. It wasn't supposed to be the last gasp of Industrial Age Management. I know because I was one of the creators... [It has become] so ugly today, to most business people in the United States, it has become a word that stands for restructuring, lay-offs, and too often failed change programmes... The rock that reengineering foundered on is simple: people. Reengineering treated the people inside companies as if they were just so many bits and bytes, interchangeable parts to be reengineered.

My own argument is that the causes of failure are inherent in Hammer's own thinking and writing. In *The Reengineering Revolution* he says, among other things:

An effective reengineer must be one part visionary, one part communicator, and one part leg breaker. (p. 48)

A sign of weakness is slapping people's wrists instead of breaking their legs. (p. 50)

The way to people's hearts and minds is not through their ears but through their wallets. (p. 48)

To catalyse potential leaders… you must play on the two most basic human emotions: fear and greed. (p. 52)

If all else fails the leader can simply demand that people contribute to the reengineering effort. (p. 36)

Nothing speaks louder than dealing sternly with those who impede a reengineering effort… extreme measures are sometimes the only way to overcome entrenched opposition. (p. 40)

And, most telling of all:

Dramatic improvements have to be paid for in some way and the coinage is usually denominated in units of human suffering. (p. 174)

This is incredible! It demonstrates a total failure to take into account the fact that re-engineering has to be implemented by the very people who will be most affected by it Change cannot be imposed on people if you wish to gain their commitment. If I feel threatened, why should I work hard to implement something that could lose me my job?

At the end of his third book, *Beyond Reengineering*, Hammer highlights the problem of what to do with the 'little people' who 'can't handle constant change, who need stability and predictability. Must they all be left behind?' He does not provide an answer and one suspects that he does not really care!

11. The core benefits are defined.

Within business process re-engineering, as with many fads, there lies a kernel of value. It is that we should think of work as a process flow and then involve the people in determining which elements add value for the customer and which 'handovers' add cost. Then combine the remaining value-adding tasks in logical order and have them undertaken in their entirety by a cohesive group of people.

But this does not mean that we should eschew specialised functions. The successful enterprise understands the difference between functions and processes and does not simply replace functional silos with process tunnels. For what do we get in tunnels? *Tunnel vision!*

Companies are not about to divest themselves of their functions, either on a macro or micro basis, and indeed they should not. Functions and specialised knowledge can be a great strength when used wisely and a great weakness when perpetuated in a rigid form. When elaborate walls are erected between functions and people rarely communicate across them you have the worst of all worlds, but when people do develop specialised knowledge and are willing to be flexible and share that knowledge you have the beginning of something which combines the benefits of both concepts.

The energised enterprise properly balances the two – it provides for the development of specialised knowledge but does not restrict it to rigid boxes which cannot be shared with others. It develops its business processes but not to the point at which process tunnel vision entirely replaces the old functional silos.

12.   **The excess baggage of the original concept is dumped or, more likely, fades away for dumping is an admission of failure, and failure cannot, of course, be admitted.**

Perhaps new executives, without the same allegiance to the concept as their predecessors, are appointed and seek to introduce initiatives of their own. In speaking of the reasons for re-engineering failures, Hammer and Stanton reiterated that, 'a common mistake is to attempt reengineering without the requisite leadership. Strong, committed executive leadership is the absolute *sine qua non* for reengineering.' With top executives rarely lasting more than a few years in their jobs, it is not surprising that the turnover of managerial fads is just as rapid!

The emergence of the kernel of value, perhaps, provides the excuse to move on to the next fad which has already been developed in those innovative companies at one o'clock, has been written up by the two o'clock academic or consultant and has been published in the three o'clock business journal!

No fad precisely follows the cycle – even re-engineering is not a perfect fit. Some, such as scientific management, take many decades to go through the cycle while others, such as time management, seem to flash through in less than ten years. Others barely reach five o'clock, in which case they do not qualify as fads. Simply, they are failed ideas.

The life of a business fad is not one-dimensional for it operates within organisations that will be at different stages of implementation. To take a current example the *concept* of 360 degree appraisal is, in 1999, in the region of stages six to seven but the *practice* for many may only be in stages three to four. The genuinely innovative companies may, often unconsciously, have started other initiatives while still on the previous journey and before the stragglers have even begun the first. The genuinely innovative are those who *begin* stage one, who establish the rules, and are able, therefore, to secure competitive advantage. Those who follow are constantly seeking to catch up!

It is easy to smile at the list of fads, sacred cows and transitory techniques, but every one will be vigorously defended. For every person who decries, say, MRP II there is another who argues that it is neither a fad nor a sacred cow but a basic tool that has brought about dramatic improvements in business performance! Equally, there are those who are sceptical of everything! When a student I read an article called *In Defence of Apathy*. Although the author's name has been long forgotten, its thrust has not – protect us from the zealots who have a mission to change the world! We need the apathetic who are not easily roused and the sceptics who do not believe everything they are told, to counterbalance the zeal of the reformers. But if all we have are the apathetic and the cynical, the first casualty will be progress!

The other great problem is that many business fads are contradictory. Were we to implement every concept advocated by the latest business books we would, among other things, be seeking to:

◆ Build a 'learning' company …or is it now a 'forgetting' company?

◆ Re-engineer …or is that now a not-to-be-mentioned word?

◆ Downsize …or is it rightsize …or do we now have to grow ourselves into success?

◆ Think globally but act locally …or just aim for a global brand …or a global brand with a local specification?

◆ Compress time …or wait for the leader to make the mistakes.

◆ Delight our customers …or give them something they had no right to expect.

◆ Practise global benchmarking …or determine the absolute best which no-one has yet achieved.

◆ Develop our core competences …or seek new fields.

◆ Decentralise …or destroy. No doubt we will soon re-centralise!

◆ Build strategic partnerships …or go it alone.

◆ Manage our knowledge workers …or make every worker a knowledge worker.

…and so on. ALL AT THE SAME TIME …with more unlisted and yet to come!

We would be going round and round in ever-decreasing circles (probably some of us are!) concentrating on the needs of tomorrow, forgetting that we also have to deliver today. Ten years ago the list would have been very different and, no doubt, ten years hence it will be different again.

Business fads do not, in themselves, energise an enterprise, although they may give rise to a short-lived burst of energy among some members. However we are only able to energise an enterprise when everyone at every level is fully committed to working together to achieve shared aims and objectives.

In my book *The Ascendant Organisation* I introduced a model which combined control and commitment leading to long-term, sustainable business success and argued that the key determinants are the quality of leadership and the quality and commitment of people. Before proceeding to the body of this book, which essentially is about leadership and commitment I will briefly recapitulate the ascendant organisation.

APPENDIX P.1: Business Fads, Sacred Cows and Transitory Techniques

The following list, while very comprehensive, will be by no means complete. Please add to it, and if you would fax me a copy of your additions (with a short explanation) I should be most grateful.

1. The grand concepts

Balanced scorecard	Ethical management	Partnership
Business processes	Excellence	Partnership sourcing
Business schools	Fordism	Re-engineering
Centres of excellence	Geopolitical	Scientific management
Change management	Globalisation	Serendipity
Chaos	Governance	Service profit chain
Chaotic adhocracy	Growth/share matrix	Shareholder primacy
Classical management	Gurus	Stakeholders
Communication	Human resource management	Strategic alliances
Competition	Holism	Strategic flexibility
Competitive advantage	Innovation	Strategic intent
Competitive strategy	Intellectual capital	Strategic partnerships
Cooperation	Intrapreneurship	Strategic planning
Core centres	Japanisation	Supply chain management
Core competences	Knowledge management	Sustainable competitive
Creativity	Lean thinking	advantage
Culture	Living company	Synergy
Customisation	Low cost producer	Taylorism
Devolving responsibility	Mergers and acquisitions	Think global-act local
Economic value added	Mission	Time compression
Enterprise resource planning	Neo-human relations	Total value
Environmental concern	Organisation development	Vision

2. Leadership

Action centred	Consolidating	Mentoring
AWWA (Ask while	Controlling	Motivational
walking around)	Enabling	Natural selection
Autocratic	Entrepreneurship	One-minute manager
Buccaneering	Followership	Servant
Bureaucratic	Functional	Transactional
Charismatic	Global	Transformational
Coaching	Inspirational	Visionary
Commanding	Management by	
Coordinating	walking around	

3. Organisation concepts

Adaptive
Agile
Ascendant
Autonomous/leaderless/
    self-directed/semi-
    autonomous work groups
BCG Matrix (dogs, stars,
    cash cows, question marks)
Bio-re-engineering
Boundaryless
Bureaucracy
Call centres
Centreless
Centralisation
Clustered
Conglomeration
Consolidation
Core/periphery
Cross border
Customer-focused
Decentralisation

De-cruitment
De-jobbed
Diversification
Divisionalisation
Donut
Downsizing/rightsizing etc.
Dynamic
Dynamic conservatism
Family
Fishnet
Flat
Flexible
Front–back
Functional
High performance
Horizontal
Horizontal integration
Intelligent
Internal contracting/markets
Joint ventures
Life cycles

Managerial hierarchies
Networks
New age
Open
Orchestra
Out-selling
Outsourced
Parallel
Portfolio careers
Primary
Seamless
Shamrock
Small is beautiful
Spaghetti
Spin-off
Strategic business units
Superior
Team
Vertical integration
Virtual

4. People management

Action learning
Annual hours
Bottom-up management
Briefing groups
Broadbanding
Cafeteria benefits
Career management
Competency-based pay
Continuous development
Counselling
Diversity
Emotional intelligence
Employability
Employee involvement
Employee opinion surveys
Employee stock ownership
Empowerment
Equal opportunity
Family
Fast tracking
Fixed term contracts
Flexible benefits

Flexibility
Grapevine
Harmonisation
Hot groups
Job enlargement/enrichment
Job evaluation
Knowledge workers
Learning contracts
Life cycles
Lifelong learning
Long-term incentive plans
Management development
Management succession
Merit progression
Non-monetary recognition
Outplacement
Performance management
Performance-related pay
Personal development plans
Personal growth
Piece rates
Portfolio careers

Profit sharing
Psychological contract
Satisfiers/dissatisfiers
Share options
Single status
Skill-based pay
Skunk works
Small group activities
Stress management
Suggestions schemes
Team working
Team-based pay
Theory X/Theory Y
Theory Z
Top-down management
360 degree appraisal
Time span of discretion
Training needs analysis
Transparency
Zero hours contracts

5. Sales and marketing

Advertising share of voice
Attitudinal analysis/
    modelling/ tracking
Brand equity
Brand tracking/switching
Buyer needs analysis
Category management
Competition win/lose tracking
Competitive benchmarking
Consumer demand trends
Customer awareness/focus/
    delight/service/retention/
    care/voice, etc.
Customers for life
Demographic profiling
Efficient consumer response

First to market
Focus groups
Geo-demographic profiling
Level selling
Lifestyle profiling
Market appraisal/leadership/
    mapping/planning/focus/
    segmentation etc.
Market research
Marketing – micro/mass/
    value/defensive/exped-
    itionary/direct/channel
Marketing mix optimisation
Marketing warfare
New product development
    gate analysis

Own labelling
Portfolio matrix
Portfolio planning
Price elasticity modelling
Price leadership
Product focus
Product life cycle analysis
Product/service envelope
Psycho-demographic
    profiling
Psychographic
    segmentation
Relationship marketing
Trade-off analysis
Unique selling proposition
Value marketing

6. Manufacturing

Agile manufacturing
Anthropocentric
    manufacturing
Automation
Autonomation
CAD/CAM
Cell manufacturing
Computerisation
Design for manufacture
Design for service
Ergonomics
Failure mode and effect
    analysis
Flexible manufacturing
Integrating quality
Just-in-time
Kaikaku (radical
    improvement)

Kaizen (continuous
    improvement)
Kanban ('pull' production
    system)
Lean production
Level scheduling
Mass customisation
MRP (Material
    requirements planning)
MRP II (Manufacturing
    resource planning)
Poka yoke (mistake proofing)
Process capability
Process time analysis
Product life cycle
Project management
Quality awards
    (e.g. Baldridge/
    EFQM etc.)

Quality function
    deployment
Quality standards
    (e.g. ISO 9000)
Simplification
Simultaneous engineering
6-Sigma
Statistical process control
Total preventive
    maintenance
Total productive
    maintenance
Total Quality Management
Twenty Keys to workplace
    improvement
Value analysis
Waste elimination
World-class manufacturing

7. Finance

Activity-based costing
Activity value analysis
Bottom line management
Cost cutting focus
Cost tables
Discounted cash flow
Economic value added
Financial engineering

Flexible budgeting
Function cost analysis
Key performance indicators
Life cycle costing
Open book costing
Open book management
Overhead value analysis
Parametric accounting

Product analysis
Return on capital
Service-profit chain
Standard costing
Target costing
Throughput accounting
Zero-based budgeting

8. Information technology

Capability maturity model
Centralised processing
Client server
Computer aided design/
  manufacturing/systems
  engineering/testing etc.
Data flow diagramming
Data warehousing
Distributed processing
E-business/-commerce/-tail
E-mail

Entity relationships modelling
Extranet
Fourth generation language
Function point analysis
Garbage in, garbage out
Internet
Intranet
Joint application
  development
Networks

Object oriented
  programming
Paperless office
Rapid action development
Relational database
Structured programming
Voice mail
World Wide Web
  + interminable,
  unintelligible jargon

9. Techniques

Activity value analysis
Assessment centres
Benchmarking
Blue-sky thinking
Brainstorming
Business improvement teams
Change management
Communication skills
Competences
Competencies
Conflict management
Contingency theory
Decision trees
Double/single loop learning
Experience curve
Facilitation
Goal alignment
Grid management

Hot desking
Imagining
Industry structure analysis
Key performance indicators
Lateral thinking
Management by objectives
Managerial grid
Mind mapping
Networking
Neurolinguistic programming
Objectives deployment
Paradigm shift
Pareto principle
Participative management
Personal development plans
Policy function deployment
Problem solving
Process mapping

Quality circles
Risk management
S-curve
Scenario thinking
Service level analysis
Seven S
SWOT analysis
T-groups
Time management
Town meetings
Trait studies
Transactional analysis
Value-added analysis
Value chain analysis
Value stream
Visioning
Work flow studies

The Ascendant Organisation

When writing *The Ascendant Organisation* I was very conscious that I might be accused of attempting to create my own business fad, but I saw it neither as a miracle cure nor as a brand new concept. Rather, it was a common-sense way of looking at businesses, recognising that we have to attend to a myriad of apparently conflicting issues, keeping dozens of balls in the air, all of which seem to want to fly off in different directions, all ready to crash to the ground. The business manager as juggler seems an appropriate analogy.

However, most of us do manage to keep the balls in the air most of the time and I tried to develop a framework which would explain how we achieve this impossible balancing act. Since then its validity has been confirmed by thousands of people who recognise that there need not be a conflict between the 'hard' and 'soft' areas of leadership and management. It *is* possible to direct and to motivate; to be demanding of people and at the same time to be caring for them; to be disciplined while encouraging innovation; to recognise the need for standard operating procedures while extolling individual contributions and seat-of-the-pants decision making; to downsize while developing those who remain; to require short-term results while aiming for long-term growth and so on.

Maybe there is a business equivalent of Adam Smith's 'invisible hand' which allows the interplay of market forces to keep everything in balance. That 'balance' I saw as the relationship between 'control of the processes' and 'commitment of the people'. One leads to the other.

The gestation of the concept is fully described in both *The Road to Nissan* and *The Ascendant Organisation* and will not be repeated here. Suffice it to say that a combined fifty years of experience came together late one evening in 1992 in a Düsseldorf bar when Rheinard Dolleschal, a trade union academic, and I were seeking to find a way through the conundrum. The key phrase for us was, 'If we are to achieve long-term sustainable success we need the right balance between commitment of the people and control of the processes.' The problem we perceived was that most practitioners and writers saw the world in terms of just one axis – the hard school of scientific management on control, and the soft behaviouralists on commitment. Even the writers on Japan seemed to ascribe their success of the 1980s either to their excellence as manufacturers (Schonberger, 1987) or to their management of people (Ouchi, 1981).

Sitting in that bar we drew a quadrant on a piece of notepaper, with one axis labelled 'Control', and the other, 'Commitment'. 'Control', we thought, is, essentially, externally imposed with top-down imposition of standards, rules, procedures and processes. Command and direction are the normal methods of determining behaviour and achieving results. 'Commitment', however, is internal, with people believing in their own values and sharing those of their enterprise. They are motivated to work to achieve their own goals and those of the enterprise.

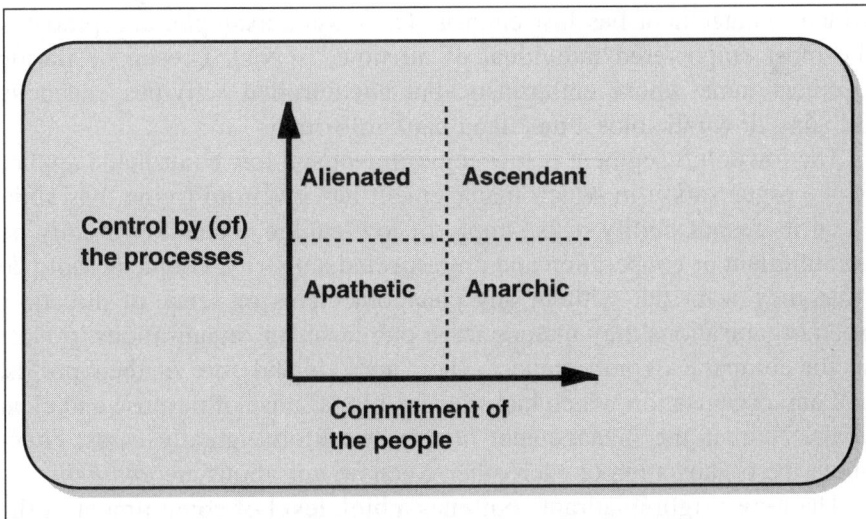

Figure 1.1   The ascendant organisation

The top-left quadrant combines a high level of people being controlled *by* the processes with a low level of commitment. An organisation in this quadrant utilises top-down imposition of standards, rules, processes and procedures with no attempt genuinely to involve people or get their co-operation. Coercion, command and direction are the normal methods of determining behaviour and achieving results. Such a style often leads to staff indulging in activities aimed at restricting individual performance or undermining the organisation.

Examples may include line-paced assembly work where individual contributions are ignored, a low-wage mass-production textile factory based on piecework, the back office of a finance company, or an insurance company in which the rule is, 'Achieve your sales target or you're out the door!' Labour turnover is high and skills development low. We called such an organisation *alienated*.

The other extreme combines high levels of individual commitment with little control or cooperation, which can lead to people doing what they, individually, think is right for themselves or their organisation but without much concern for any corporate objectives or for others. We called this *anarchic*.

Such organisations may include sales companies operating on the edge of the legally acceptable, brokerages working on commission, creative businesses in which it is everyone for themselves, or any organisation in which management has lost control. The classic example, and probably the most empowered individual of all time, is Nick Leeson of Baring Brothers fame whose enthusiastic but uncontrolled activities ended up bringing down the oldest merchant bank in Britain.

The lower left segment is low commitment and low control and applies to the organisation in which management has given up trying, has abdi-cated its responsibility or is simply of low calibre. There is virtually no commitment or cooperation and no respected authority. People broadly do what they want but without any clear objectives or sense of direction. Such organisations may include large public sector organisations, private sector companies comfortable in their markets and sure of their profits, and any organisation which lacks leadership, a sense of purpose and clear goals. Neither the management nor the workforce greatly cares, either about the organisation or each other. Such organisations are *apathetic*.

The upper-right quadrant combines a high level of commitment of the workforce and high control *of* the processes. And that is the trick – the substitution of the word *by* with the word *of*. People throughout the enterprise, instead of being controlled *by* the processes have control *of* the processes. You cannot overestimate the importance, and difficulty, of this change.

This is the 'invisible hand', for *because* people control their own processes and are responsible for maintaining and improving them, they are committed to them. We called such organisations *ascendant*.

Ascendant organisations are positively led by people who care about all the stakeholders and who seek to align the goals of the organisation. They have understood shared values and a sense of purpose which permeate all behaviour and ensure equity of treatment throughout. Ascendant organisations aspire to provide security of employment for their core workers and high levels of training and development for all. Individuals, instead of having every task determined for them, are able to influence or determine how the job is done, and often what that job should be.

Responsibility is genuinely devolved allowing individuals, within the accepted framework, to be innovative and make their own inputs. The enterprise is able to respond flexibly to changing pressures. It combines the best of all cultures and can appear almost anywhere – provided the leaders are committed and set the example.

The ascendant organisation is defined as follows:

> **The ascendant organisation combines high levels of commitment of the people with control of the processes to achieve a synthesis between high effectiveness and high quality of life leading to long-term, sustainable business success.**

In the definition we use 'effectiveness' rather than 'efficiency' for the latter is too narrow. 'Effectiveness' combines productivity, quality and profitability and means that you can sell what you provide. It reaches out to suppliers and to the market place. It requires high-quality investment, research, and product and service development. Above all it requires high-calibre and highly motivated leaders and people committed to shared values and goals.

The Ascendant Organisation sought to demonstrate how 'control' and 'commitment' might be combined and included considerable grass-roots detail. This book is much broader in scope. It brings in much that I have learned from my consulting experience and is more concerned with 'commitment' than 'control'. It shows in much more detail how to develop an enterprise that will score highly on the commitment axis. Above all it is concerned with everything that flows from 'leadership' and to this we will now turn.

2

Energising Leadership

The old world was simple – we used to compete on price; then the Japanese came along and started beating the pants off us on quality; then we tried to differentiate ourselves on service (remember the 'old days' when we thought it was enough to 'delight your customers!'), and then found that everyone had the same idea; now we try to provide customers with a service they have no right to expect!

The new world is much more complex. High quality, which we thought would give us a competitive advantage, is now no more than the entry price to the race. Everyone who has survived is up there. We all read the same books, attend the same conferences, go to the same trade shows, quickly learn about new technology and processes, Nothing is secret for long. Today, we have no alternative but to compete on *price* and *quality* and *innovation* and *design* and *time* and *service* and anything else you can think of.

We used to believe that the scarcest resources were land and money but with the world capital markets ready to lend to anyone, anywhere who can demonstrate a market for their products and services (£10 million in ten minutes is about the norm for the finance director of a medium-sized company with a good track record) we recognise that there are only two factors which really count – the quality of leadership and the quality of people – and it is their combination which determines success or failure

Even in previous less complex worlds, this has always been the case. But today, if we want to reach this state I call ascendant, then high quality leadership has to provide something else. *There has to be that vital spark which, like a bolt of lightning, can strike an organisation, producing a sustained injection of power and energy which generates sustained performance far beyond anything previously dreamed of. From the lightning strike things happen which create long-lasting star-bright performance.* It is that lightning strike which makes the difference.

Figure 2.1   Energise your enterprise

Most charismatic leaders provide that spark. Adolf Hitler and Winston Churchill were charismatic leaders – although Hitler was the incarnation of evil and led his nation to defeat, whereas Churchill's lone stand against him eventually led to the Allies' victory. Margaret Thatcher and Theodore Roosevelt were genuine leaders. Who can doubt Nelson Mandela's right to sit at the very top of the list alongside Martin Luther King and Mahatma Ghandi (lovingly referred to by our guide on a recent visit to India as 'the father of our nation'). For many years, Nelson Mandela, Mahatma Ghandi and Martin Luther King, had no formal authority – just great moral authority because they had 'right' on their side. On the other hand, what about Waco's David Koresh who inspired his followers to mass suicide?

In the business world, Lee Iaccocca of Chrysler, Bill Gates of Microsoft, Andy Grove of Intel, Herb Kelleher of Southwest Airlines, Akio Morita of Sony, Max De Pree of Herman Miller, Ted Turner of CNN, Percy Barnevik of ABB, Soichiro Honda of Honda, Jack Welch of General Electric, Richard Branson of Virgin and Anita Roddick of Body Shop are among those frequently cited as role models. Others such as Robert Maxwell (a Hitler of the business world!) may not now be seen as a role model, but for a time he was, and for better or worse he did lead Maxwell

Communications in a very positive way. Rupert Murdoch of News Corp. is criticised by many – usually by media rivals and sports fans – but who can doubt his vision and business acumen which has led his multimedia company to its pre-eminent position. But you do not have to be at the very top to intimidate – we can all cite examples of 'little Hitlers' at every level of an organisation, people who lord it over their department or section, all in the name of strong leadership, but who in reality are no more than old-fashioned gang bosses or are demonstrating their own insecurity.

The great difficulty with our preoccupation with 'leaders as heroes' is that almost by definition, heroic leaders are different; they are special. They make for great copy but are very much creatures of their time and place, and although it may seem easy to read lessons from their examples, those lessons often contradict each other and are not transferable. Was Hitler really a great leader? Churchill, virtually alone, inspired a nation to resist Hitler before the rest of the world joined in, but both before and after the Second World War he achieved very little.

In the business world, Lee Iaccocca is now virtually *persona non grata* at Chrysler and Anita Roddick's star no longer flies high in the sky. Soichiro Honda's successor, Nobuhiko Kawamoto, took over a financially troubled company whose products were determined by engineers and whose collegiate style slowed decision making to a snail's pace. By focusing on the market and imposing a dose of top-down decision making he turned the company round to the success it is today. Percy Barnevik's successor as CEO of ABB, Göran Lindahl, trimmed back on the portfolio of businesses assembled by his predecessor, cut 10,000 manufacturing jobs in Europe and North America and, the greatest sacrilege of all, scrapped elements of ABB's much-vaunted matrix management structure in favour of clear lines of leadership for its core businesses.

What will happen at Virgin when Richard Branson steps aside? Who else could, or would want to lead a disparate group selling, with varying degrees of financial success, airline and railway seats, condoms, cola, wedding dresses and financial services? Branson seems much more an entrepreneur than a person who enjoys managing established companies, and within a few months of his departure, the disparate partners in Virgin's numerous alliances are likely to go their own way, and the Virgin Group as such will disintegrate.

Some leaders – Clement Atlee, Harry Truman, Lord Simon of BP, David Montgomery who replaced Maxwell at the Mirror Group – are not particularly charismatic (nor do they seek continuously to publicise themselves), but it does not matter. They have other talents which energise. Toshiaki Tsuchiya of Nissan would not say 'boo to a goose' but he was wise – with a tough edge – and we would walk through fire for him. Some leaders have fought their way to the top or have turned round an ailing country or company; others founded their own company and, through their determination and drive, succeeded where the great majority fail. Their styles range from dictator to democrat, their personalities from bully to laid-back and their methods from bureaucrat to entrepreneur. There is no pattern.

Further, there is no one style that is right in all circumstances. In their *Harvard Business Review* article, 'The Ways Chief Executive Officers Lead' (May-June 1996), Charles M. Farkas and Suzy Wetlaufer reported the results of their two-year study into leadership styles. Their most significant conclusion was:

> **We found that in effective companies, CEOs do not simply adopt the leadership style that suits their personalities but instead adopt the leadership approach that will best meet the needs of the organisation and the business situation at hand.**

The styles range from the long-term strategists to those who concentrate on values and individuals; from those who seek to build up the technical expertise of the organisation or implement procedural controls to those who believe their prime responsibility is 'continual reinvention'. Enterprises such as banks which are subject to strict regulation and financial controls do not necessarily need the charismatic, freewheeling, change agent CEO. Farkas and Wetlaufer argue that 'personality' is just one element of effective leadership and often not the decisive one. The truly happy CEO is the one whose personality matches the situation! They say:

> **Herb Kellerher, Southwest Airlines' humorous, down-home CEO, probably could not work in a company that didn't require a human-assets leader. Assertive and demanding, Stephen Friedman, former managing partner of Goldman Sachs, would likely champion change at any organisation.**

All of this is not so very different from good old situational leadership!

Most of us, though, will not become the heroic, transforming chief executive of a major corporation, the top-level strategist or the creator of a successful new enterprise, and the incessant concentration on such people is often no more than a wish-fulfilment exercise – but that does not mean that we cannot exercise leadership.

We all have a part of our enterprise we can lead, whether it contains one person or ten thousand! We need to recognise that:

> **As soon as you have:**
>
> - **One person you can influence**
> - **One process over which you have some authority**
> - **One facility on which you have some control**
> - **One budget line on which you can have some impact**
>
> **You can exercise leadership.**

Without leadership *throughout* the enterprise the top-level leader will have but a short-lived impact, whatever his or her style or whatever the enterprise demands; but if we can harness the potential leadership energy of everyone that impact can be magnified a thousandfold.

To energise our enterprise we need energised and energising leaders not only at the top but at all levels: people who can create the environment in which others give of their own energies, use their full potential and go beyond their comfort zone to achieve their goals and set evermore demanding targets. Above all we need to recognise that everybody can have a part of the enterprise in which *they are not a small cog but top dog*. We need to recognise and create the environment in which:

- ◆ **Everyone can be a hero in their own enterprise**
- ◆ **Everyone can be the chief executive of their own facility, process or budget line**
- ◆ **Everyone can be the manager of their own mini-enterprise**
- ◆ **Everyone can innovate**
- ◆ **Everyone can lead an enterprise unit of one**
- ◆ **Everyone can lead an innovation team**

if only we could open up our own minds to the talent that is lying there, unused.

I am not going to present yet another theory of leadership – no four box models or three intersecting circles, valuable as they can be. Nor do

I assume that leadership can be taught or learned from a book. No-one can *teach* leadership. You can teach only that which already exists – management skills – but you can put people into situations from which they can learn, give some general principles and help avoid some of the silliest mistakes.

Apart from the very few 'naturals', most people who end up leading do so as the result of long preparation; by learning from others – both good and bad; by first following effectively; by gaining a wide range of experiences and learning from their mistakes; and very often by being thrust into early responsibility. Many successful leaders praise specific individuals who greatly influenced them and enthuse about the tough job they were given at an early age. Of course, we never hear of those who were broken by being given that tough job too soon!

So, what are we concerned about? Essentially, with the leadership style that seeks to energise people at all levels throughout the enterprise, and the fundamental leadership qualities necessary for such an endeavour. Let us begin by sharing a definition of the type of leadership that will energise our enterprise.

There are hundreds of different definitions of leadership – many such as 'Management is about doing things right : leadership is about doing the right things' are 'nice' but teach us very little. I used in *The Ascendant Organisation* that given by Murray Steele and Anne Brown in their excellent book, *Leadership – The Philosopher's Stone of Management* (1990) but it needs to be developed for the energised enterprise, in which leadership is displayed at all levels. This is a description rather than a definition:

> **Leadership is about creating the strategy, the values, the sense of purpose and the goals of the enterprise, then living them so that all members are inspired by them and come to share them. It is creating the environment in which leadership can be displayed at all levels; and in which all people are valued, can perform to their full potential, establish their own goals, successfully implement them, and innovate. It is ensuring that the gains are sustained and that the enterprise is continuously improved.**

There are numerous other elements which could be included (which is why there are so many definitions), but let us break it down and begin the exploration.

Create the strategy, values, sense of purpose and goals of the enterprise, then live them so that all members are inspired by them and come to share them.

The concepts of strategy, values, sense of purpose and goals will be explored in depth later but whether we speak of the total enterprise or a small section of it, a lack of clarity will guarantee failure! This responsibility cannot be ducked, but wise leaders recognise that they do not have a monopoly of wisdom and that *create* does not mean *dictate*. They involve people before they reach a conclusion, they listen, decide and then behave in the way they talk. It is only when people see that their leaders 'walk the talk' that they begin to trust them. *People listen to what I say but believe what I do!*

Create the environment in which leadership can be displayed at all levels.

The chief executive creates the environment for everyone but particularly for top managers – and if top managers are not energised what hope is there for everyone else? Top managers create the environment for middle managers. Middle managers create the environment for the first-level managers; and first-level managers create the environment for operational staff. Time and time again when discussing their responsibilities, business leaders almost casually use phrases such as 'creating the environment' or 'creating the conditions in which other people can achieve'. Most successful leaders instinctively understand that they cannot do everything themselves but only rarely do they recognise that 'As soon as you have one person...'.

Mike Reilly, president of automotive components supplier Calsonic International Europe, says:

> **There's no way I can achieve everything we need to do by myself. I see it as my job to create the environment which makes it easy for others to achieve – and if I fail in this, we all fail in everything.**

Mike seeks to live by this premise. He recognises that his most important task is to appoint good people who have an empathy with the strategy and values of the enterprise and give them headroom to do their job. If he fails in that, there is no way the company will be a success – and he knows it.

Essentially this means devolving real responsibility and authority which has unfortunately been called 'empowerment'. A mistake of many of those who advocate so-called empowerment is to see it as an alternative to direction. 'Empower our workforce' is a popular rallying cry, but empowerment is a word which is both narrowly understood and understood narrowly; that is, only a small proportion of those who use it really understand it, and it is interpreted too narrowly. We do not need an alternative to direction: we need a combination of direction, support and devolved responsibility. And this shift has to be a gradual process. We cannot move from total direction to total devolved responsibility in one go – the managers, the staff and the organisation will not be able to handle the shock.

Using the terms of the ascendant organisation model, total direction can lead to alienation, whether you are on a line-paced final assembly operation or work in modern-day direct sales; and total empowerment can lead to anarchy whether you are an advertising agency or a market trader. You cannot take either to its extreme without creating major problems. The element which is usually missing is *support*, and the balance between direction, devolved responsibility and support constantly changes. This changing balance is illustrated in Figure 2.2.

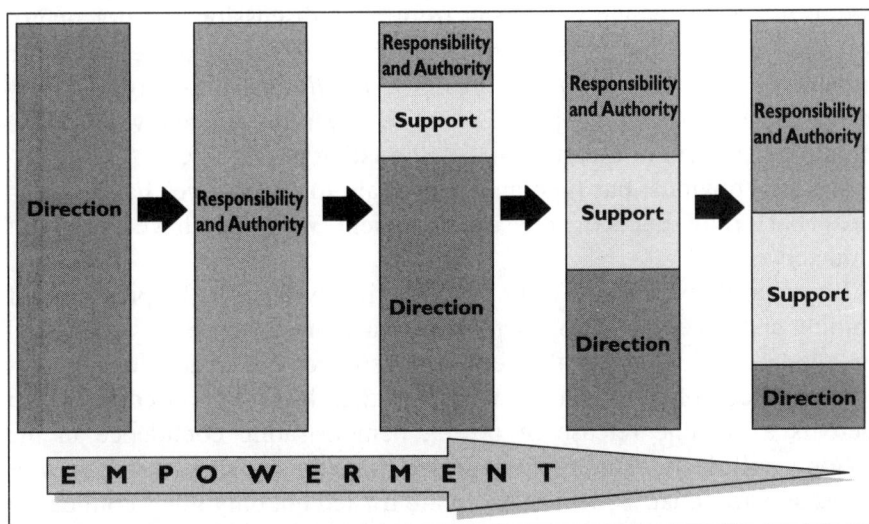

Figure 2.2 Leadership throughout the organisation

The 'traditional' company in the left-hand column relies almost totally on high levels of direction with virtually no devolved responsibility and authority. Managers are Taylorist, separating thinking and planning from doing; breaking jobs down into simple definable tasks and allowing no discretion on how they might be done. But they hear that delegation responsibility and authority is 'a good thing', that delegating a task not only takes some weight off their shoulders but somehow can motivate their subordinates. Of course, to them there can be no halfway house and it all has to be achieved within three months, so the first thing is to say something like, 'That part of the job now belongs to you. Do not come to me with any problems – just get on and do it!' You have to sink or swim, and if it goes wrong you know you are in big trouble. The poor subordinates take on the job but find that they cannot cope because they have no real authority to do anything. Often, they sink.

The real breakthrough comes when the boss realises that with delegation must come *support*.

> ## The less the 'direction' the greater must be the 'support'.

And it is support which is missing from most discussion and practice of so-called empowerment. As we progress across the columns, reducing the amount of direction, *but never losing it totally,* we must continuously increase the amount of support. Let me re-emphasise, there always has to remain an element of direction – the alternative is anarchy.

It seems obvious, but time and time again top executives have said to me, 'That's right, that's the missing ingredient. We should have thought of it ourselves!'

But what do we mean by support? Obviously there is the provision of training and development opportunities to acquire the necessary skills and knowledge, and ensuring the required resources are available, but it is both more complex and more subtle than that. Real support comes when there is a genuine release of power, demonstrating confidence in the person's abilities to handle the new situation and showing trust in him or her as an individual. To feel that you are trusted not only gives confidence but places a great responsibility, and an obligation, on you to ensure that the trust is not misplaced and that it is used wisely.

Support also means being there and readily accessible when needed; providing an open communication and information channel and recognising that asking for guidance at the appropriate time is a strength not a weakness. Being prepared to listen and to act as a sounding board will always provide vital support. It is about providing the framework within which they will operate; it is about providing help and advice; it is agreeing goals and discussing progress; it is providing a high level of recognition and feedback; it is about encouraging people to admit mistakes by discussing them constructively; it is ensuring that they can see that their work impacts on you and on others; it is about discussing their ideas in an open and non-threatening way. Above all it is knowing when to stand back and let them get on with it and encouraging them to create the same environment for others.

Devolved responsibility and authority have to reach all the way through the organisation – if it stops at one level you can be certain that it will not proceed any further, that the blockage will eventually blow back and affect not only you but those above you.

The other significant objection to 'empowerment' is that it seems to be about 'giving' and we know that that which is given can be removed. Instead of feeling pleased with ourselves when we give responsibility we should seek to create the environment in which people *take* responsibility.

The Eurocrats have a word, 'subsidiarity', meaning that no decisions or actions should be taken at a higher level if they can more appropriately be taken at a lower level. It goes beyond delegation and empowerment. Under subsidiarity the *right* belongs to the lower level not to the higher. Although there are often vigorous Eurocrat debates as to its application, its importance to us is that if we wish genuinely to energise our enterprise we must ensure that:

> **Responsibility for any decision or action lies at the lowest or most peripheral level at which it can be effectively managed.**

Nothing gave me greater pleasure than having someone working for me come and tell me that he or she had *taken* a new responsibility – it may even have meant encroaching into an area that I had previously thought was mine. When you have confidence in yourself and in the people working for you it is not that it just does not matter, it means that you have truly been able to develop a climate of trust and mutual confidence.

All people are valued, can perform to their full potential, establish their own goals and successfully implement them.

'Valuing' means recognising the intrinsic worth of all people, not by proclaiming 'Our people are our greatest asset' but by treating everyone with respect and dignity, by avoiding the culture of first- and second-class citizens, and by recognising worth in a way that is appropriate and meaningful to them as individuals. This does not mean having some great financial pay-out. Sometimes it is no more than, 'Thanks, that was a brilliant job you did there.' Other times it may be, 'Let's go down the pub. The drinks are on me.'

In fact, we do not want the person who is only motivated when there is the chance of the pay-out. If people only offer creative thinking when they believe they are going to get something out of it you have failed. More of this later when we discuss Innovation.

Manufacturers speak of the seven wastes – the wastes arising from overproduction, transportation, inappropriate processing, waiting, defects, unnecessary motions and unnecessary inventory. But there is an eighth waste, and it causes greater losses than the other seven put together.

Waste No. 8:
THE WASTE OF HUMAN POTENTIAL

The waste of human potential arises when managers fail to realise they are not using people's abilities to the full, or worse, when they do realise but do nothing about it. In so many organisations, people switch off when they come to work or use their intelligence to thwart the system. Enabling 'people to perform to their full potential' is vital if we are truly to energise our enterprise.

Benjamin Zander, conductor of the Boston Philharmonic Orchestra, pronounced one of Tom Peter's justifiably favourite quotations, when he said:

> I set as the goal the maximum capacity that people have – I settle for no less. I make myself a relentless architect of the possibilities of human beings. (Peters, 1997: 144)

Establishing their own goals and successfully implementing them

When the right environment has been created, establishing goals is comparatively easy, but ensuring that these goals are aligned throughout the organisation is much more difficult. We will return to this in Chapter 4. But 'successful implementation' is about achieving results and it is here that life becomes difficult. Developing our values, sense of purpose and goals takes less than a percentage point of the total time – it's a demanding intellectual exercise. But if that is all it is, if we then sit back and think our job is done, everything will collapse. Translating words into deeds takes (about!) 99.73 per cent of the time, and is the tough part.

Innovate

This is so important that it has two chapters to itself – I will say no more here.

Sustain the gain

No part of the process is easy but, once we have achieved something, sustaining the gain, while less dramatic, is almost the most difficult task of all. This is where so many change programmes break down. So many things can go wrong – a change of personalities (one of the reasons for our success at Nissan was that the top team stayed together for ten years – the *power of continuity* is totally disregarded in much of the West; the German middle-sized businesses are an exception), redirected interest, a waning of enthusiasm, lack of ownership, reverting to type and so on. Sustaining the gain can be boring; it does not have that spark that makes life exciting. Inspirational leaders do not like the steady state. It requires different qualities, which is why so many innovators (and revolutionaries) move on or move out once the initial task is complete. The big question is, 'How do we continue to energise the enterprise in the steady state?' or, the even bigger one, 'How do we ensure that we never have a steady state?'

Equipping the company continuously to improve itself

This is the most difficult task of all. It requires the leader to create an enterprise in which innovation is the norm, one in which no-one is satisfied with the *status quo*, where change is led from the top but is driven at all levels from within – not by outside consultants or external events. How do you maintain a high level of dissatisfaction throughout the enterprise?

Not dissatisfaction of the whingeing type but constructive dissatisfaction, because however good you are you can always improve.

The Qualities of the Energising Leader

It is easy and somewhat trite to list 'The Qualities of Leadership'. It has been done many times before and I include such a list not with a view to adding anything that is particularly new but for the sake of completeness and, perhaps, to pull out those qualities that are particularly relevant for the energising leader. I emphasise that the list is incomplete (as, in any case, they always are) for it omits certain fundamental qualities which will emerge when we come to discuss The Heart of Leadership in Chapter 4.

◆ First of all must come that grouping of qualities which centre around... I guess the best word is 'energy' – knowing what you want to achieve and having the single-mindedness, passion, courage, deter-mination, drive and perseverance (and any other such dynamic words as you can think of) to get there; it is about identifying with your enterprise and from this identification comes credibility and trust. It is about wanting to make things happen – I know no energising leaders who are motivated solely by money, most want to *achieve* (and as we will see when discussing values, very occasionally it is possible to imbue the whole enterprise with the desire to achieve).

◆ Energising leaders are powerful communicators – they are willing and able to put over their messages in a way which is clear, open, approp-riate and meaningful to their specific audience. They never talk down to or patronise people. They recognise that real communication is a two-way process and they *listen*. They frequently go to people in the environment rather than always expecting people to come to them. (Much more on communication in Chapter 4).

◆ Energising leaders analyse logically, think rationally but are not afraid to use intuition. A leader who is always seen to go by the book will inspire no-one. The intuitive decision based on years of accumulated knowledge is not guesswork – it is wisdom!

◆ Energising leaders have the moral courage, when necessary, to make their own decisions – to do what they know to be right – perhaps con-trary to the advice they receive. Part of this relates to intuition but it goes beyond it and requires self-confidence and strength. General Sir Peter Inge, when Chief of the General Staff, deliberately echoed one of the acknowledged great military leaders, Field Marshal Slim, when he said:

I believe that moral courage is the single most important quality for a successful leader... The funny thing is that the more you use your moral courage on small issues the easier it becomes to use it on big issues. The less you use it on small things the more difficult it becomes to use it on big issues. (*Management Today*, November 1993)

Of course, if you go down your own route and are regularly seen to be wrong you are in trouble – in the military world you may lose your life!

◆ They know when to do nothing – not in a 'I do not know what to do' sort of way but in a way which shows that they are not going to panic or be pressurised into doing something just because 'doing something' gives the appearance of action, when it may be the very worst response. I call it 'positive non-action'.

◆ They set consistently high standards of personal integrity, honesty and ethical behaviour and ensure that nothing less is acceptable throughout the enterprise.

◆ They also, set consistently high standards for the quality of the product or service making clear the standards by which they will evaluate performance. As soon as someone in the company says, 'We'll let that one go, we need the sale' you've lost it.

◆ An energising leader is both leader of the team and a member of it. The leader who is seen to be working with others to achieve shared goals will secure respect far beyond anything achievable by the 'Do as I say' merchant. More of this in Chapter 8, Real Teamworking

◆ They are willing to coach and support people. They are there when needed. They go in to bat for them. They are their champion. They help people through the difficult times but are also be prepared to take the tough decision when necessary. They do it but do it right.

Others will observe how they treat those who cannot handle it, and if the leader gives only cursory consideration to the needs of others they will lose respect. But when they do help and there is no response – and they then do nothing about it, they will also fail in the eyes of others.

◆ Energising leaders give prompt feedback and recognise good performance in the appropriate way, and I'm not talking about financial rewards. They provide positive feedback when things go well as well as criticising when things go wrong. Remember the power of, 'Thank you – that was a great job.'

There are many other qualities – no doubt you can add a dozen – but the important thing is not the length of the list but the *feeling* it gives. When you *feel* that a successful enterprise is not just about making a good product or providing an effective service you will be on your way, for you will know that it is about the quality of leadership and the quality of people. Those qualitites you personally can add to the list are far more important than anything I can provide. The writer of a book has no monopoly of wisdom.

Listen to John Gardner, former US Health Secretary, on leaders:

Leaders can serve as symbols of the moral unity of society. They can express the values that hold the society together. Most important they can conceive and articulate goals that lift people out of their petty preoccupations, carry them above the conflicts that tear a society apart, and unite them in pursuit of objectives worthy of their best efforts. (cited in Caulkin, November 1993)

Much of what follows will be concerned with values and goals, but first we turn to the leader as a strategist.

3

The Leader as Strategist

My colleague, David Jackson, got it right when he said in his book, *Dynamic Organisations:*

> **Many believe strategy is about what happens in the future. Strategy is *here and now* [my emphasis]. This misconception leads people away from action into interminably long planning cycles.**

One of Jack Welch's early actions when he took over at General Electric was to dismantle the corporate strategic planning group. He pronounced the corporate strategy to be the now celebrated, 'No. 1 or No. 2 in every market we serve.' That is all the strategy GE needed!

When speaking of the leader's role as a strategist I begin then with an approach influenced by David Jackson's words and Jack Welch's actions:

> **To determine today the strategic goals for tomorrow, and lead the actions which will ensure their achievement.**

All else, including the processes and practices, approach to customers, investors, staff and the community, flows from those few words. The broad strategy may range from:

> **Move into the market, maximise short-term profit by taking advantage of everyone and everything, and get out as quickly as possible.**

TO

> **Achieve long-term, sustainable business success by maximising value to our suppliers, customers, shareholders and staff.**

Both, and all the permutations between, are legitimate business strategies.

You may not think much of the first statement, but for many businesses it is close to the real world. Think of all those so-called 'Christmas Wonderlands', full of tacky decorations and cheap and nasty gifts, that descend on us, taking over empty shops in October, only to vanish after their 'mammoth clear-out sale' in January. No doubt, from February to September their owners are involved in some other in-and-out enterprise. Compare them with one of the truly wondrous stores of the world, The House of Käthe Wohlfahrt, an all-year-round Christmas shop in Rothenburg ob der Tauber, Germany, whose delights and quality are unimaginable. Its strategy, expressed in its own words, is:

> **Beautiful works of art specially for Christmas.**
>
> **Made by hand with a great love for detail, they make our Christmas dreams come true.**
>
> **KÄTHE WOHLFAHRT,**
> **We carry German Christmas traditions out into the world.**

Go to Rothenburg, itself one of the best-preserved mediaeval towns in Germany, and experience Käthe Wohlfahrt's wonderland – you will not be disappointed.

However much we may disapprove of the tacky, temporary Christmas stores, there can be no doubt that they have a legitimate business strategy and meet a need; and if they do that, who are we to criticise them for taking the opportunity? Although these are the extremes, who can doubt that in the Anglo-Saxon world many companies, particularly small businesses, tend more towards the in-and-out end of the spectrum (hoping for the white knight to come along to buy them out), and may laugh themselves silly at Käthe Wohlfahrt – 'A handcrafted Christmas store! What about their cash flow?' There are not too many Käthe Wohlfahrts about – and it is in an all-year-round tourist town.

The second point about this approach to strategy is that it can apply at all levels of the enterprise. People at lower levels may be more circumscribed and have shorter timescales, but this does not mean that a section of half a dozen people cannot have what for them are strategic goals. Wouldn't it be great if the supervisor of the ladies' shoe department of a fashion store were able to say:

Our strategy is to concentrate on achieving high levels of customer satisfaction and to ensure that our customers are always able to buy what they want when they want it.

That may not sound very much, but in a business in which it is difficult to buy summer shoes any later than mid-August, the second part, in particular, is a major strategic shift. From such a strategy certain goals and actions might emerge. For example:

Our goal is to become the strongest performing department both in customer satisfaction and in percentage growth in cash sales measured over the three-year period from 1 April 1999 to 31 March 2002.

To achieve this we have determined that our annual sales growth should be 7.5 per cent in real terms year-on-year, and our customer satisfaction index should improve by 10 per cent per annum. The necessary actions include:

1. To complete by end-March 1999 a full review of performance in 1997 and 1998 to ensure that we have valid base data from which we can measure future performance improvements.

---

2. To measure the relative proportion of sales coming from year-round and seasonal fashion ranges, and to determine the peak-sales period for seasonal fashion shoes.

3. To ensure that the customer can always buy what she wants when she wants it, record the number of requests we receive for seasonal fashion shoes after the suppliers have ended deliveries.

4. To work with our suppliers to ensure that we do not run out of stock when customers are still requesting a particular range.

5. To implement training programmes to ensure that all staff acquire a full understanding of:

Shoe fitting
The properties and care of shoe materials
Sales techniques
Customer service
Displays
Relationships with suppliers
And so on...

I suspect that very few of us know anything about selling shoes in a fashion store – certainly I do not – but you can see that it's not too difficult to work up a strategy for such a mini-enterprise. And once you have developed your strategy, the goals and actions will flow – and they will be actions to which the departmental staff are committed.

They may not seem much like strategic objectives to those sitting in a lofty managerial position, but for the people at the operational level they certainly are. Who says operational staff cannot develop strategies? They may be shorter term and more tangible, they may sound like goals to you and me, but it's all part of a process which gets everyone thinking that their part of the enterprise is their own mini-enterprise. Even the words, 'mini-enterprise' may seem strange, but work on it; you may even decide that 'enterprise' has no need of the prefix. It's not the precise words that are important – it's the commitment they convey, and if you or the people concerned want to use other terminology that feels right for you then please do so. But do not lose sight of the eight ball.

But in any such discussion we necessarily begin at the top, and at the end of the spectrum which speaks of long-term sustainable success –

although we cannot deny that the in-and-out merchants might well be highly energised.

The new millennium has a fascination for business executives and I have lost count of programmes with titles such as Vision 2000, listing goals such as 'Delight the customer', 'Become a learning company', 'Achieve zero defects' and so on – all fad phrases which fool some of the people some of the time. Towards the end of 1995 I led a study tour to Japan comprising senior executives from top British companies who were seeking to understand long-term strategic thinking. We found that most Japanese companies were also stuck in the 'Vision 2000' mode. But one company was different.

The president told us that the prime reason for their continuing success was that they have long worked to a fifteen-year strategic horizon which they review at five-year intervals. (Of course, they also have shorter-term goals which complement the long term.) Their 1995 review had concluded:

> **By 2010, market leadership will be with the company which *determines* the materials and technology.**

They could have extrapolated from current knowledge, but recognised that everyone can do that. As a result they have established partnerships with researchers at some of the best universities throughout the world and have shifted a significant proportion of their in-house resources from five-year applied research to long-term pure research. At the least they will have the inside track, and at best will determine the technology and materials.

Microsoft, when announcing in 1997 its investment in a major new research facility in Cambridge, England, was asked what it would be researching. The guarded reply was, 'Certainly not Windows 2000!'

This is the difference between leadership within the current rules and leadership by determining what those rules will be; between bench-marking to be among the best and innovation to be the best; between operational effectiveness and strategy, between continuous improvement and radical innovation and between remaining in your comfort zone and ener-gising for the future.

Many will argue, 'I can't think fifteen days ahead let alone fifteen years!' (Some may even be thinking, 'fifteen minutes!') Life is unpredictable and fifteen years is a long time: but it is precisely because life is unpredictable that we must seek a long-term strategy! Maybe not fifteen years but how about ten – or five – or three? (Please, do not go lower than three!) There are companies that do have such perspectives and, if they get it right, they will be the companies which, not only will still be in business, but will be in the lead in 2015.

It is very clear from all of this that strategy is not about detail, nor about tightly defined planning and control systems. It used to be. Remember the *annual strategic* plan – that's a contradiction in terms if ever there was one. It started at the top and every business unit then had to have its own mini-version which was reviewed at the top and matched with the plans of other functions; and subsequent performance was closely monitored by the Strategic Planning Department. In my time as a director of British Gas in the early 1980s we spent more top management time on the strategic plan than on any other activity. It was just about the most sterile process ever.

No company can have a detailed long-term strategic plan based on the premise that, somehow, events and people are controllable and all you have to do is put in place the right systems and structures to make events conform to the plan. However, it can have a strategic direction that evolves through continually changing circumstances, through which the mid- and shorter-term goals can be determined and measured and which supports and is supported by the financial horizon of the organisation and its investors.

Strategic planning, in the way it used to be conducted, is not only an oxymoron but the very antithesis of strategic leadership.

Henry Mintzberg, the distinguished writer on organisation and planning, said in 1994:

Strategic planning is not strategic thinking… It causes managers to confuse real vision with the manipulation of numbers… the most successful strategies are visions not plans… Planners should make their contribution around the strategy making process, not inside it.

Planning is about calculation: leadership is about commitment.

What Mintzberg meant was that the planners (if you have any) should bring some of the information (about demographic trends, global warming, market shifts and such like) to the door, and then let the strategic leaders use that information as just one part of their decision-making process.

Often it is a matter of gut feel about the right way to go. You cannot prove it – you just know.

◆ Paul Girolami of Glaxo did not seek to *prove* that the company needed to prepare for a new and dramatically different health care environment.

◆ Lord King and Sir Colin Marshall of British Airways did not seek to *prove* that BA would succeed by creating the world's first truly global airline.

◆ Herb Kellerher of Southwest Airlines could not *prove* that it would succeed by introducing what was virtually the totally opposite strategy to BA – low-cost, short-haul flights between mid-size cities, then by adding 'amuse, surprise and entertain' to its already great reliability. BA is now jumping on the band-wagon with its own low-cost, short-haul company – Go. Time will tell if it can succeed in both markets.

◆ Percy Barnevik was not able to *prove* that dividing ABB into hundreds of self-managing businesses was the key to success.

When we were determining Nissan's business philosophy and practices, one of the most infuriating questions from the Japanese (who always have to 'know' before they move, and if they do not 'know' are unlikely to do anything – which accounts for a lot!) was, 'How do you *know* it will work?' I started by trying to explain, but after many frustrating attempts and failures ended up by saying something like, 'Twenty-five years of experience with a track record of getting it right!' The one-time President of IBM, Al Williams, called it the 'smell test'.

The most successful strategic thinking and actions capture what the leaders learn from all sources: from the accumulation of long experience; a comprehensive understanding and grasp of the business, the recollection of previous occurrences; from conversation and the observation of seemingly insignificant events; from feelings; from small clues as well as from hard data. It is emotional as well as logical – a synthesis of the hard and the soft. It is an understanding of how people behave that alerts you to a trend, a problem, an opportunity, a solution or a new direction. It enables you apply your experience, allowing you to go from A to Z in one mental leap without having to spell out every intervening B to Y. It is

POSITIVE INSTINCT

Positive instinct is far removed from guesswork. It is assembling all possible information from all possible sources and then adding that extra undefinable ingredient which ensures that you just *know* the right way to go. What is the undefinable ingredient? If I could tell you it would not be undefinable! For the vast majority of us it comes with experience – for a few it is there without experience and they become the entrepreneurial founders of their own businesses. They become the millionaires or the bankrupts – and some become both!

You may determine that you are not in this game; you are not the free-wheeling entrepreneur nor do you have or need the resources to indulge in pure research, the opportunities to gain the experiences that facilitate global thinking, or the experience and confidence to let your positive instinct determine your strategy. I do not seek to tell you what that strategy should be – it may be, perfectly legitimately, to follow behind, letting others make the mistakes, for we know that the first to market does not always get it right. You may believe that the leader is often exposed and the personal price of experimentation high. The conservative, test-it-to-death, follow the leader, market research, focus group mentality is safer.

High-profile experimentation and the use of positive instinct may result in your getting to the market twelve months earlier, gaining large 'first to the market' profits; or it may lead to high-profile failure. 'Is it not safer,' you might ask, 'to keep our heads down and keep our jobs?' You know that being first does not guarantee success – it may adversely impact on your current account, whereas doing nothing or following the leader has less dramatic results. 'Let us concentrate on cutting our costs – growing the business requires too much effort and is too risky.'

Those of us who take this view of life are *denominator managers* – but what we need if we are to energise our enterprise are *numerator leaders*.

The terms, 'numerator' and 'denominator' were first used by Gary Hamel and C K Prahalad in *Competing for the Future* (1994) but let me explain them. The equation making for corporate performance can be presented as follows:

$$\frac{\text{Numerator}}{\text{Denominator}} = \text{Performance}$$

where, in the simplest of terms, the numerator is about net income and the denominator is about costs.

As in any such equation, P can be enhanced either by increasing N or by reducing D – but for years we have been persuaded to demonstrate our corporate virility by concentrating almost entirely on controlling D, the denominator, mainly by cost reduction. We have sought to reduce our costs by declaring vast numbers of people redundant (using, of course, the 'downsizing' or 'rightsizing' euphemisms); we have pressured our suppliers to improve their performance and reduce their prices; we have attempted to go 'lean', often concentrating solely on 'labour productivity' whether measured as units produced or sales achieved and we have slashed our cost and asset base in whatever way possible.

Most of us gave little thought to the numerator. Growing our income takes time and effort. It requires a long-term commitment to getting our business strategy right; it means investing for the future, developing the people, innovating in products, services and processes, understanding our actual and potential customers' changing needs, growing existing markets and developing new markets. It requires us to seek to create extra value for our customers. The results are not immediate.

Reducing the denominator, however, gives us the sense of doing something – or at least being seen to be doing something. De-layering and downsizing, we believe, are macho and result in dramatic, short-term productivity and labour cost improvements. Squeezing the suppliers makes us feel good. *But the benefits are finite.* There is a limit to the costs you can take out – although as the Japanese have shown us with their 'Squeeze the dry towel dry', there always seems to be a little more. *But what good is increased productivity when you have no saleable product and cannot keep up with, let alone lead, the market?*

However productive you are, you must always remember that customers do not purchase 'productivity' – they purchase products and services. For years, when talking about Nissan's leadership and management philosophy and practices I used to end my presentations with a slide of the cars, and said something like:

We've spent the last hour and a half talking about our philosophy and practices, but please remember – all of this is only a means to an end. Customers do not buy philosophy – they buy cars! However good our philosophy and however effective our practices if, for whatever reason, they do not want the end product we go out of business.

Perhaps, in such a situation, when collecting your redundancy cheque or when switching the lights off for the last time as the last person out of the building, you can console yourself by saying, 'We were one hell of a productive company!' *In any case, whoever was energised by cost-cutting?*

Growing the numerator is much more difficult. The fact that the results are not immediate is perhaps why the Anglo-Saxon mentality favours the alternative approach. But when you get it right the benefits are long-lasting; they create an enterprise which can look to growth based on a solid foundation, and to long-term sustainable success. And, the biggest plus of all, *the benefits of increasing the denominator are potentially infinite* – there need be no end to growth. Or, more accurately we can go on for as long as we wish to. We can continually develop the people and secure the benefits of a truly energised workforce; we can invest in our facilities and have the confidence to develop all our resources; we can move into new markets, we can innovate and invest for the future.

The results of the denominator approach, in British manufacturing industry at least, have been dismal. Starting from an appallingly low base in 1979 our output per person rose by 78 per cent by 1994 – a greater improvement rate than all other industrialised countries – due primarily to a decline in manufacturing employment of one-third (2.3 million). However, absolute productivity levels remained low against international competitors, but the then government delighted in reporting how well the country was doing. They kept quiet about the facts that from 1973 to 1992 real output increased by a derisory 1.3 per cent (*The Economic Journal*, January 1996) and that our competitors were also improving on their much higher base. These figures are not plucked out of the air. They are the sum of the performance of UK manufacturing businesses.

Stephen Roach, chief economist of Wall Street's Morgan Stanley, and the man credited with coining the word 'downsizing', recognised this when in May 1996 he said in the company journal:

> **Surging profits, sustained low inflation, improved competitiveness and a record run in the stock market are all unmistakable by-products of spectacular improvements in business efficiency. But it is increasingly apparent to me that these are the results of plant closures, job cuts and other forms of downsizing that are not recipes for lasting productivity enhancement... Tactics of open-ended downsizing and real wage compression are ultimately recipes for industrial extinction... If you compete by building you have a future. If you compete by cutting you don't.**

Look at the example of one of the United States' most celebrated slashers and burners, Al Dunlap, nicknamed Chainsaw Al or Rambo in Pinstripes, whose philosophy is that any business that cannot be fixed within twelve months cannot be fixed at all. His prime method is to cut jobs – 11,000 in Scott Paper, and then after joining household appliance manufacturer Sunbeam in 1996 he shut down or sold off two-thirds of its 18 plants declaring 12,000 employees, half the total, redundant. Then after bitter wrangling inside the boardroom over inflated revenue and profit figures he was told to go. Sanford Jacobs, professor of management at the University of California commented in 1998:

> **At Scott Paper and later at Sunbeam, lay-offs occurred before other alternatives were explored. Employees bore the brunt of efforts to improve performance. In the short term the approach can yield almost miraculous results. But as time goes on, the liabilities of the low road become more apparent. If and when new hiring occurs, [wise potential recruits] will keep their distance. This is hardly the recipe for long-term business success.**

The fundamental truth is that companies that are perceived as being good employers, who are believed to treat people well and in the downturns handle problems in an understanding way are always able to recruit good people and when the quality and leadership of people are the only factors which make a real difference the conclusion is obvious.

Of course, none of this means that the numerator-led enterprise in its quest for long-term sustainable success can ignore the need to control its costs today. Poor performance today may mean that there is no tomorrow. It is often by improving operational effectiveness that you develop the strength, the space and the time to work on the numerator. We are seeking the power of 'both... and' not the conflict of 'either... or'.

But there is another associated element that comes into this discussion. The energising numerator leader knows the difference between *future income foregone* and *current income lost*. This a difficult concept so let me give an example. IBM forewent (if that is the right word) future income when it failed to launch a laptop computer until 1991, by which time Toshiba had launched some thirty different models. Not every one was a success and in the five years before IBM's launch Toshiba withdrew more models than most other companies launched, but during this period it built the knowledge and strength that enables it to maintain market leadership to this day.

In simple terms, when we become obsessed with preserving our current account we greatly endanger our future income and profitability. But in so doing we encourage safety first and the result can be atrophy – a wasting away through undernourishment. The alternative creates a major attitudinal change throughout the enterprise. You work on growing the business rather than cutting your costs. You concentrate on the numerator rather than the denominator. You become an energising leader and create an energised enterprise. *You move to the heart of leadership.*

4

The Heart of Leadership

It is easy to come up with a list of positive qualities of leaders – I included some in Chapter 2 – and there are numerous 'models' and assessment techniques – action-centred leadership, situational leadership, the Blake-Mouton grid, Myers-Briggs, and so on. There are thousands of books and articles describing 'what leaders do', listing the traits of the successful, and providing anecdotes about the charismatic.

There cannot be anything new to say, can there? Hopefully, there is. Our starting point is the need to energise our enterprise. What are the fundamental qualities of the leader who aims to energise the enterprise? Or to use the corollary, what do 'followers' have the right to expect of their leaders? Both questions are apposite, for once you accept the premise that leadership can exist at all levels of an enterprise you must also accept that the vast majority of us are both leaders and followers – at the same time. Max De Pree, in his beautiful book *Leadership Jazz* (1992), introduced the concept of 'followership' in which the leader is dependent on the members, but even he did not pick up the fact that the vast majority of us can be both a leader and a follower *at the same time*.

Before developing the description of leadership given in Chapter 2, I used to say that the difference between management and leadership is:

Management is about the organisation and development of resources whereas leadership is about getting people to do what you want them to do because they want to do it for you.

And, somebody wisely added at one seminar, '...and for themselves'.

The development of the somewhat more wordy description does not make the earlier definition wrong; in fact there is, as we will see, much to applaud in it. The difficulty is that by itself it is one those aphorisms like 'Management is about doing things right, whereas leadership is about doing the right things' which does not give us very much guidance as to what we need to do. Therefore I ask you to reflect both on the examples of well-known leaders cited earlier and on your own experience, and ask yourself the fundamental question, *'What qualities do certain individuals possess and give to me that makes me accept them as genuine, energising leaders?'* Or, to put it the other way round, *'If I aim to be recognised and accepted as a genuine energising leader, what qualities should I possess and give to others?'* These are very difficult questions, for we are seeking to go beyond superficial descriptions of behaviour and definitions of types and styles to reach the *heart* of leadership of an enterprise, which is something very different from being at the *top* or *centre*.

The word 'heart' has all sorts of implications about loving, caring, sharing values, being genuinely involved, long-term relationship and so on. As I was writing the first draft of this chapter on 3 May 1998, British Prime Minister, Tony Blair, was in the middle of his six months presidency of the European Union and was chairing the meeting of Heads of States agreeing the European Single Currency, from which Britain opted out. Tony Blair was therefore at the top and in the centre of the European Union. Few would suggest that he was at its heart.

It is in the nature of the beast that there are no 'one-size-fits-all' answers, and there will always be the mould-breaking individual who follows none of the rules but is universally recognised as an outstanding leader. But through personal experience, discussions with people at all levels and analysis of my analytical questionnaire, 'Leadership and Management of People – Measuring up to the Best', there are four fundamentals which, in various guises, repeatedly come through.

'If I am to accept someone as a leader I must... '

> ■ **RESPECT THEIR ABILITY**
> ■ **HAVE TRUST IN THEM**
> ■ **SHARE THEIR GOALS**
> ■ **BE INSPIRED BY THEM**

These are not 'either... or', they are 'both... and'. Each one has to be present. Each one affects the others and in turn is affected by them. Each one is as important as the others, and there are few aspects of behaviour which impact on only one quality. Consider the possible outcomes if all four are not present:

You do/are	But you do/are not	As a result
Respect their ability Have trust in them Share their goals	Inspired by them	You will not be motivated to work with great enthusiasm
Have trust in them Share their goals Inspired by them	Respect their ability	You will have little faith in their grasp of the business, nor in their ability to get the job done and meet the goals
Have trust in them Respect their ability Inspired by them	Share their goals	You will have little confidence in the direction of the enterprise; they may be other peoples' energising leader but not yours
Respect their ability Share their goals Inspired by them	Have trust in them	You may feel they are in it for themselves and you cannot rely on them to stick in there when the going gets tough or another opportunity arises

Think of people you know who are in positions in which they are supposed to exercise leadership and ask yourself if you regard them as real, energising leaders. Assess them against these four qualities. Do you respect their abilities, trust them, share their goals and are you inspired by them?

Ask of yourself as a potential energising leader (we are still talking about leadership at all levels) what do you have to do to *earn* respect, trust, sharing and inspiration?

It is *earn* which is important. Whatever our position or however grand our title, acceptance of our leadership is not there as of right. And even when we have earned that accolade, it can be lost in a moment. We spend years building a reputation but a single foolish act or statement can destroy everything we have achieved.

But the $64,000 question is, '*How* do you earn respect, trust, sharing and inspiration?' There is no simple answer, no magic ingredient, no tablet of stone which can be handed down, but there are *behaviours* which if followed can make it more likely that we will be accepted, and if not followed will make it almost certain that we will be rejected.

The four qualities are inseparable but as it is impossible to speak of everything at once let us attempt an artificial distinction and begin with respect for ability.

RESPECT FOR YOUR ABILITY

As a real leader you are respected for what you know and what you do. You become a leader by doing the work of a leader – apart from those very few 'naturals' – *you learn by doing*. But it is rather like an onion – as you peel a layer, another appears. What is it that you do?

The starting point, and probably the easiest to understand, is sheer technical ability – your ability to do the job, your knowledge of the techniques, your grasp of the business. It is from this that real security comes. Whatever your other attributes, if people take the view that you do not know what you're doing you've lost it before you begin.

Reflecting on those energising leaders I have worked for and with – Bob Schleif of Continental Can Company, Toshiaki Tsuchiya and Ian Gibson of Nissan, Gero Panskus of The Panskus Team, Gianni Ravazzotti and Battista Errera of Ceramic Industries, Mike Reilly of Calsonic, Albert Hickman of Thorn Lighting, Anne Wright of the University of Sunderland (and now chief executive of the University for Industry) – most of them are unknown outside their immediate circle but every one of them understands their business inside out. They understand the processes, the product or service, the market, the customers and their suppliers.

Hermann Simon, in his brilliant study of successful German companies, *Hidden Champions* (1996), tells the story of Reinhard Schmidt, CEO of Dürr, the world's leading suppliers of car painting systems. Simon had read an article about the difficulties experienced in an American car plant because the workers were using hair sprays with metal particles that settled on paint surfaces. He continued:

> **I cut out the article and sent it to Reinhard Schmidt. Schmidt wrote back to me: 'I know about this problem because I have been in that plant. The current equipment is from a competitor who can't handle the problem. We have a solution and the next time it will probably be our turn.' That's closeness to customer: a CEO of an $800 million company in Stuttgart not only knows about a specific local U.S. problem, but he has been there and experienced the problem and has a solution for it. (pp. 109–11)**

That is understanding your business.

Because of this such leaders know what resources (in the sense of ability and skills, information, facilities, financing, authority, time and so on) are needed to allow people are able to perform superbly. I reflect on those who do not have this knowledge and understanding – regrettably, no names – they will never become energising leaders – not in a month of Sundays!

Only rarely do we hear of women who are regarded as genuine energising leaders, so as an example let me add a name to the select but growing group.

When I was a governor of the then Sunderland Polytechnic, we were selecting a new Rector. There were those who, for various reasons, opposed appointing Dr Anne Wright, an English literature academic, to head up what was then regarded as a technical institution. However, comparing her with candidates with the so-called correct technical background (and gender!) we concluded that in view of the problems that needed to be addressed and the leadership, constructive thinking and actions required to bring the Polytechnic into the modern era, there was no contest.

The new leader had to be a person who would earn respect for her ability, and in *that polytechnic at that time* such respect would come from a combination of academic credibility and the ability to understand and lead the necessary changes. Anne Wright had real academic credibility, and was the only candidate who really understood the nature of the inherited problems and the change processes that were needed if the institution was ever to become anything more than a third-rate backwater. As Vice-Chancellor and Chief Executive of what is now the University of Sunderland, Anne Wright succeeded magnificently as a leader at the heart of the enterprise.

She recognised that some of the senior academics saw themselves as having no managerial responsibilities. As a result academic freedom had degenerated into anarchy. Most Heads of Schools were unwilling to accept the necessary changes and left by a variety of ways, to be replaced by people attracted by Anne's vision of the future, her drive and credibility. The new, energised team was able to develop and lead the long-term strategy, establish the values and sense of purpose and determine the goals for quality, numerical growth, and for the development of a totally new campus.

These goals have been achieved and in the process she earned the respect of everyone in the university, throughout the academic world, in the local community, and from government. The university is still not in the first division – that accolade will take decades to earn – but it is a university of which people are becoming proud, which is beginning to attract high-calibre academics, and in the new St Peter's Campus has high-quality, state-of-the-art facilities that are the envy of many of the more established universities.

Anne Wright was both at the top and the heart of the enterprise, and the lessons are clear for energising leaders at all levels – you gain respect for your ability to do the job both in its narrow sense of technical capability but also because you can do what leaders do! The balance between 'hands-on' practical performance and 'doing what leaders do' will vary considerably not only by position but also by the needs of the day. Go back three or four paragraphs and note that we determined the criteria we thought necessary *in that polytechnic at that time.* The successor to Anne Wright may require different specific skills but the leadership requirements are very much the same.

When appointing a first-level manager, who will often need to possess a high degree of technical capability, the leadership balance may well be loaded towards that end of the spectrum. In Nissan our approach to appointing first-line supervisors has always been to look for *technical aptitude* (as opposed to task-specific skills) and then emphasise *attitude.* We seek people who have both the aptitude to learn the task-specific skills and who will be the genuine leaders of the team. As I say at virtually every seminar and presentation (hopefully it will soon be unnecessary) one of the fundamental problems of many businesses is that they appoint the best 'doer' to the first level of management rather than the person who combines technical aptitude with a high level of leadership potential.

My first experience of this new approach was in the late 1970s when we were appointing supervisors at the newly established Continental Can Company in Wrexham, North Wales. About half came from the industry bringing their technical expertise with them, and half were local people who had the right technical aptitude but were, we judged, excellent leaders. For the first year those with specific task knowledge were ahead; after a year the local 'leaders' had learned the technical part of the job but their leadership attributes had pulled them ahead. It was this experience which gave me the confidence to insist at Nissan that we gave much greater emphasis to leadership than task-specific skills when appointing our supervisors.

EARNING TRUST

We trust people, not organisations.

In a 1997 survey of business leaders conducted by Amin Rajan and Penny van Eupen of the Centre for Research in Employment and Technology in Europe, the top-rated leadership requirement (with a 75 per cent rating) was:

The ability to inspire trust and motivation.

(Visioning came second, listening skills third, strategic thinking fourth and interpersonal communication skills fifth.)

This is much more difficult to achieve and as we peel through the layers it brings in a number of other attributes which are equally difficult to define. For me, the most important are:

Deliver what you promise
Care for the people and the enterprise

I sometimes ask groups of top executives, 'Put your hand on your heart and ask yourself the question, "Am I trusted throughout my organisation?" Think about it for a few moments, and if the answer is "Yes", raise your hand.' It is difficult and probably unfair but generally only about ten per cent do raise a hand. Sometimes, if we have the opportunity, I ask them if they would be prepared to break into small groups to share their experience and concerns with their peers from other companies. There is no compulsion and no reporting back and I only become involved if unanimously invited, but it is a powerful learning experience from which can begin a total change in behaviour and leadership style.

More frequently I ask business audiences, 'Apart from the obvious crooks, who do you least trust?' You can be certain that the answers will include:

Politicians
Journalists
Lawyers
Consultants
Public relations advisers
Commission-earning sales staff
Financial advisers
Agents
Bosses
and so on

When I then ask why they do not trust such people the answers are invariably on the lines of, 'They never mean what they say', 'They promise but do not deliver', 'They're only in it for what they can get out of it' and so on. People are not stupid. For the most part we quickly discover the phonies, we know the difference between gestures and commitment and we remember the promises that are not carried out.

We see politicians visiting deprived areas, making eloquent statements about creating employment, renovating the housing stock and so on, and then going away to make equally eloquent statements elsewhere about the need to rein in public expenditure.

We note the hypocrisy of journalists who purport to seek the truth but are really only interested in the angle, who dress up any salacious story as being in the public interest and whose own lives would stand little scrutiny.

We are wary of chief executives who say, 'Our people are our greatest asset' but who have no compunction about downsizing when the balance sheet demands it; who make casual promises and then promptly forget them, who award themselves and the top group large salary increases and favourable share options while preaching pay restraint for all others.

We deeply distrust all those who profess to act in our best interest but are primarily concerned with the commission they will earn by selling us an insurance policy, legal advice, a house, an automobile or double glazing.

In all cases their public promises do not match their deeds and this is disastrous, for the public promise can be so powerful when properly used.

I believe in the power of the public promise. Ian Gibson, Nissan's second managing director, and I have stood on platforms before every member of staff and said,

We guarantee that no-one will lose their employment because of productivity improvements.

We could do that because the number of staff and the demand for the product were about in balance; it did not mean that we were immune to the vagaries of the marketplace. It was not contractual but it was 'written in our blood'. It came from two directors who were absolutely committed to the concept that if we expected people to contribute to the continuous improvement process we had to give something back – and that 'giving back' was security of employment.

People will not work to improve performance if they believe that it will result in them losing their jobs. And saying it in public meant that we were deliberately putting ourselves into a position for which we could be held accountable. If we reneged on such a promise our credibility, which we had spent years earning, would disappear in a moment. But being seen openly to give such a promise helps build the trust, and delivering on it when the going gets tough secures it.

Promises can, however, be much more prosaic. Doing what you say you will do is effective at all levels, whether it is the CEO promising that no-one will lose their employment because of productivity improvements or a first-level supervisor promising to sort out a salary query. Failure to deliver has exactly the same effect. 'It's no good asking her, she says she will do something but then forgets all about it!' 'It's no good listening to what he says – he's always quick with his promises but nothing ever happens'. Successful delivery does not always achieve an immediate positive response, but over the years you build a reputation as someone whose word can be trusted and who gets things done.

Successful energising leaders are prepared to make such promises and deliver on them, not just because it is the best way to get the job done but because they *care* about the enterprise and empathise with the people.

Empathy with people is not usually on lists of leadership qualities but in the energised enterprise it is crucial. It means that leaders have a real understanding of the problems affecting people throughout the enterprise. It means caring, not in a superficial 'people are our greatest asset' way, nor in believing they can do no wrong, but because it is the right and natural thing to do. It means recognising that everyone in the enterprise is an individual, each with his or her own aspirations, concerns and needs. Empathy results in leaders understanding the impact of their decisions on people and taking actions that support constructive relationships, whether it is the elimination of illogical differences in treatment or simply talking with people at the grass-roots level in a way which emphasises their importance.

Empathy can make the difference between passive obedience and active loyalty.

Nissan (UK) is one of the leanest automobile manufacturers in the world and by far the leanest in Europe, but in most lean companies, with all the talk of eliminating waste and increasing labour productivity, the one element that is left out of the equation is the impact of ever-reducing waste and ever-increasing labour productivity on the people who are subjected to it! Most companies dress it up by talking about 'working smarter, not harder' but the reality is that as waste is eliminated (any activity that does not add value is waste) and people move towards spending 100 per cent of their time adding value, the pressure on them can, in fact, increase even although each individual activity may be less strenuous.

I discussed this fully in the second edition of *The Ascendant Organisation* but in simple terms I came to realise that there is what I call 'the pressure equation':

$$\text{Pressure} = \text{Frequency} \times \text{Effort}$$

This means that the pressure on an individual is the result of the effort, mental or physical, required to perform a task multiplied by the frequency or pace with which that task is performed. As the amount of effort reduces and a person's task becomes easier he or she *must* perform it more frequently – if not, all the benefits accrue to the individual and none to the company. Performing a simple task more frequently can result in the pressure being greater than a complex task performed infrequently. We do not know for certain what the outcome will be, but the real problem is that most managers do not care!

Let me give a simple physical example.

An assembler has a difficult task during the course of which he has to lift a total of fifty pounds. He performs this task every ten minutes – six times an hour, meaning that each hour he shifts 300 pounds. Along comes an understanding engineer who redesigns the job so that the weight he has to lift reduces to twenty pounds. But as a result it is determined that the easier job can be performed more frequently, say 15 times an hour. The total hourly amount shifted remains at 300 pounds.

Who is to say whether or not the pressure has increased? Under the old way he may have been able to squeeze in some personal relief – under the new way such opportunities may disappear. Under the old way he may have been in danger of straining his back – under the new way he may be in danger of repetitive strain injury. Under the old way he may have been able to switch off – under the new way he will be on the go the whole time. Under the old way the job may have had some semblance of interest – under the new way with its more frequent repetitions it may simply become monotonous.

Such an example may seem trite but I cannot overemphasise the importance of understanding this equation. It took us a long time in Nissan, but while not initially expressed as succinctly, the impact on people of moving towards 100 per cent of their time being spent adding value *was* appreciated by the leaders of the enterprise. We realised that when you are operating at low levels of efficiency, say 40 per cent, a shift to 50 per cent does not place too great a strain on people but when you are at 90 per cent then seeking to move to 95 per cent can have a dramatic impact. As a result we put into place a policy which said:

> **The ergonomics of building a car will be a fundamental factor in the original design, engineering and specification of the product, facility, tooling and processes. Such factors will be included in all changes, improvements and *kaizen* activities.**

(See Chapter 8 for a discussion on *kaizen*.)

The practical actions that followed were both preventive and remedial (see Wickens, 1998, *The Ascendant Organisation,* revised and updated edition, pp. 47–52 for a more detailed description) and challenged some of our sacred cows, but their impact was huge – everything we did was aimed at reducing the pressure on people. Supervisors and managers were then formally assessed on their performance towards this objective.

That is what I mean by caring.

Ask yourself if you can give similar illustrations from your own experience. The pressure equation applies just as much to mental work as to physical, and in many practices such as call centres and the back offices of financial institutions the parallels are highly appropriate. In senior positions the frequency may be lower but the mental effort considerably greater. We are all subject to the pressure equation and when the result is too high, that is when we are damaged, either physically or mentally.

Trust is however a two-way process. Appointing good people and genuinely devolving responsibility are two of the most difficult and most important tasks for any leader. Learning what you do *not* need to know is even more difficult and requires tremendous trust and confidence in those working for you, but when achieved, such trust can permeate the whole of your part of the enterprise. On occasions I took pride in telling Managing Director, Toshiaki Tsuchiya that I did not know the answers to his detailed questions and that I would ask the appropriate person to come to talk with him. That tells people you have confidence in them, that you trust them and that they can make decisions without your having to know, and it inspires them to greater things. It works both ways, for you need to trust those working for you for them to trust you. Leading and following are inextricably entwined. The motto of the Royal Military Academy, Sandhurst is *Serve to Lead*. They have got it right!

SHARING GOALS

How often have you heard cries such as:

Nobody told me what we were supposed to be doing!

One person tells me one thing, then someone else comes along and tells me something else!

The bosses have no idea what it's like down here. They set impossible tasks and then give us a kicking when we do not achieve them!

Quite honestly, I'm not interested in all this stuff about being world-class and achieving the best quality. As long as I am paid – that's all that matters to me.

The goals of an enterprise are the tangible expression of its values and strategy. We have already discussed strategy and will turn to values in Chapters 5 and 6. However, values and strategy are fine but unless we develop shared, tangible goals which are widely known and frequently reaffirmed the values and strategy may well drift away. Using the fashionable terminology of recent years I have often asked conference audiences and top management seminars to explain the difference between vision and mission, and it does not take long for confusion rather than clarity to reign. Which, I guess, is the prime reason why seeking to define vision and mission has not had too much impact on businesses. However, everyone understands what a goal is – a target to be achieved.

Sometimes that understanding comes out of adversity – 'If we do not win the order we're all out of a job' – but such understanding is short-lived and no basis for long-term sustainable success. At other times it comes from a powerful chief executive who is a brilliant communicator. Jack Welch set his famous goal for General Electric, 'Become No.1 or No. 2 in every market it serves.' 3M UK speaks of:

To provide and deliver on time, products and services that conform to agreed specification in line with customer requirements.

Dräger, the German world leader in incubators says simply, 'Top position: We want to stay ahead!' (Simon, 1996: 29)

The great thing about a top-level goal is that when properly expressed it is clear to everyone – you know what you have to do and how long you have to achieve it. You also know *when* you have achieved it.

One of the most famous goals of all time was set by President John F Kennedy in 1961.

> **This nation should commit itself to achieving the goal, before this decade is out, of landing a man on the moon and returning him safely to earth.**

Although often referred to as a mission, JFK actually used the word 'goal'. 'Mission' had not been thought of in 1961 and his language was simple, direct and readily understandable. He used the word 'should' because he was seeking to persuade Congress to provide the funding, but so persuasive was he that Congress had little alternative but to agree. Kennedy's brilliantly communicated goal ensured that everyone knew what was expected of them and by when, and success or failure would be clear. How often can you say that about so-called mission statements? Latter-day commentators and advocates of missions and visions would do well to study the simplicity, directness and power of JFK's language. And that power continued even after his assassination in 1963.

The goals of JFK and Jack Welch each came from the drive of one man – they were BIG goals, and when you are the president of a country or the chief executive of a company you are in the position to set the challenges for your whole population. And they can work – provided that such a style is one with which the leader is comfortable, that the leader can communicate it effectively, and that it is right that the enterprise should seek to be the biggest and the best!

James Collins and Jerry Porras in their excellent book *Built to Last* eulogise what they call BHAGs – Big Hairy Audacious Goals. They praise the audacity of companies such as:

◆ Boeing, which from 1952 successfully transformed itself from being a military aircraft manufacturer to becoming a major player in the commercial aircraft industry. (Boeing is in the late 1990s implementing some 48,000 redundancies – nothing fails like success!)

◆ Cigarette manufacturer Philip Morris, which in 1952 held only ten per cent of the market but set itself the goal of becoming 'the General Motors of the tobacco industry' (before General Motors became a 'dog'), and

◆ Sam Walton's Wal-Mart (Wal-Mart is one of those companies which manages to feature in virtually every American business book – and is the one o'clock starting point for numerous business fads) in which the founder set ever-increasing goals which took it from a five-and-ten-cent store in Newport, Arkansas in 1945 to the largest retailer in the world by the early 1990s.

Such powerful goals make good stories in business leadership books (they rarely mention those entrepreneurs whose goals are about simply survival or 'Be successful and sell up and retire!') and can temporarily enthuse the vast majority who stand not a snowball's chance in hell of emulating the Sam Waltons and Jack Welches of this world.

Most such goals talk of being Number One (surely, not *everyone* can be Number One!) but even if you do not want to build your enterprise into being the biggest and the best in the world, there can be no doubt that establishing clear goals can have a major impact – or they can be just another list of weasel numbers which satisfy the planners and the chief executive, but are little known and rarely shared throughout the company. Consequently they have little impact on the business, and are long forgotten by the time the target date comes along! Sometimes they are changed too frequently, on other occasions they are too soft and attaining them has little impact on the business, or they may be too tough and end up by demoralising the non-achievers. Often they end up as bookshelf or bottom drawer plans.

When your company is in bad shape how many 'hockey-stick projections' do you see, that is, a downward slope for the next three years followed by an upward shift towards the end of the planning period? Most such goals are wishful thinking and by the time the reference date arrives those responsible have probably moved on and the planning document is deep down in someone's filing system!

Below the grand 'Be Number One' statements the process is more serious and precise. The BICC Group in 1993 set clear goals for its worldwide cable making business:

Scrap:	**2 per cent**
Rework:	**Zero**
Manufacturing inventory:	**Reduce by 80 per cent**
Delivery performance:	**98 per cent on time**
Productivity:	**Double**

In 1997 Calsonic compared its radiator plant with its sister operation in Japan and established the aim for the year 2000 'To achieve the same level of performance as Atsugi'. To know precisely what they were aiming for they published their key goals showing sister plant, Atsugi's performance in 1996, their own current performance and their target for 1999.

Subject	Item	Measure	Atsugi	Calsonic current	Calsonic 1999
Quality	Customer defects	Parts per million	1.5	408	10
	Process defects	%	0.9	8	0.8
	Supplier defects	Parts per million	19	1010	50
Cost	Labour productivity per year	% improvement	114	115	115
	Scrap	%	0.4	1.6	0.4
	Machine downtime	%	1.3	3.6	1.3
Delivery	Overall equipment efficiency	%	83	63	83
Safety	Lost time accidents	Per annum	1	4	0
Morale	Kaizen team participation	% of workforce	96	13	75
	Solutions per team	No. per year	4	0.5	3

For the outsider the detail is not important, but look at the gaps between where they are now and where they want to be and imagine the effort that will be needed to close them, remembering that Atsugi will not stand still. But the important point is that *inside the company* everyone knows what has to be achieved. For example Atsugi is currently sending only 1.5 parts per million defects to its customers against Calsonic's 408! Imagine the amount of work required to achieve the goal of ten defects per million! Atsugi's suppliers deliver only 19 defects per million parts supplied; Calsonic's suppliers send it 1010! Imagine the amount of work required to achieve the goal of 50 defects per million. To get there requires the whole company to be energised.

But knowing what is to be achieved and achieving it are two very different things, particularly when the people in your enterprise have spent years erecting Chinese walls (or Iron Curtains), often barely speaking to each other and when they do, limiting information to the minimum possible. A critical task in an energised enterprise is to break down these divisions, to share the goals and to get everyone working together to achieve them; in short to ensure that *the goals are aligned throughout the enterprise.*

It is easy to set performance goals at the top of an organisation and cascade them down as did BICC and Calsonic – good old Management by Objectives (MBO) – but *aligning* is very different from cascading. It is much more difficult and significantly more time consuming, but when done properly can have an extraordinary impact. It is about shifting the perspective so that the goals of the enterprise and the goals of the individual are working to the same end. Gaining the commitment of everyone, not only to the top-level goals but also to the goals of their part of the enterprise, is the real prize. Goal alignment is another piece in the energising jigsaw and, while eventually it permeates all levels of the enterprise, it must start at the top.

We are all used to Management by Objectives but look at Figure 4.1.

Goal alignment occurs when people at *all* levels of the enterprise and in all functions and divisions *work together to define and achieve their shared goals.* Look at the arrows – they point both up and down, indicating that people at the lower level do not just receive goals from those above but that they can contribute to defining and amending the goals of those at the higher level. This is the fundamental difference with MBO. Under goal alignment the process is two-way. It can be called catch ball. But it also differs from management by objectives in other ways, see Figure 4.2.

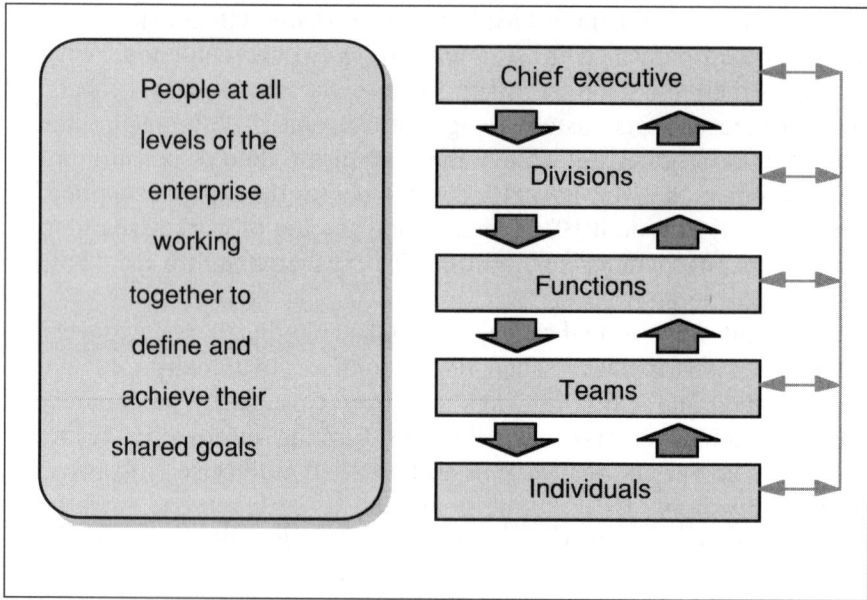

Figure 4.1   Goal alignment

Figure 4.2   Goal alignment and MBO compared

Goal alignment is concerned with *how* the results are achieved; about helping rather than on pinning blame; it is about discussion rather than dictation.

It is not easy. It requires weeks of painstaking discussions in which people at all levels meet and bounce ideas off each other. And by discussion I do not mean some two minute meeting based on, 'I've drawn these up. Anyone got any problems? No. Right, we'll run with them. Do not say I didn't give you a chance!' I mean a genuine two-way exchange with ideas bouncing between the levels, defining and refining the goals to make them tough but realistic and achievable and, at the same time, gaining commitment to clear time-bounded measurable targets and progress indicators. You have to establish these before the event so that everyone knows whether or not they have succeeded, not some fuzzy, after-the-event, 'We think we did OK on that one', based on opinion rather than fact.

But it is more than that. On the right of Figure 4.1 you can see other linkages, less clearly defined, which are meant to indicate that people at any level can talk to people at any other level and in any other function or division *without necessarily having to go through the intermediate level.* Many will hold their hands up in horror at this, and I do not suggest it as the starting point; but is it not reasonable to aim for a time when it becomes possible for any person to speak directly to any other in an open and non-threatening way?

It means discussing the *how*, so that everyone understands the part they will play; what the priorities are; who will take the lead in which area; whether innovation teams are required and who will participate. It requires an appreciation of whether assistance is required from outside the group and who should be brought in. It also requires an appreciation of how the goals fit in with 'higher' goals and how they will impact on the 'lower'. What you are seeking is an appreciation of other peoples' goals, how they interrelate and whether you need or can give assistance. You can't go merrily down your own path at the expense of fouling up everyone else.

Going back to the top-level goals there are some fundamental questions. How do you know that they are the right goals for the enterprise? Are they shared by the top team? In seeking to get people to commit to the goals of the enterprise could it be that you are asking them to unite around something that is too soft, too tough or fundamentally wrong? And if this is the case could you not be doing more harm than good, having people happily marching together to destruction? All this goal definition is good stuff but if it is taking you in the wrong direction is it not better that you never start the journey?

These questions were prompted by an experience in 1994 when I sat with the board of directors of a company which manufactures printed circuit boards. Naively, I asked them if they could tell me their key goals. This should not be too great a problem (I thought) because the managing director had previously shown me their agreed written statement and my question was no more than a memory test. After three hours of fairly unstructured and sometimes acrimonious debate they just about reached agreement on ten goals, of which only three coincided with the MD's list, three were in the same area but with the specifics changed, and four were totally new! There has to be a better way.

That better way is a goal definition and alignment exercise. Over the years I have found that the following process works superbly:

Step one

Ask each member of the top team individually to write down around ten financial and non-financial measures they consider should be included in their company's top level key performance indicators (KPI). These are the ten measures they believe really matter, so that just by looking at them they should be able to get a good appreciation of the health of their enterprise. At this stage they do not have to specify the targets, only the broad areas. Share their lists by having each person in turn calling it out with the facilitator recording them on the flip chart. Ensure that the top person present goes last!

Let me give a real example of one company's initial listing of possible KPIs:

Sales level	First to 'Own Label' market	Units packed per period
Employee turnover	Reduction of overheads to sales	Data integrity
World class manufacturing rating	New product success rate	Fixed costs
Standard margin	RM costs	S&M costs
Return on sales	Customer perception	Environmental
Stock-outs	Right-first-time delivery	RTM costs
Warehouse inventory	Supplier quality	Time to market
Product development costs	Sales growth	Quality improvements
Market share growth by category	Customer service	Production efficiency
GMP vs competitors	Customer satisfaction	Sales trend
Reduce production plan changes	Percentage share of Group turnover	Staff costs
Logistics costs	Forecasted orders on book	Labour utilisation
Staff skills	Cash flow	Right-first-time performance
Rejects	Supplier efficiency	Supplier costs
No. of product launches	Product obsolescence	Return on capital employed
Absenteeism	Debtors days	Cost of sales/average stock
Operating expenses/cost of sales ratio	Credit period taken	Accuracy of sales forecasts

This from a company in which the managing director had already defined what he considered to be the key performance indicators!

With the obvious duplicates being previously eliminated the eight top managers between them came up with 51 different possible KPIs! (Experience shows that this initial number will about 60 per cent of the maximum possible, that is with eight participants the maximum number of different KPIs is 80 and the minimum ten. The actual number will be close to 50). Chief executives are always astounded! (In another exercise, twelve members of the top team came up with 74 different corporate key performance indicators – they had recently gone away for a weekend 'State of the Nation' session and the managing director expected that based on these discussions the maximum number would have been about twenty!)

When I then told the group that if they end up with more than ten top level KPIs they will have too many, not a few eyebrows were raised! But this *must* be the end result, for if your KPIs are to be meaningful you cannot have dozens of them – all you then do is cause confusion and disseminated effort.

Clearly some are more properly departmental goals, there are overlaps and some lack clarity or are meaningless departmental jargon, but at least everything is out on the table; everyone knows what the others consider to be important. With this sharing of opinion there comes the beginning of understanding.

Ask them then together to go through the initial list distinguishing the top level from the departmental, eliminating the overlaps and so on. I do not intend to take you through every detail but you will find that as people replace their functional or divisional hat with a corporate hat it is not too difficult for them to reduce the list by half (but do not throw away your rejects – you will need them later) and with a little more effort end up with say fifteen or so. Do not force them below this number – the 'surplus' will later fall out quite naturally.

Divide them into groups of about four people, with each group taking half of the indicators. If possible ensure that each group has someone with specialist knowledge about each of the remaining indicators, and task them with defining a specific measure for each indicator and then determine where they are now against that measure and where they aim to be within three years. This will be difficult for they are unlikely to have enough information, but the task is designed first to make them question the indicators (from which there will be further fallouts) and second to enable them to determine the information they need.

The groups report back to a plenary session, share their understanding and views and seek agreement on the top level KPIs and the broad measures to be used.

That is enough for one day, but it does not end there. Remember the two-way arrows. Discuss the outcome with the next level down, get their views and be prepared to listen, learn and amend when appropriate. Work on the indicators and make sure you have them right and that the measures and goals are meaningful and motivational. Also, work out who has the lead responsibility for each indicator and specifically determine what others need do to help – previously this would have been difficult but having gone through the process and having achieved an unheard of level of understanding I guarantee you that it will all fall into place!

The company with its initial 51 indicators came up with the following nine KPIs:

Key Performance Indicator	Current	Target 1998	Target 1999	Target 2000
1 Sales growth from existing customers	£22m	£25m	£28m	£30m
2 Return on capital employed	39.9%	41%	46%	50%
3 Return on sales	6.9%	9.0%	11.0%	50%
4 Delivery of right quantity at the right time to the right place:	91%	93%	95%	98%
5 Cost of factory and customer rejects as percentage of sales	0.7%	0.6%	0.5%	0.4%
6 Stability index: Attendance x staff retention	72%	75%	78%	80%
7 World class manufacturing index (Twenty Keys score)	35.5	40	45	48
8 Materials spend with core suppliers	50%	60%	70%	75%
9 Stock holding: Raw materials	5 wks	4.5 wks	4.0 wks	3.5 wks
Finished goods	9 wks	8.0 wks	7.8 wks	7.5 wks

We need not bother with the detail and you or I might not fully agree with the indicators – I would have preferred to see a more tangible measure of customer satisfaction and something on the training and development of their staff, but in the end it has to be the company's list, not the consultant's. The point is that the top team worked together to develop its KPIs and as a result the commitment is total and considerably greater than the previous indicators which had been established by the managing director and handed down with but cursory consultation.

The objective however must be to ensure that these goals are shared throughout the enterprise and at the end to have them available to all, continuously updated and preferably on-line so that anyone can tap into a PC anywhere in the business and find out immediately how the business is performing against its KPIs. But before you get there you need a few more stages. But do not worry, it is just more of the same.

Step two (and three and four...)

It is too simple to say 'Repeat the process at every level in the enterprise' but the principle is right. Those people directly reporting to the top team will already have had an involvement, but their task now is to take the top KPIs as their starting point and led by their boss, who participated in the earlier stage, conduct a similar exercise in their own functions, divisions and so on

This step is not, however, a simple handing down of the tablets of stone for, as the upward arrows in Figure 4.1 indicate, it is vital that those at the lower level have the opportunity to comment on the initial goals determined by the top group. Observations along the lines of 'You must be crazy if you think that is attainable' is one of the more polite responses! This is the catch ball process which is difficult and painful, but which is vital if the higher level goals are to be both realistic and shared. This does not mean that they should not be stretching goals – the world is full of easy goals we know we will achieve, and 'impossible to achieve' goals. The trick is to get the balance right. And when people are prepared to listen and, when appropriate, modify the original that is when the goals start to make sense.

The second objective is for the lower level then to go through a similar process to determine their own KPIs which will enable them to contribute to the top goals.

In effect, at each stage the higher level in conjunction with the lower level determines 'what' needs to be achieved, and the lower level in conjunction with its lower level determines 'how' it will be achieved. One level's 'whats' become the next level's 'hows'.

It sounds complicated doesn't it? But give it a try and you will find that the complex words on paper translate easily into a process which will be readily understood by all people at all levels. But much more important than that, you will find yet again that with involvement comes commitment and ownership. For goals are useless until they are shared and aligned. Then they become so powerful that their achievement almost becomes a self-fulfilling prophecy.

Note: Those readers who have heard of or gone through the process known to the Japanese as *hoshin kanri* (policy deployment) will recognise much of the foregoing. But you will also know that it is an extremely difficult and sometimes painful process. Having been on the receiving end it is not a process I would wish on anyone and for my own work with companies I developed the simpler and more direct approach described above.

INSPIRING PEOPLE

This is the most difficult of all. Effective leaders can inspire people to achieve great things but very often they do not know how they do it.

When discussing leadership with top managers I often ask them to assess whether or not they believe they inspire people throughout the enterprise. They score themselves on a scale of 1 to 10 on three given statements, with 1 and 2 covering the left-hand statement, 3 to 8 covering the middle and 9 and 10 the right-hand statement:

Top managers are seen as 'the grey suits'. They/we are not much known and their/our impact on people is minimal.	Top mangers are known, and are thought to be effective, but do not inspire people to achieve great things.	Top managers are known throughout the enterprise for positive leadership, vision and drive. They/we inspire extraordinary performance from others.

This is but one of 26 leadership characteristics. The ensuing discussion is often very difficult but the results are powerful – particularly when people at other levels undertake the same assessment and we then compare the results! This final step of bringing everyone together has to be treated with caution, and is not always the smart thing to do, but if everybody has the courage to speak and listen in an open, constructive and non-threatening way the learning experience is powerful and the subsequent behaviour changes profound.

As always there will be the 'naturals' – some leaders *are* born, but most of us have to build on what we have and learn; but if we are to inspire people what is it that we have to learn? Also, do we not read of different leadership styles for different situations? Did not Hersey and Blanchard, writing in 1982 about situational leadership, tell us that in different situations we have to direct, coach, support or delegate? But like all such models its value lies in providing a focus for analysis, not in providing a prescription for everyday behaviour. Real life is not divided into neat compartments in which we consciously switch from one mode to the next. In real life we either say, 'This is me – you take me for what I am' or we subconsciously mix everything up while trying slightly to modify our behaviour according to the circumstances; rarely do we adopt the pure version of a single style.

There is no contradiction in directing, coaching, supporting and delegating all at the same time. All that practically happens is that the emphasis changes slightly. Anyway, Hersey and Blanchard were more about effective management than inspirational leadership!

When we break it down to its most fundamental level I would put forward the view that:

> **Leaders inspire when they know what they want to achieve, communicate it effectively and ensure that others want the same thing.**

It's almost going back to my earlier definition of leadership, but it is somewhat more complicated than that!

One inspirational leader is Albert Hickman, Operations Manager of Thorn Lighting of Spennymoor, County Durham, who from 1988 has led the transformation of a British manufacturing company which previously had ineffective leadership, an inflexible workforce, outdated employment practices and antiquated manufacturing technology and processes into a company genuinely able to compete in the world marketplace.

Thorn Lighting's story well illustrates the power of inspirational leadership. The company's deteriorating competitive position in the mid-1980s led a new top team to conduct a thorough business review, which concluded that the company needed 'to move rapidly to a market-led culture dedicated to satisfying customer demand' and that if it was to achieve this goal there had to be changes in every aspect of the business.

One element of this was to move to so-called world-class manufacturing and this was Albert Hickman's baby.

Albert recognised that if the goal was to be achieved it would require a fundamental change of attitude throughout the company and the big challenge was to inspire people. He asked, 'How do you get 1100 people to understand where you want to go and get them to change attitudes and traditions held over 40 years?' Although in retrospect the process looks neat and tidy it did not appear that way at the time, but in all such processes the vital first step is to *show* commitment at the top. Says Albert Hickman:

It was vitally important for everyone to see *and more important feel* that there was a genuine and sincere commitment from the people leading Thorn Lighting towards a long-term philosophy of continuous improvement. It was equally important that everyone was committed to the need for change and for us the breakthrough came when we recognised that *the more you educate people the more they are receptive to change.*

Albert is passionate about education. One of his favourite one-liners is:

IF YOU THINK EDUCATION IS EXPENSIVE – TRY IGNORANCE!

As I have continually emphasised such commitment does not come from fine words, nor is it possible to put subsequent actions into discrete, sequential boxes – many things happen at the same time. But Thorn Lighting's explanatory sequence is:

1. **Gain commitment at the top**
2. **Create the environment for change**
3. **Understand world-class manufacturing**
4. **Educate for change**
5. **Establish the manufacturing policy**
6. **Create a steering committee**
7. **Team build**
8. **Educate the workforce**
9. **Implement pilots**
10. **Implement large scale introduction**
11. **Continuously improve**

I will conclude this book with a generic model for energised change and it begins with *understanding*. For Albert Hickman the really crucial stages were to gain commitment at the top, to *understand* world class manufacturing, to educate for change and to educate the workforce. So often companies begin a change programme without really understanding what it is about nor what it entails and, as a result, they are surprised at the amount of hard work it takes and cannot believe that the outcomes are not what they initially thought they would be. Thorn Lighting did not make this mistake.

Albert Hickman and the production managers, engineers and senior trade union officials attended seminars run by Richard Schonberger and visited companies such as Black and Decker, IBM, ICL and Nissan. They became inspired by what they saw as being possible to achieve. Later, production staff studied Schonberger's videos and were given training in JIT, preventive maintenance, statistical process control, continuous improvement and problem solving methods. But alongside this they worked on the 'soft' areas – three layers of management were eliminated to improve communications; team briefings were introduced; they threw out the stop watch; months of negotiation ended restrictive demarcation practices and paved the way for flexible working; the troublesome bonus scheme was eliminated and a new productivity payment scheme introduced; 1000 people went through a team-building programme and learned the early lesson that they had to create the environment at work which reflected their new-found spirit. They also learned that *everyone* has something to offer.

Throughout this process Albert Hickman led from the front, being seen to challenge the *status quo*, and the top team walked like they talked, and in particular stayed true to their fundamental belief that it is people that matter. Within their aim to become 'a world-class supplier of lighting solutions' their eventual Mission Statement said:

> **By involving all employees in the process of continuous improvement, we will exceed our internal and external customers' expectations, providing quality products and services at a competitive price, ensuring the profitable long-term growth of the company.**

Thorn Lighting conducts regular anonymous 'climate surveys' among all its staff and a typical comment from the latest survey said:

We feel genuinely involved and firmly believe we contribute to the success of the business. That makes us feel important.

For Albert Hickman, that is what it is all about – ensuring that everyone *is* important. When you accompany him on the shop floor the overwhelming feeling is one of pride – his pride in the people and they in him. He is no shrinking violet – he knows everyone and they know him, and you can feel the warmth between them and the mutual respect. When he talks of Thorn Lighting you can *feel* the enthusiasm and commitment. Recall the earlier comment about his wanting people to feel the genuine and sincere commitment of the leaders – it is there in spadefuls.

But Albert also constantly challenges – the *status quo* is unacceptable – you can always do better. He likes to try ideas out on people and when going through the major change programme he ensured that all the ideas were discussed with people from the shop-floor and they were listened to. 'It's getting people to buy into it.' Now, he frequently has informal chats with the trade union shop stewards and asks them what they think of an idea. This is not a weak manager trying to get the blessing of a powerful trade union but a strong leader confident in himself who regards it as entirely reasonable that constructive representatives have a valuable contribution to make.

Let us look at an example which comes from different angle. You cannot earn acceptance of your inspiration unless you put yourself about – properly. The managing director of a company I work with, regularly put himself about on the shop floor – he thought he was great at 'managing by walking around' – but as far as the troops were concerned, 'You only see him down here when there's trouble.'

One day, when running an Effective Communications programme for the top managers I invited this MD along to the wrap up session. It went well, he was in a great mood and intuitively, at the end, I suggested that as everyone was together he might like to say something about the issues facing the company and give us his thoughts about the way forward. Without any pre-warning or rehearsal he spoke brilliantly for half an hour, covering areas he had never discussed before, demonstrating a clarity of purpose previously unseen, even by the top group. Their response was tremendous – for the first time he had really shared something important and they felt genuinely inspired. They were emphatic that he simply had to put that same message over to everyone in the company. It took some persuading, and a lot of coaching, but the eventual outcome was again brilliant. He fielded high quality questions in a confident and open manner, and judging from subsequent comments, ended up with the beginning of a respect and trust that previously had been denied him.

We need to remember that the majority of people do not have many opportunities of seeing their chief executive in action. But if they are to develop trust and confidence in their leaders, let alone be inspired by them, what better opportunity can there be to demonstrate that they have a grip on the business, that they understand the key issues and can point the way forward in a way which shows their ability to relate to the staff? Virtually none.

One managing director said to me, 'I know what you mean but I just haven't got the time.' What he really meant was that it was low on his priority list and he didn't have the inclination. Sometimes, when all else fails, you just have to shame people into doing things they would prefer not to – and this includes CEOs. Sometimes, even they are frightened of getting up on their feet to address large numbers of people, 'I'm the CEO – people expect me to be an effective speaker and I can't put myself in a position in which I dry up. My credibility will go down the tubes.'

Think of it. When company chiefs say that they do not have the time or inclination to communicate, they are telling you – and signalling to everyone else – that they have got their priorities all wrong. We've always got the time to do those things we believe to be important and enjoy doing. If it is a real difficulty, provide training and support, then with practice and experience, confidence will come. It's great to help it happen.

Moving from the specific to the general, are there any lessons to be learned from Albert Hickman and my non-communicating MD about earning acceptance of your inspiration? (Of course there are or I wouldn't ask the question!)

First is the need to have a clear vision of what you want to achieve. You can express it in different ways – providing the direction and focus, knowing your goals, establishing the standards and so on, but they all mean very much the same. This does not mean that everything must be determined in detail – indeed inspirational leaders are those who encourage others to put the flesh on the bone. Inspirational leaders set challenging goals for themselves and the enterprise, and *demonstrate a determination to succeed*. They do not give up. They are not deflected by short-term adversity. They are never satisfied with the existing way of doing things or the current standard achieved, and constantly seeks innovation in all areas of the business.

They communicate effectively both in what they say and what they do. This does not mean they are always grand orators, although the ability to speak fluently and effectively is a skill which can greatly improved with proper training and experience – Toshiaki Tsuchiya did not even speak English but no-one was ever in any doubt as to what he wanted for Nissan – and when he was on the shop floor or with suppliers his deep understanding of the processes and the business virtually communicated itself.

But for the inspirational leader communication is multidirectional and it reaches both inside and outside the enterprise. The effective communicator can relate to customers, suppliers, shareholders and staff throughout the enterprise. I love using a slide which brings out everything that real communication is about and likens it to a family group who:

> **Talk together**
>
> **About what is relevant**
>
> **For you and your group**
>
> **Not written or rehearsed**
>
> **Not from 'on high'**
>
> **But from the heart**

Think of a family – mother, father and children – talking at the breakfast table. They do not discuss the state of the world using business-level language; they talk about matters relevant to them. It is not written or rehearsed but from the heart. That is what real communication is about and it is how real communication in a business environment should be conducted. It is not about great presentations with sexy visuals, elegant videos or corporate newspapers – it is about taking the time to relate to people openly and honestly in a way you both understand. When you have such a system in place it then becomes easy for 'the great message from on high' to be slotted in on those few occasions on which it is needed.

Toshiaki Tsuchiya and Albert Hickman genuinely care both for the business and the people, and this communicates itself to everyone with whom they come into contact. Being prepared *to go to* people, not always expecting them to come to you, is a trait exemplified by the late Princess Diana. She was prepared physically to touch those to whom other Royals never got close; she was prepared to talk to people in their language, not expect them to talk in hers. Having been with her and with other members of the Royal Family and having seen them talk with different types of people one clear characteristic she had above all the others was that she genuinely cared and was able to communicate this caring – much more in her private actions than in her public utterances. As much as anything it was this which inspired those she met.

Not many leaders enjoy such a natural ability – but you can work on it. You can be open and honest in everything you do and say; you can be approachable so that if people believe it important that they speak to you, then you can make sure that it is seen to be important to you. You can always make the time to do those things you consider to be most important. Do you make the time to talk with people many layers below you in your hierarchy?

You can also learn to listen. One of the most profound documents I have ever seen comes from the training programme for people who wish to become Samaritans. While I have rephrased it slightly it is still not 100 per cent applicable to a business context. However, I did not want to adulterate it too much as it is so beautiful in its original. Read it carefully:

AM I LISTENING TO YOU?

I *am not* listening to you when:

I do not care for you

I say I understand before I know you well

I have an answer for your problem before you've finished telling me what your problem is

I cut you off before you've finished speaking

I finish your sentence for you

I am critical of your grammar, vocabulary or accent

I am dying to tell you something

I tell you about my experiences, making yours seem unimportant

I am really communicating with someone else in the room

I refuse your thanks saying I haven't really done anything

I *am* listening to you when:

I come quietly into your private world and let you be you

I really try to understand you even if you're not making much sense

I grasp your point of view even when it's against my own convictions

I realise that the time you give to me is very important

I allow you the dignity of making your own decisions even though I may think they are wrong

I do not take your problem from you, but allow you to deal with it in your own way

I hold back my desire to give you good advice

I give you room to discover for yourself what is really going on

I accept your gratitude by telling you how good it is to know I have been helpful

---

Now read it again. Translate it into your own business context and ask yourself how listening in such a way can help you do your own job. I would be inspired by a leader who practised such behaviour and have yet to find anyone who is not moved by it.

How you translate your values, strategy and goals into actions can inspire – or fail to inspire. The Japanese are fond of saying that *how* you do things is often more important than *what* you do, and I can understand their thinking. We have already discussed strategy and goals, and to some degree have put the cart before the horse. Let us now turn to values and sense of purpose.

5
Values First

One of the most persistent business fads over the last few years (now approaching ten o'clock on the 'fad cycle') has been our love affair with so-called culture, vision and mission. In *The Ascendant Organisation* my chapter on this topic was titled 'Culture, vision, mission – whatever you call it', suggesting that our working lives have become imbued with this mixed-up, vainglorious pot-pourri. And when you add in motherhood and apple pie statements, something on goals, a bit of strategy, a statement of principles and so on, the result is to confuse rather than clarify. Rarely do they inspire and never do they energise

I spoke of 'culture', arguing that every organisation has a culture, whether it likes it or not. The chief executive who proclaims, 'We do not bother with this culture stuff, we know what we've got to do. We all work hard to make a profit or we go out of business!' is, in fact, directly expressing the company's culture; for culture is not about what you say, it is about what you do. The fact that you 'have no culture but simply work hard to make a profit' *is* your culture.

The managing director of a drop forging company complained to me of the years of accumulated garbage on the shop floor (it really was the most disgusting workplace I have ever seen); the antiquity of his equipment (some was 100 years old and, to say the least, was not working too well); the uncooperative attitude of the staff; the vast piles of inventory before, during and after processing and their poor profitability. He lamented, 'I know what needs to be done but I can never get people to snap out of their lethargy and do it!'

That MD was directly expressing his company's culture, emanating from his lack of leadership, and while his cry from the heart may seem somewhat distant from the oft-quoted leaders of exemplar companies, it was not a million miles from the everyday reality of many managers.

'Vision' and 'mission' are also overused words. How many companies do you know which have 'Mission Statements' reproduced on glossy laminated sheets displayed in the reception area and carried around on plasticised $3'' \times 4''$ cards? Usually they have been written by the CEO or a small group of top managers and handed down like the tablets of stone. They often mix up top-level corporate platitudes such as 'We are on a journey to excellence', 'We aim to be world class in all we do', and 'We intend to be No. 1 in customer satisfaction' with broad homilies such as 'Our people are our greatest asset' and 'The customer is king'. Rarely are the corporate goals broken into targets and measures which are meaningful to people at the operating level. Just what does 'world class' mean to an assembly line worker or the processor of insurance claims? Come to think of it, what does it mean to top managers? Within your own company, try to find a shared definition – you will have some difficulty.

Further, such statements are usually prefixed by '*We*', with the originator assuming the right to speak on behalf of everyone in the organisation. The fact that the chief executive aims for the company to be 'world class in all we do' says nothing to the front liners. The chief executive often believes that *saying* 'We' *achieves* 'We'. Nothing could be further from the truth.

People are, in the long run, inspired by actions not by words, and rarely are those apart from the top management inspired by the written mission statement; rarely do others deeply and instinctively relate to it, and even more rarely does managerial behaviour consistently reflect the words on the laminated card. We are so influenced by the publicised success stories of a few high-profile, self-selected companies that we tend to believe that everyone behaves this way – they do not! Further, we believe almost everything that is written about these companies, forgetting that most of it originates from top executives who have a vested interest in promoting success; from academics who do not wish to upset those who have given them cooperation, or from consultants who wish to publicise their own achievements. Rarely do we question the *depth* of implementation and acceptance, and even more rarely do we hear from those on the receiving end – the people at the operating level.

Having read scores of mission statements and experienced the lack of awareness and non-implementation at operating level of the words on the paper, the only possible conclusion is that they have, for the most part, singularly failed to inspire.

How then do we reach the point where people at all levels share an *understanding*, are *inspired* by, are *committed* to and *behave* in accordance with 'the way we do things around here'?

Understanding comes from involvement, not from receiving handed down tablets of stone or from isolated examples of inspirational behaviour. Then, with understanding comes the recognition that rarely is there one all-embracing statement that can be meaningful to everyone at every level – it does not exist. But the search is not a waste of time. When undertaken properly it is a powerful exercise of trust and the very process can begin to energise your enterprise.

One of the major problems is that the searches conducted over the last two decades have begun in the wrong place. 'Understanding' cannot be achieved if the search begins with an attempt to *define* our wish list of culture, vision and mission. These things cannot be *defined* – they have to be *discovered*. But there is something else. Deeper down, lying behind strategy, culture, vision and mission are our *values*.

> **Values are the small number of central and enduring principles that guide all aspects of our behaviour.**

When in late 1984 we were thinking about how we wanted to manage Nissan, we visited many companies including, as one would expect at that time, IBM. One of the most significant learning points was that that IBM had a coherent and shared set of values, the need for which had been clearly set out some twenty years earlier by Thomas J. Watson, Jnr, son of the founder. He put it brilliantly when he said:

> **I firmly believe that any organisation, in order to survive and achieve success, must have a sound set of beliefs on which it premises all its policies and actions. Next, I believe the most important single factor in corporate success is faithful adherence to those beliefs... Beliefs must always come before policies, practices and goals. The latter must always be altered if they are seen to violate fundamental beliefs. (Watson, 1963)**

Watson's *beliefs* were, in fact, values, and for him it was all about respect for the individual and 'How well the organisation brings out the great energies and talents of its people'. Translating the words into practice, IBM's later booklet, *Employment at IBM – Principles at Work* said:

> **Concern for the individual cements the foundation of our personnel philosophies in full employment, promotion from within, equal opportunity, pay for performance, and single status... Our challenge is to keep our practice in line with our principles.**

For IBM, the basic values were all about people, which may be one of the reasons it later took its eye off the ball called 'product'. But values are not always solely people-related.

Akio Morita, joint founder of Sony, in his book *Made in Japan* wrote of the early days of the Sony spirit as 'a statement in which we believed', and very obviously still do. He continued:

> **We first said Sony is a pioneer and that it never intends to follow others. 'Through progress, Sony wants to serve the whole world,' we said and went on to say that in doing so the company would be 'always a seeker of the unknown.'...We also said this: 'The road of a pioneer is full of difficulties but in spite of the many hardships, people of Sony always unite harmoniously and closely because of their joy of participating in creative work and their pride in contributing their own unique talents to this aim. Sony has a principle of respecting and encouraging one's ability and always tries to bring out the best in a person and believes in him and constantly allows him to develop his ability. This is the vital force of Sony.' (Morita, 1987)**

The story of Johnson and Johnson's response to the 1982 Tylenol crisis is well known. Seven people in Chicago died as the result of someone lacing Tylenol bottles with cyanide, and J&J, rather than implementing a minimum and piecemeal response quickly removed *all* Tylenol from the entire US market, and involved 2,500 staff in an effort to alert the public, all at a cost of some $100 million. A potential disaster for the company turned into a public recognition that here was a company that was prepared to do the right thing. Its actions were a direct and inevitable reflection of a company which lived its values.

J&J calls its values 'Our Credo', and first among its values from its earliest expression in 1943, are its customers:

> **We believe that our first responsibility is to the doctors, nurses and patients, to mothers and all others who use our products and services.**

The second responsibility is to:

> **Our employees, the men and women who work with us throughout the world. Everyone must be considered as an individual. We must respect their dignity and recognise their merit.**

The third is to 'the communities in which we live and work and to the world community as well', and fourth is to 'our stockholders'. Only a company which *genuinely* puts its customers first, as opposed to mouthing the platitude, would have taken such an action.

Richard Branson, Chairman of the Virgin Group begins with Johnson and Johnson's number two. Speaking of Virgin Atlantic Airways he said to the Annual meeting of the Institute of Directors in 1993:

The basic principles are that people matter and that small is beautiful... We give top priority to the interests of our staff; we give second priority to the interests of our customers; and the third priority to the interests of our shareholders. Working backwards, the interests of our shareholders depend upon high levels of customer satisfaction, which enables us to attract and retain passengers in the face of intense competition. We know that the customers' satisfaction which generates all-important word-of-mouth recommendations and repeat purchase, depends upon happy staff, who are proud of the company they work for. That is why the interests of our staff come first.

Richard Branson is a great publicist for himself and his enterprises – for many people Branson with his open-necked shirt, woolly sweaters and beard *is* Virgin and his style of dress sends out a powerful message about his style of leadership. He is the best known and most admired entrepreneur in Britain, but in expressing his values in this way he did himself and his companies less than justice. Without doubt one of the fundamental values of Branson is *constantly to challenge the existing order*; to enter established 'stuffy' markets – airlines, rail transport, financial services, contraception, soft drinks and so on – and present products and services in a way which clears away the clutter and makes them simple and understandable, so that they address directly and appeal to the needs of the potential customer.

Bill Hewlett and Dave Packard, founders of Hewlett-Packard set out their own core values from the very beginning – trust and a deep respect for the individual, and a dedication to affordable quality and reliability, a commitment to the community and a view that the company exists to make technical contributions for the advancement and welfare of humanity. These values have stood the test of time and while they are now expressed slightly differently, the commitment remains absolute.

Sunrise Medical Inc., a health care products company, has expressed what it sees as its seven enduring values. I paraphrase:

- **We are committed to offering products with genuine superiority in quality, innovation and value.**

- **Our goal is to achieve perfection in customer satisfaction.**

- **We believe in the dignity and worth of every individual.**

- **All of us together are stronger and wiser than any of us individually.**

- **We must earn an attractive return for our shareholders.**

- **We will improve the welfare of all those who use our products, and advance the progress of society.**

- **We will act with integrity and character. Faced with moral choices we will do the right thing.**

Having worked with Sunrise Medical executives I know that they seek to *live* their values. And how about the last one? Can you truthfully say that your own company would *live* by such a value? Sunrise does.

Ciba-Geigy does not refer to values as such but in a brilliantly produced multicoloured, unstuffy document, *Leadership and Teamwork*, it comes very close. Look at what it says about individual responsibilities:

> **We, as individuals**
>
> If we are to achieve our demanding goals, each of us must excel both professionally and personally, exhibiting such qualities as vision, courage, human concern, and a sense of reality.
>
> We endeavour to steadily develop professional competence and personal qualities, and to bring them to business.
>
> The visionary person thinks innovatively and with an eye to the future, recognizes interrelationships, and keeps the long-term objective in view.
>
> The courageous person stands by his convictions, taking the initiative and assuming responsibility even when a situation appears difficult or controversial.
>
> The concerned person is open, honest and fair towards others, takes their concerns seriously, and supports them in their development.
>
> The realistic person perceives the constant changes in the world about him and takes them into account objectively.

Some of that extract does seem too top down but it means a lot to Ciba-Geigy people – they do try to behave in that way and when you translate those individual precepts into the behaviour of the enterprise it is not too bad at all.

You may feel more cynical about BT's values statement. In 1991 BT's Chairman, Sir Iain Vallance, decided that the company had to start putting the customer first, and restructured the business so that the customer-facing parts of the company moved to the top of the pecking order, above functions such as finance and personnel which previously had a dominant role. Vallance also defined a set of values which he hoped would reinforce the new focus:

We put our customers first

We are professional

We respect each other

We work as one team

We are committed to continuous improvement

This exhibits everything that is wrong. It seems to come from one person who speaks in terms of 'We' as though everyone was already committed. However, very few people knew what they meant, so over the next 18 months some 35,000 managers (yes, 35,000) went through workshops designed to help them understand these values (if values they were). Some three years later in 1994 BT withdrew its ten-month-old performance pay system for its then *26,000* managers because of its excessive cost. David Scott, BT's Industrial Relation Manager, was not too worried about the impact on morale, '[We] have to lose managers in the next financial year anyway'. So much for the values!

In Nissan we never discussed values as such, but our company philosophy statement was very close. However, in a 1998 discussion with Managing Director, Ian Gibson we thought they might look something like:

> ◆ Build cars of the highest possible quality and achieve ever increasing levels of customer satisfaction.
>
> ◆ Achieve mutual trust and cooperation between individuals at all levels.
>
> ◆ Encourage and value individual creativity and innovation.
>
> ◆ Develop all people to the maximum of their potential
>
> ◆ Always achieve the goals

We thought long and hard about the first, for quality like profit may be a goal not a value, and many companies, if the market suddenly decides that it wants 'pile it high, sell it cheap', instead of 'high quality, high value' will readily switch. But we concluded that for Nissan, 'high quality and customer satisfaction' *is* a value. Whatever may happen in the market, for Nissan this value will be just as strong in twenty years' time as it is today. But such a value is nothing without the commitment and contribution of the people; three others therefore focus very much on the people, and are values in themselves. They came from within us – they were not conditioned by what we perceived as being fashionable, we did not attempt a profit and loss equation with different values as the variables: they are what we believe in, deep down and for ever.

But we felt there was another value that was not thought of when we were developing the company's philosophy and which came out of our subsequent behaviour – 'Always achieve the goals'. Within the company there developed the phenomenon that everything we set out to achieve we achieved. Initially this was an outcome, but gradually this record of success took on a life of its own and, we believed, became a value in itself. At every level of the company this commitment to achieving whatever goals may be set, whether they are externally or internally generated, is absolute and tremendously powerful. It becomes self-reinforcing and it certainly is a major factor in the energised enterprise. Perhaps it *is* the energised enterprise.

But, we may have got it entirely wrong, for they are the *professed* values of two of the so-called founding fathers of the company and may not coincide with the perception of others, those on the receiving end, which would be based on their judgement of *actual* behaviour. However, because such a profession came after fourteen years of behaviour that has attempted to live the values, we hoped very much that people throughout the company would agree that our deeds had matched our words, but until they participate in the discovery process, the nature of which I will shortly describe, I do not *know.*

We can see from all of this is that there is no one set of values that is right for all companies under all circumstances. For some companies, innovation is the fundamental value, for others it is putting the customer first, for others it is putting staff first. Some organisations will be much more abstract, talking about respect, integrity, truthfulness and so on. Very few mention profit or other financial targets as a value. When it does occur it is seen as the outcome of all activities, or as the *raison d'être* of the organisation. However, this does not mean that, for example, 'maximise value for our shareholders' cannot be *the* value – for some companies it is there upfront and may be held so strongly at the expense of all others and all behaviour is directed to this end that it becomes *the* value. The Hanson Group in its 1980s heydays may well be an example. In principle there is nothing wrong with this, although I doubt if 'maximise shareholder value' is something that many people would be willing die for!

The critical point then is not what the values are but that they are shared by all people at all levels in the organisation and that everybody behaves in accordance with those values. To achieve this, policies, procedures and in particular the behaviour of the top people have to relate to those values.

As previously stated we did not use the word values when setting up Nissan in the mid-1980s – we spoke of *Our Company's Philosophy*. However, whenever asked to list the most important factors contributing to its success, that process is close to the top. By clearly defining what we stood for we were able to develop our procedures and practices, our business principles and our people principles, so that they dovetailed with that philosophy. The full philosophy statement is given in Appendix 1 to this chapter but a couple of examples show how the philosophy relates to the formal agreement reached with the trade union:

Philosophy	Trade Union Agreement
We aim to build profitably the highest quality car sold in Europe. We want to achieve the maximum possible satisfaction and ensure the prosperity of the Company and its staff.	The objectives of this Agreement are: ■ to develop and maintain the prosperity of the Company and its employees ■ to establish an enterprise committed to the highest levels of quality, productivity and competitiveness using modern technology and working practices and to make such changes to this technology and working practices as will maintain this position.
Flexibility – We will not be restricted by the existing way of doing things. We will continuously seek improvement in all our actions.	To ensure the fullest use of facilities and staff there will be complete flexibility and mobility of employees. It is agreed that changes in technology, processes and practices will be introduced and that such changes will affect both productivity and staffing levels.

On rereading Nissan's 1985 philosophy statement it is clear that the language is of its time. Contrary to my current strictures we used the word

'We', and wrote those dreadful words, 'We recognise that people are our most valued resource'. There is much else in the *expression* of the values that might now be changed but the *actual* values remain as strong today as they did in 1985 – and that is a vital point. The details may change – indeed if they do not you will be caught in a twenty-year time warp – but the fundamentals remain as vital now as they were when we put them together. The phrase 'flexibility within a consistent framework' applies to values as much as to every area of business.

Re-emphasising, much more important than words on paper is behaviour, and to help ensure that this matches the values Nissan still gives every new starter a copy of the philosophy statement. But it is not just handed out with the mass of other documentation. Each one is individually addressed, and signed by the managing director and they are distributed by a director of the company who takes new starters through the philosophy in great detail explaining its genesis and how the principles are practised. New starters, who usually bring with them the baggage of belief that directors of companies are some sort of special beings who never consort with those at the operational end, are amazed that 'such important people bother to take the time to meet with the like of us'. Although we never thought of it in this way I guess it is the directors seeking to demonstrate that in Nissan no-one, and everyone, is special – perhaps an unspoken value in itself. This, of course, is only the beginning – but what a beginning! At the very least it demonstrates that the most senior people in the company believe in it and it provides the benchmark by which subsequent behaviour can be judged.

And this benchmark is vital, for we quickly realised that by expressing our philosophy so openly and upfront we were establishing a standard by which we would be judged. Paradoxically, however, that very expression makes it easier to live up to, particularly when you genuinely believe in it. It provides the guidelines by which you can assess your own policies, procedures and practices *before* they see the light of day. It also provides the standard by which actual behaviour can be measured – if you believe that, say, innovation is a fundamental value it is vital to include innovation as part of your performance management programme.

It works all the way down the line. The original philosophy was developed by a group of some twenty British directors and managers, and the great thing is that once you have a shared set of values you are able to select others who share those values. Other managers and supervisors were selected by the original group, and they in turn selected people who they felt would fit. This does not mean you are selecting clones (and you must always seek to avoid such temptation), so one of our criteria was, perversely, to select people who could make individual contributions in their own way. We also said:

> ## NEVER SELECT SECOND BEST!

It's easy to select someone because you need a warm body to do a job right now! But we all know that you can live to regret it. Delay an appointment rather than go for someone 'we think can manage' because you will be stuck with him or her long after the immediate need has passed. Build up your talent bank – it will be one of the best long-term decisions you ever make.

But it also meant that as far as possible we selected out those who were inflexible, who did not wish to make individual contributions or innovate, who did not want to communicate effectively and who saw their job as 'heads down – do not make waves'. The message must be:

> **If you want to create an energised enterprise it helps a hell of a lot if you begin with the right ingredients!**

Why give yourself the task of rolling the stone uphill?

No-one should feel guilty about seeking to build a company comprising people who have an empathy with the company's way of doing business – people who share its values. Similarly, although you cannot do it all at once, no-one in an established company should feel guilty about selecting new people or promoting only those who will reinforce its values, particularly when those values have been only recently discovered and expressed. Indeed, with regard to internal promotions, only promoting those who are committed to and behave in the new way sends out a very powerful signal that things are now different and that it is not just talk.

We must acknowledge however that a company with strong values is not a comfortable place for those who are non-sharers. Indeed, the stronger the values and the associated behaviour, the easier it may be for the believer, but the more difficult it is for someone who does not fit. Proctor and Gamble, Disney, Hewlett-Packard, Ford, Mars, Unilever, Nordstrom, Marriott Hotels, The John Lewis Partnership, Nissan and Marks and Spencer are just a few of the companies recognised as having strong values and strong matching behaviours. If you do not like the purity of Disney's 'pixie dust cleanliness', John Lewis's 'paternalistic partnership', Nissan's 'continuously improving quality' or Nordstrom's demand on its staff that they be aggressively dedicated to the customer, you get out of the kitchen – or are helped on your way!

In Nissan, despite our best efforts we did not always get it right; there were people at all levels – from a Japanese director to shop floor manufacturing staff – whose attitudes and behaviour were not compatible with the way we all needed to behave. Some, with help and time were able to respond. Others who through no fault of their own (it was 'our' fault for making a poor selection decision) were unable to make the transition, went: the vast majority recognised the mismatch and left under their own steam, but a few were helped on their way.

Expressed like this, it may seem to be harsh, but think of the alternative. Whatever your business, can you seriously consider hiring someone who is totally out of kilter with your way of working? You just do not do it. Empathy is an integral, though often unspoken, part of most selection procedures and the higher you go the more important must be this 'fit' – unless you want someone to come in and change everything! So we all do it, but we do not all speak of it!

Only a very few enterprises have the luxury of seeking to *determine* their values unhindered by years of behaviour, and even fewer bother to use this glorious opportunity. For most of us our values creep up on us – as with culture we all have values whether or not we are aware of them. And as we will see those values may be negative as well as positive. If we want to move forward with everyone sharing positive values we must *together* first *discover* our existing values and then *together determine* what we wish them to be. We now turn to the discovery process.

APPENDIX 5.1: Nissan's Philosophy Statement

OUR COMPANY'S PHILOSOPHY

As a company we aim to build profitably the highest quality car sold in Europe. We want to achieve the maximum possible customer satisfaction and ensure the prosperity of the company and its staff.

To assist in this we aim to achieve mutual trust and co-operation between all people within the company and make NMUK a place where long-term job satisfaction can be achieved. We recognise that people are our most valued resource and in line with this spirit believe that the following principles will be of value to all:

People

• We seek to delegate and involve staff in discussion and decision making, particularly in those areas in which each of us can effectively contribute, so that all may participate in the efficient running of NMUK.

• We will develop and expand the contribution of all staff by strongly emphas-ising training and by the expansion of everyone's capabilities.

• We firmly believe in common terms and conditions of employment.

Teamworking

• We recognise that all staff have a valued contribution to make as individuals but, in addition, believe that this contribution can be most effective within a teamworking environment.

• Our aim is to build a company with which people identify and to which they feel a commitment.

Communication

• Within the bounds of commercial confidentiality we will encourage open channels of communication. We would like everyone to know what is hap-pening in our company, how we are performing and what we plan.

• **Objectives**

• We will agree clear and achievable objectives and provide meaningful feed-back on performance.

Flexibility

• We will not be restricted by the existing way of doing things. We will contin-uously seek improvement in all our actions.

6

Discovering Your Values

While there will always be exceptions to the rule, particularly when an organisation is headed by a charismatic founder–entrepreneur or by a powerful change-agent chief executive, for the vast majority of us *values are discovered and then expressed* – they are not invented by a group of senior executives, nor can they be imposed on an unreceptive organisation. While, in the previous chapter, we have seen examples of companies that have attempted to define their values, the vast majority have not – but this does not mean that they do not have values.

Like all discoveries, they are there without our knowing it, although often we instinctively feel 'there is something there'. They are not thought up based on an analysis of other companies' values, they are not copied from 'The Book of Best Values' – they are already within us and our company. Once discovered, they exist unchanged over many years; for if we feel the need to change them regularly they are not values – even though their expression may be modified over time. The values of an enterprise are what it stands for; they are shared by all and provide the inspiration for all members. And the discovery process is a fundamental building block for energising your enterprise.

This process of discovery is vital and will bring with it many surprises – both along the way and at its end. In particular you will almost certainly find that the values as displayed by your behaviour are not what you would profess or wish them to be. But you can only discover your true values by making and sharing the journey.

This journey must be led (but not dominated) by the formal leader of the enterprise, for ultimately he or she will be responsible for the final expression; but others on that journey are not simply passengers and, to extend the metaphor, the role of navigator best belongs to a facilitator from outside the company. It is not something which can be the sole prerogative of top management; indeed, it must not be. Shared values cannot be discovered by a senior management working group, shut away, pouring over a draft statement prepared by one of their number – all that will do is reinforce their belief as to what their values are or ought to be, giving virtually no thought to what their values really are, as demonstrated by their behaviour and perceived by everyone else.

However, as you attempt to share the discovery process you will also find that it is virtually impossible to begin with a completely blank sheet of paper. People, the vast majority of us, who have never thought this way will have great difficulty in coming up with more than a few 'value words'. Undoubtedly, buzz words such as 'customer first', 'innovation', 'honesty', 'integrity' and 'trust' will quickly spring to mind, but the well will rapidly run dry. The temptation is to ask someone to come up with a few thought starters, but the great dangers with this are that, with the best will in the world, the unfortunate person will produce a list of platitudes, which will be very similar to that of the senior executive draft and which will confine rather than open up the parameters of the debate. We all know that in any group the person with the pen at the flip chart can control the discussion.

So, how do we proceed? And what beyond the broad definition, are values? Is profit a value? What about productivity, customer service, market share, quality and so on? Are they measures or values? To enter such a debate too early can confuse rather than clarify. Market share, for example, was always regarded as fundamental to Japanese companies but after the bursting of their financial bubble it is amazing how quickly it was replaced with short-term profit. In fact, it was never a value but a goal. Even quality, which will be thought by many to be a value, might be discounted as companies come to realise that it is now simply the entry price to the competition and is 'expected' rather than 'desired' by the customer. When supermarket chain, Tesco, first opened its doors, 'Pile it high, sell it cheap' was its marketing strategy; today, 'High quality, high service' is the basis of its success. Tesco would claim that its current policy is a value: would it have said the same thing of its original practice?

All such 'goals' are important but customer emphasis may be very different in five years time and, if it is, companies will adapt accordingly. But values go beyond your immediate response to the market place or to your competitors. So how do you discover them without beginning with the managerial draft or the blank sheet of paper?

The answer is simple but its practical application is anything but. *If you want a genuine discovery process you must involve people at all levels of the enterprise*, for managers need to learn what their true values really are as demonstrated by their behaviour, rather than their professed values. And, if you want to energise your enterprise, full participation is vital.

You are energised when you 'own' something, when you truly believe in it. We all resist change unless it is our idea: but when it is, we want it to happen as soon as possible and we want other people to believe in it. Of course, in very large companies 100 per cent direct participation is difficult to achieve but through the communication process we must try.

Let us have a look at this discovery process. Run your eye down the list of some possible values words:

Caring	Freedom	Optimism
Challenging	Fulfilment	People first
Commitment	Genuine	Pride
Compromising	Growth	Productivity
Continuous improvement	Harmony	Profit
	Honesty	Quality
Cooperation	Humour	Radical
Creativity	Individuality	Reliability
Customer first	Innovation	Respect
Customer led	Inspirational	Security
Development	Integrity	Service
Diversity	Justice	Shareholder value
Empathy	Leader	Teamwork
Enjoyment	Leading edge	Traditional
Ethical behaviour	Learning	Trust
Excellence	Openness	Truthfulness
Flexibility		

No doubt you can think of many more. But pause a moment. They are all what you might call 'positive' words, or if you are less generous 'motherhood and apple pie', or if you are less generous still, 'wet and soggy'. At least, most people would agree that they are 'a good thing' even though some might argue that they are not all appropriate in a business environment. Whenever someone is asked to discuss values it inevitably centres on so-called positive values.

But for every such word, for every positive value, there is an opposite; for caring read uncaring, for commitment read non-commitment, for co-operation read non-cooperation and so on. Consider the following list, which again is far from complete:

Aggression	Dictatorship	Reactionary
Anarchy	Disrespect	Resigned
Apathy	Exploitation	Resistant
Autocracy	Favouritism	Restrictive
Budget-led	Follower	Secretive
Chaos	Insecure	Selfish
Cheating	Non-commitment	Self-serving
Closed value	Non-cooperation	Shareholder
Compromising	Paranoia	Short term
Conformist	People last	Slow
Confusion	Pressure	Suspicion
Control	Privilege	Uncaring
Cynicism	Profit	Unreliable

If your behaviour is perceived as being in line with the negative words (Note that some, for example profit, appear on both lists and others are debatable – is 'traditional' positive or negative?) then, irrespective of what you believe or would wish, *they are your values*. I repeat yet again, values are not what you profess but what your behaviour tells people, and can be negative as well as positive. I have worked with one privately owned company which professed openness but never gave out any financial information, which professed teamworking but was seen by the staff as being dictatorial. In fact, while the owner-manager professed many of the 'positive' values the perceptions of the staff consisted entirely of words opposite to those in the first list, plus half a dozen from the second!

It is for this reason that if we are to achieve a true discovery of our values and if we want to energise our enterprise, *staff at all levels must be part of the process from the very beginning*. If they are not, management will simply perpetuate the self-deception under which they currently labour, and staff cynicism will be even greater for having been subjected to a charade.

THE DISCOVERY PROCESS

There is no magic formula. You will be venturing into the unknown, but hopefully it will be an unknown that, with a wealth of experience behind you and a good navigator, will not be too frightening – even though there will be a few unpredictable events and the eventual destination will contain a surprise or two.

Bring together a representative cross-section of people from all levels, functions and business units of your organisation. Around 16–24 is about right. You may need more than one session if you are very large.

Step One

Introduce the concept of values using these chapters, if you wish.

Step Two

Do not begin with a managerial draft, or with a blank sheet of paper. We have already seen what this can lead to. Perhaps using my lists as your starting point, brainstorm your own additional positive and negative values words and phrases, adding those which strike a chord with your organisation – particularly negative words which otherwise might not see the light of day. As with all brainstorming sessions everything called out is worthwhile and there is no discussion at this stage – there is great danger in analysing too much too soon – there will be plenty of time for that later.

Step Three

Ask everyone individually to select the half-dozen words they believe most accurately describe their perception of the current values of their organisation as demonstrated by the behaviour of the top people and those around them. Ask them to think about what is rewarded and what is frowned upon. Remind them that these individual assessments will be anonymous, they will not be collected and can be taken away with them. This part of the exercise should take no more than ten to fifteen minutes.

Step Four

Divide participants into groups of four. These groups must be as homogeneous as possible with priority being given to ensuring that people of the same level are together: top managers with top managers, operational staff with operational staff, financial people with financial people and so on. *The purpose is to pull out differences of perception, not to hide them* and you do not want operational staff to be overawed by having to discuss such matters with top executives. For the most part they will simply clam up. We aim to deconstruct before reconstructing.

The task for each group is to reach broad agreement on not more than eight perceived current values, still without being too precise. You may wish to determine the technique to be used: discussion and debate, voting, pairing (whereby two members seek to agree with each other, then those two seek to agree with the other two), and so on. The essence is openness and frankness, so emphasise that you are not seeking an average or the lowest common denominator. If there are irreconcilable differences let them come out; if one person has a strongly held view and will not withdraw it is better that it be expressed and made known rather than be sat upon or smoothed out. Allow one to two hours for this stage. A good facilitator will quickly be able to judge the optimum time.

Step Five

Ask the groups to report their conclusions to a plenary session. You will find that values not included in the original lists will emerge. I use as an example the results from a type of organisation with which most readers will be unfamiliar – the Barnsley Alcohol and Drug Advisory Service, a group which has gone through a period of rapid growth and a change of leadership. We divided ourselves into four groups, one from management, one from the administrators and two groups of counsellors. Their initial list of perceived values was as follows:

Managers	Administrators	Counsellors (2 groups)
Innovation	Unreliable	Budget led
Humour	Humour	Confusion
Flexibility	Commitment	Creativity
Self-serving	Genuineness	Short term
Suspicion	Aggression	Unreliable
	Reliability	Under-valued
	Flexibility	Reactive
	Individualism	Insecurity
	Honesty	Resistant
		Diversity
		Humour

They surprised themselves at the preponderance of negative values *as demonstrated by their behaviour*. The only common perceived value was 'humour'! Not surprisingly, the counsellors came up with the highest proportion of negative values, but even among managers two of the five were negative. Note the inclusion of both 'reliable' and 'unreliability' in the administrators' list – clearly someone was not prepared to massage his or her view.

Lynn Rogers, the new director, commented that by concentrating on actual behaviour rather than some theoretical wish-list it brought a totally new dimension to her own thinking.

It is here that top mangers can begin to feel uncomfortable, for the results can imply that they are wearing rose-tinted spectacles, have failed to walk like they talk, are out of touch or have bred a cynical workforce. Middle mangers are often confused as they constantly receive conflicting messages from all directions and operational staff tend to be cynical, although they generally describe it as being realistic!

Step Six

This is where the skills of the facilitator really come in. Discuss the results. The task is not to reach 100 per cent agreement for you will be discussing perceptions, and perceptions linger long after reality has changed. Nor should you at this stage seek to flesh out the 'single words' (although, inevitably you will begin to do so). The real task is to achieve an understanding of the other person's view and that comes from sharing those perceptions; from discussing the response to, 'What do you mean by...?'; and by responding positively to, 'Can you give me an example of...?'; and by debating issues such as, 'Is profit really a value or is it the *raison d'être* of our business?'. It provides an opportunity for people to listen to one another – a facility denied to most of us most of the time – but which can be helped by a good facilitator. The managing director of a leather goods company said to me after one such session which was addressing manufacturing performance, 'Do you know, that's the first time I've really listened to my middle managers.'

The facilitator will, of course, seek to narrow the areas of difference, eliminate some of the extremes and secure agreement on those words which really are values. For example the Barnsley group agreed that neither 'reliability' nor 'unreliable' were values and then came up with the following list of their current values *as determined by their own behaviour*:

Confusion	Diversity	Self-serving
Resistance	Fragmentation	Frustration
Humour	Budget led	Suspicion
Flexibility	Innovative	Personal growth
Insecurity	Reactive	Honesty

Not everyone will agree with everything on the final list, there are contradictions and some may still not really be values, but the important point is that whole group will have begun to get an idea of what values are and will have a greater understanding not only of the others' points of view but will also better understand their own.

Step Seven

This is the big one! Ask the question,

What do you want your company's values to be?

Start from the position you have reached but also go back to the list of positive values words and phrases. As at the very beginning, ask everyone to come up with their individual answers, and then divide them into groups of about four. But this time make the groups multi-level and multifunctional and task them with reaching agreement on not more than half a dozen fundamental values that they all share. They will astound themselves at how easy this is and then, when the groups report back to the plenary session, they will surprise each other with their high degree of commonality. Again, it is possible that 'new' values will emerge.

The Barnsley Alcohol and Drug Advisory Service people came up with the following list. There were three groups and the numbers show how many times each value was mentioned:

People first	3	Customers first	1
Innovation	3	Fulfilling potential	1
Commitment	3	Honesty (personal and interpersonal)	1
Respect	2	Quality	1
Ethical behaviour	2	Relationship with funders	1
Excellence	2	Continuously improve	1

Step Eight

In a plenary session, led by the facilitator, seek to pull together these desired values into a manageable number – usually four to six – of the really fundamental values (but do not get too hung up if it rises slightly higher – it will eventually find its own right level), and then seek to put flesh on the bones. This is where the real debate begins. The biggest issues for the Alcohol and Drug Advisory Service centred on whether 'Excellence' was an outcome or a value, and whether and how 'Relationship with funders' should be included. The conclusions were that 'excellence' was an outcome, and that however politically desirable it might be to include something about 'Relationship with funders' it was not fundamental enough to be have a value to itself!

The agreed values of the Barnsley Alcohol and Drug Advisory Service were:

> ■ **Our clients come first in everything we do. We will always respect and value their dignity.**
>
> ■ **We are committed to enhancing the quality of life of people affected by their own and others' use of substances.**
>
> ■ **We will combine continuous improvement in the quality of existing services with a constant search for new methods for the benefit of clients.**
>
> ■ **We recognise and value the contribution of all staff (full-time and volunteers) enabling them all to develop to their full potential.**
>
> ■ **We always seek open, trusting and understanding relationships between all people – management, staff, volunteers, clients and funders.**

You may argue that they should have got there in one – they need not have gone through such a process to determine the obvious – *but you would be wrong.* They were not obvious *before* we began but it is great that they were obvious *afterwards*, for that means that everyone is in agreement. But in any case, for the Barnsley Drug and Alcohol Advisory Service agreement at all levels on the first two values – 'The client comes first' and the concern for 'the quality of life of people affected by... *others*' use of substances' – came as a complete revelation. The counsellors were not originally convinced that the managers shared the first, and no-one had previously given serious consideration to the second.

You cannot reach such a conclusion by having a couple of managers sitting together. But much more important you would not have the same level of understanding nor would you have had the participation and achieved the ownership by people throughout the enterprise.

Leave it there for a week or so – you will have achieved a lot in one day. But this is by no means the end of the journey of discovery for, so far, only a small proportion of the population will have been involved.

Step Nine

Give all members of the group the time and resources to discuss the outcome with their colleagues (if 'Openness' is one of your values you will have little choice but to do this), and get them to discuss questions such as 'What do we mean by...?', 'How will these values affect our behaviour, our relationships with each other and with our customers, suppliers, investors and the community?' Involve as many people as possible, aiming to make everyone an 'insider'. Learn from what you hear, further opening your own mind. Then reconvene.

Step Ten

At the second session ask for second thoughts, pulling in the knowledge and insights gained from the consultation process – it is not too late to change – and then refine the initial conclusions. Amazingly, the Barnsley Alcohol and Drug Advisory Service decided that they did not wish to change one word, which meant that we had either achieved first time perfection or that the participants had bullied their colleagues into submission – which they didn't. But this is unusual and in most cases you can expect minor modifications.

Note also the use of 'we', for having involved and gained the commitment of people at all levels you can now genuinely use that word. It is no longer a few top managers purporting to speak on behalf of those who have no voice. You have worked together to achieve the foundation for everything you do and against which your actions can be judged. They contain the mental energy of a wide group of people and the communication process has already begun.

Some of your results may seem a little 'motherhood and apple pie', while others may be revolutionary, but all have major implications for your behaviour, both internally and externally. However, it is only a beginning, and although there will now be many ambassadors, the chief executive must be the greatest ambassador of all, continually talking with people at all levels, always seeking understanding, strategies, policies and actions that are in line with the values. But the CEO must also continue to learn. Every meeting, every discussion will add to the body of wisdom and maybe, after several months, there will need to be minor adjustments. Do not worry about that. It's all part of the learning process.

If you have got it broadly right you will have the foundation for everything that follows, but if you then stop, believing that you have achieved something wonderful, you will quickly find that you are just a percentage point or two along the road. It will have been an interesting exercise but your efforts will have little long-lasting benefit.

Step Eleven

The most difficult step – implementation, sustaining the gains and continuously improving – is about to begin. Your values must translate into modes of behaviour, into goals and measures by which your progress can be assessed. As Lynn Rogers said:

I ended the session extremely aware that we were at the *start* of something and that the real reflection, discussion and action had to happen in the organisation.

Also remember the negative value words brought out at the beginning of the exercise. By working on the new positive values you will begin to eliminate many of the negatives but you cannot assume that this will automatically happen without effort. So go back and address them, asking what you have to do to eliminate the negative behaviours. You will then find, as did the Barnsley group, that working on the negatives also helps create the positive – they become mutually reinforcing.

It will not be easy but the process will help you move to the next stage – generating a sense of purpose.

7

A Sense of Purpose

A sense of purpose is arguably
the most important and satisfying force for an
individual and an enterprise.

It may seem a strange phrase to use in a business context. The prime definition of 'purpose' is 'a goal to be attained' but 'sense of purpose' does not
appear as a derivative phrase even in the *New Shorter Oxford English
Dictionary*. But think about those people you know who have a sense of
purpose – they seem to put so much more into their lives and get so much
more out. And it is the same for people in an enterprise – when they have
a sense of purpose they both give and receive so much more. It seems so
obvious and right when we are trying to create an enterprise with which
people identify and in which there is mutual commitment.

When we speak of a sense of purpose we mean something bigger than
a goal:

We aim to achieve a goal but we seek to
fulfil our sense of purpose.

The goal of fun runners in a city marathon is to reach the finishing line,
but their sense of purpose may be to conquer their fear or to prove to
themselves and others that they have the dedication and determination to

achieve the maximum of their potential. The elite athletes may aim to win but their sense of purpose is to show that they are the best. When I am at the top of a severe black ski run my goal may be to reach the bottom in one piece but my sense of purpose is to conquer my fear. When I write a book my goal may be to meet a deadline but my sense of purpose is to share ideas and to influence the behaviour of people within enterprises. The goal of pilgrims is to reach the shrine but their sense of purpose is to achieve spiritual fulfilment.

We may or may not achieve our tangible goal but it does not always matter, for fulfilling our sense of purpose is different from and beyond the tangible. I may not reach the bottom of the black slope or meet my deadline, the fun runner may not reach the finishing line but we can still fulfil our sense of purpose. However, the elite athlete or the pilgrim will be unfulfilled if he or she does not achieve the goal. Consider your personal goals and aspirations. Does one depend on the other? Then transfer your thinking to your business environment and ask the same questions. You may be surprised at the answers, but maybe you also need a little more understanding.

The story of the three mediaeval stonemasons is fairly well known. A traveller observes three stonemasons chipping away at blocks of stone and asks each in turn what he is doing. They reply:

1. 'It's obvious, isn't it? I'm trying to cut this stone.'

2. 'I'm carving a stone for the foundations of the building.'

3. 'I'm helping to build a cathedral.'

The meaning is that work can be interpreted on different levels, with the third stonemason having the broadest perspective – he has sight of the goal. Up to now the story has always ended there – but it need not, for I would add a fourth stonemason who, when asked what he is doing, answers humbly:

4. 'I am helping create an edifice on earth to the glory of God'.

Who would doubt that my fourth stonemason has the greatest sense of purpose and that he both gives more and receives more, that his work has a deeper meaning?

Our sense of purpose goes beyond what we are actually doing and beyond the tangible end product. In a business context our immediate goal may be to make a profit by manufacturing a product or providing a service but P. Roy Vagelos, Chief Executive of pharmaceuticals manufacturer Merck and Company put it well when he expressed its long-standing sense of purpose, saying in *Values and Vision: A Merck Century* (Merck, 1993):

> **A century from now, I believe we [will] feel the same esprit de corps... because Merck's dedication to fighting disease, relieving suffering and helping people is a righteous cause – one that inspires people to dream of doing great things. It is a timeless cause, and it will lead Merck people to great achievements during the next hundred years.**

Sunrise Medical was expressing much more than an immediate, tangible goal when stating:

We will improve the welfare of all those who use our products and advance the progress of society.

It is seeking to move onto a higher plane beyond the daily task and monthly targets. It is lifting its eyes above the immediate horizon. Sunrise Medical staff may have achieved a goal when they make 'an attractive return for our shareholders', or when they have improved productivity by 2.5 per cent, but how many are genuinely *fulfilled*? How many will sweat blood for such targets? How many are truly dedicated to them? The answer is obvious – 'Very few'. You have to *care* about fulfilling your sense of purpose, even if it is difficult to express in words. It is often much more abstract but, if people can unite around a sense of purpose, its power and energy will be far greater than any tangible measure.

You might argue that it is easy to have such a sense of purpose when you are in the health care business, but it can apply to all enterprises. Henry Ford while much admired has also been much maligned. But he had a sense of purpose. He wrote:

Power and machinery, money and goods, are useful only as they set us free to live. They are but means to an end. For instance, I do not consider the machines which bear my name simply as machines. If that was all there was to it I would do something else. I take them as concrete evidence of the working out of a theory of business which I hope is something more than a theory of business – a theory that looks towards making this world a better place to live. (*Ford on Management*, 1991, p. 1)

Ford did not simply see himself as a manufacturer but as someone who was seeking to improve the quality of life of his fellow human beings. When announcing the Model T he said:

I will build a motor car for the great multitude. It will be large enough for the family but small enough for the individual to run and care for. It will be constructed of the best materials, by the best men to be hired, after the simplest designs that modern engineering can devise. But it will be so low in price that no man making a good salary will be unable to own one – *and enjoy with his family the blessing of hours of pleasure in God's great open spaces.* [my emphasis] (ibid., p. 59)

AT&T's Bob Allen inherited a strategic plan that spoke of loading more traffic onto the existing telecommunications network and developing products aimed at meeting the growing information and communications business. Such words are goals, they do not give a sense of purpose. Instead he spoke of building an enterprise:

dedicated to becoming the world's best at bringing people together – giving them easy access to each other and to the information and service they want and need – anytime, anywhere.

The big challenge in that statement is 'anytime, anywhere'. It is a 'break out of your boundaries' statement. It is about using initiative, being innovative, giving freedom to do your own thing. Of course there has to be back-up and support and goals and measures. Freedom without any form of control or direction leads to anarchy but it is the freedom and the opportunity to break through the boundaries to become the world's best at brining people together that gives the sense of purpose.

Bob Allen's deceptively simple statement achieved more to change the *feeling* within AT&T than a myriad of strategy documents. But it also led to the recognition that the tools and technology had to be in place. Part of acquiring the tools and technology was major investments – $7.5 billion for NCR and $12,6 billion for McCaw Cellular. A sense of purpose does not come cheap!

In Nissan when we wrote:

Our aim is to build profitably the highest quality car sold in Europe.

did that give a sense of purpose? In retrospect I think not; it is a value and a goal. Only rarely is it possible to express a sense of purpose in words but 'you know it when you feel it'. A visitor to Nissan, Sunderland commenting on the energy he felt said, 'It's hard to pin down but I've never felt anything like it.' One Customer Service Director from a car hire company asked if he could package it and take it away with him.

Another top executive from a consumer goods manufacturer asked, 'What do you have to do to make people work with such enthusiasm?' My response was something like:

> **If you talk of making people work you are starting with the wrong mindset – you have to create the environment in which people want to work like this, so that there is no other way. The only motivation that is worth having comes from within. It is not imposed – it comes from people knowing that the management actually cares about them; that their contribution matters and is valued; that they are treated with respect; that they are not second-class citizens – work at that for several years and you might create the atmosphere.**

'It's not easy is it.' he responded! Maybe he was seeking the instant formula for 'Always achieve the goals'.

When you visit a company you often just *know* that it is special but it is very difficult from the two hour snapshot to understand why. I get that buzz from Calsonic's exhaust systems plant in Washington, Co. Durham – everyone knows what they are doing and why; they work effectively but are not frenetic. Information is everywhere in a relevant and digestible form; the factory floor is spotless, systems and procedures are in place and are observed because they *belong* to the people doing the job. But the whole is greater than the sum of the parts – there is a sense of purpose about the place and you feel it when talking to the people. Even though it has not been spelled out – it is shared. You can see things happening but you cannot *see* the thinking and commitment that lies behind the practical. That lies deep within people.

In fact, although we are seeking something that truly unites people, to search for the right words may even be counter-productive. People will not unite around a few words unless they encapsulate strong emotions. Consider the power of 'We will overcome' – not just the words but the feelings, emotions and determination they convey. And most such expressions emerge or are latched on to – they are not consciously produced. When the Liverpool pop group, Gerry and the Pacemakers, recorded the song from Carousel, *You'll Never Walk Alone* they could not have thought that they were creating an anthem which would inspire not only the supporters of Liverpool Football Club but create a sense of purpose for a whole city.

On a more prosaic level, in mid-1997 I was working with a group of supervisors from ball-bearing manufacturer NSK-AKS with the aim not only of developing them but in so doing to significantly improve the performance of their company. We had some difficulty in expressing our feelings beyond the immediately tangible until one day at the whiteboard, arising from a comment by one of our group, I wrote:

> **TOGETHER, WE CAN MAKE
> THE DIFFERENCE.**

Together we had discovered our sense of purpose. Immediately everyone knew that it was right for us.

Perhaps it easier to generate a sense of purpose in a crisis situation. 'Change or die' can be very powerful and focus our energies for a short period of time but it cannot be maintained for long. You either change or you die. If the latter, there is nothing left anyway and if the former, we can quickly return to our comfort zone but *whoever has a sense of purpose when they are comfortable?* 'Let's just stay as we are' is not conducive to making the hairs rise on the back of your neck!

A sense of purpose is so extraordinarily difficult to write down that maybe you should not even attempt to do so. A lengthy statement can sound like a rehashed mission statement and something which is short and pithy may appear to be no more than a short-lived advertising slogan. Unless instilled by a powerful or charismatic founder-leader a sense of purpose can only *emerge* and, maybe, someone will find a form of words but if they do not, it does not matter. And that is when we come back to process and behaviour.

The very process of discovering values in the way I have described can help create the environment in which a sense of purpose can emerge but it is leadership and constantly-reinforced behaviour that really counts. A leader around whom people can unite can be a powerful force. The first few years in a start-up company can create a tremendous drive and sense of purpose and having been at the heart of two such projects I know well the inner drive that causes everyone to work long hours and give of themselves far beyond the norm. But most of us do not have the inspirational leader or the thrill of a start-up. So how can we create this sense of purpose, this energy which will unite everyone and which creates this inner drive?

We have, in fact, already started. We have spoken of energising leadership and have discussed the process of discovering our values. No statement from on high can impose a shared sense of purpose but I guarantee that during the discovery of your values someone will ask the questions:

> **What are we really here for?**
> **What is our purpose?**

Let the debate flow, raising issues such as 'What really gives you satisfaction and fulfilment at work?' You are seeking something beyond goal achievement but you want to avoid both the clichés of the behavioural scientists and pseudo-psychological mumbo-jumbo. There is no guarantee that a sense of purpose will emerge but at least you will have started people, at all levels, thinking. For some companies there will be an instant realisation; for others it will grow steadily and for many it will never happen.

Marriott has attempted to put its sense of purpose into words: 'Make people away from home feel that they're among friends and really wanted.' It has lived with them through the evolution of the company from A&W Root Beer to its chain stores, airline catering and international hotel chain. In mid-1997 I was staying overnight at the Swansea Marriott Hotel.

The weather was wretched so I decided to have dinner in the hotel's restaurant. The meal was good but was rather spoiled by the fact that on five occasions I was asked if I was enjoying it. Every member of staff had no doubt been through the same customer service training programme – 'Smile, and make the customer feel that you are interested in him personally.' The result was somewhat mechanical, considerably over the top and not a little irritating.. After all, we now *expect* good quality and friendly service as a right – it is the starting point, not the finishing line.

However, when putting on my glasses to read the dessert menu, a lens retaining screw sprung out, probably onto the floor; the lens dropped onto the table and I became a one-eyed menu reader! I went down on my knees looking for the screw and within seconds a waitress was there. She asked the problem and joined the search. We were soon joined by another member of staff – three of us on our knees in the middle of a restaurant looking for a tiny screw! We failed, but the waitress said she would see if the electrician was still around – he might have a replacement. Unfortunately, he was not on duty. After the meal I had another search and this time was joined by the restaurant supervisor, but again without success. She then said that they would be happy to take my spectacles to a local optician first thing in the morning to get them fixed. Unfortunately, I had to leave early and quickly purchased a pair of off-the-shelf reading glasses from a supermarket.

Making guests welcome and treating them as individuals is clearly a shared sense of purpose among the Swansea Marriott Hotel's restaurant staff. Its customer service training programme resulted in them going over the top in their mechanical response, but when it really mattered their actions could only have come from people who genuinely cared. When it really mattered they genuinely walked the talk. There was nothing phoney or mechanistic about their responses to an abnormal situation; they were not just going through the motions. They clearly had a sense of purpose that had evolved from their values, and that cannot be measured. But if you have developed your values and have a sense of purpose such responses become second nature. You do not think about them – you just behave in the way that comes naturally.

A sense of purpose and an energised enterprise go hand in glove and as we proceed, ideas may well emerge which provide the spark that is right for you.

8
Real Teamworking

In many organisations 'teamworking' has now replaced 'family' as the desirable corporate glue and it is lauded as the magic answer to many corporate ills – although, as always, the results only rarely match the promise. But however much senior executives may publicly proclaim 'We're one big team in this company' there can be little doubt that many secretly agree with the apocryphal maxim attributed to film director, Michael Winner:

> **TEAMWORKING IS A LOT**
> **OF PEOPLE DOING WHAT I SAY!**

Judging from the reaction whenever I use this slide, this approach does not go unnoticed! Michael Winner's most celebrated films are the 'Death Wish' series – a title which, when related to teamworking, is somewhat prophetic!

It may seem an obvious point, but how can you expect real teamworking to develop when the chief executive is a follower of Michael Winner's maxim; when macho individualism and 'strong' decision-making are the paths to success; when the top managers have got there by climbing over someone else; and when the chief executive and the top group is the worst imaginable example of a team.

Bill Hayden, when chief of all of Ford's European manufacturing operations once told me, when the body framing section had been on strike for a week over a so-called failure to involve them in a changed practice (We'd been discussing it for only three months!), 'You bloody tell 'em they're going to be involved!' It seemed somewhat of a contradiction in terms, but Bill, despite his many positive characteristics, was not known to be at the cutting edge of tolerance. His words were not unlike those of the chief executive who says, 'Get teamworking in this place by the end of next month.' It just does not happen like that, especially when there is no change at the top.

One of the great difficulties is that 'teams' and 'teamworking', because they are in such common use, are terms which are capable of a myriad of interpretations. As with 'innovation', we talk together thinking we mean the same thing but eventually find we have totally different interpretations. Look at the confusing plethora of terms that have been used:

HOT GROUPS   SMALL GROUP ACTIVITIES

MULTIFUNCTIONAL TASK FORCES   QUALITY CIRCLES

CELL WORKING   CONTINUOUS IMPROVEMENT TEAMS

PROJECT TEAMS   CUSTOMER-FIRST TEAMS

PROBLEM SOLVING GROUPS   SKUNK WORKS

PROCESS TEAMS   INNOVATION TEAMS

Self-managed work teams   SUPER-TEAMS

SEMI-AUTONOMOUS WORK GROUPS   VIRTUAL TEAMS

HIGH PERFORMANCE TEAMS   LEADERLESS GROUPS

Figure 8.1   Team types

The mind boggles! Some of the words and phrases have value, but others seem to have been developed merely to put a sexy title on to a trendy article or book based on the usual 'research', that is a questionnaire completed by twenty to thirty self-selecting respondents plus half a dozen 'in-depth' interviews, which 'prove' either that teamworking is the greatest thing since sliced bread, is endemic throughout 75 per cent of organisations and has had a major impact on performance, or that its impact is minimal and that it has barely penetrated even those organisations that claim to have implemented it.

The trouble is that many top executives believe that saying, 'We're one big team in this company' actually means that everyone shares this view. Some are convinced that sending people on team-building courses during which, among other things, they attempt to cross a five metre-wide river with a three metre plank of wood, a couple of barrels and a length of rope, will build long-lasting teamworking back at the ranch. In early 1997, ICL took its top 50 directors and country managers on a one-day team-building exercise at Donnington Park race track where they assumed the roles of Grand Prix pit stop crews. Said Human Resources Director, Mark Birchenhough:

This was not just a fun day for the top people. We used the car as a metaphor for our customers. We said, here's a problem which the customer wants us to solve quickly and correctly. He doesn't care how we do it, he just wants it done. This sent a powerful message to our top people which said that customers want seamless and speedy interaction with their suppliers and that the only way to achieve this was by working as a team. (Creelman, 1997)

ICL has been expounding customer service for as long as I can remember so to find in 1997 that it has to send its top executives on a *one day* team-building exercise to get over that message is astounding; then to believe that one day would make any difference is even more astounding. No doubt it was a great day out, but then as Mark Birchenhough said, 'It was not just a fun day for the top people'.

But do not get me wrong – for some, such exercises are great fun, and the therapeutic value of off-site, residential sessions can be tremendous with the best work being done late at night when a few drinks have relaxed inhibitions. (My *Ascendant Organisation* and the title of this book both came out of such sessions.) So if a company wants to take people away for a few days, great – but let us not confuse the purposes. In any case, for others the artificial and macho nature of many such exercises can readily become competitive and destructive, and often their relevance to the real world is limited. I have yet to find a company which, a couple of years down the road, has experienced any long-lasting, significant impact.

Similarly, encouraged by Japanese practice, many think that gathering a group of people together to perform a task, and asking them to begin by selecting a name for themselves, will create a team. Doesn't 'The A Team' sounds much more dynamic than 'Accounts Payable'? (Virtually every company that goes down this route ends up with an 'A Team'. The producer of the celebrated television series has a lot to answer for!) To some it may well sound more dynamic – until it becomes embarrassing, and they last six months at the most. When executives make such a suggestion, first ask if they are not being somewhat patronising; and if they persist, then suggest that they give a similarly dynamic sounding name to the top management team. Do unto yourselves as you would do unto others. Rarely does it go any further.

Many, encouraged by popular writing, believe that teamworking is about those groups of wonderful people from different sections and different levels who come together to solve those intractable problems with which the rest of us have struggled for months; or who bring a new product to market in a third of the usual time! Some of the titles given to such practices are included in the graphic, but if you are not included in a skunk work or hot group what does it say about you? How do you feel about being excluded from the inner circle? Such groups work for a time because they are special, but if they become the norm they miss the input from the great unwashed, they become isolated and out of touch. They may well become real teams, for being treated as something special can have a great motivating effect (Elton Mayo taught us this some 70 years ago), but if they are the only teams in town they will have no foundation and you will have failed to achieve one of the fundamental principles of leadership – ensuring that all people throughout the enterprise are developed to their full potential.

Another great problem comes when we confuse teamworking with work groups. Work groups have long been with us – manufacturing cells, process-based groups, airline cabin crews, military platoons and the company board are but a few examples of work *groups* now commonly called teams. This is more than just a semantic distinction, for many organisations attempt to create teams simply by changing the structure, thinking that introducing cell manufacturing, or re-engineering will, in itself, create teams. (When you think of it, the principles of cell manufacturing and re-engineering are no different.) It will not. Changing the structure and then calling the resulting group a team does not create a real team.

Work groups and teamworking are different – a group of people who work together is not necessarily a team. You can have a group of totally interdependent production line workers, a self-managing group of insurance claims processors or a project group who have to live in each other's pockets, and they may be terrible teams. You can have a group of salespeople out on the road who see each other but once a month, or the ground and aircrew of a fighter squadron who have no real knowledge of what the others do, and they may be a brilliant team.

So, what do I mean by real teamworking? It is very simple.

> **A REAL TEAM IS A GROUP OF INDIVIDUALS WHO WORK TOGETHER TO ACHIEVE SHARED GOALS.**

The key words are *together* and *shared*, for it is comparatively easy to establish 'a group of individuals who work to achieve a goal', but totally fail to establish real teamworking. For real teamworking, both *together* and *shared* have to be present. Most of us have experience of sports teams in which, while there is a shared goal, the players do not work *together* to achieve it – such teams are the losers. In the business world it is much more difficult to define let alone share the goals. And when you cannot define and share, how on earth are you going to work together to achieve them?

And let us not forget 'individuals'. One of the starting points of the energised enterprise is that every member is an individual and that the leadership task is to create the environment in which those individuals *want* to come together for a common purpose. The Japanese begin with the group – the West begins with the individual. For the Japanese, team-working is the natural order; Westerners have to work at it.

Recognising individualism means appreciating that every person is different and will bring his or her own talents, contributions and peculiarities to the party. This does not mean filling the place with those whom Tom Peters calls 'WEIRDOS' and 'WOW-ERS', people who break all the rules and win. Usually, it seems, they are freewheeling, Californian entrepreneurs. I guess, if you are a freewheeling, rule-breaking, California-based entrepreneur then in that society you are pretty normal! And that is what most of us are – 'NORMAL'.

My idea of normality is different – heaven help us if the world was full of weirdos! Just as most of us are not like JFK, Richard Branson, Percy Barnevik, Lee Iaccocca or Tom Peters, most of us are not weirdos or wow-ers. But the great thing is:

> **When normal people develop into a real team WE are capable of achieving the abnormal**

And that is what really counts! WE – you, me and 99.99 per cent of the rest of us – are capable of achieving the abnormal. As the group of supervisors discovered:

> ## TOGETHER, WE CAN MAKE
> ## THE DIFFERENCE.

At the macro level, real teamworking can mean everyone working together for the success of the enterprise. At the micro level, a small team may work together to achieve the targets, develop a new product or make life easier. It can also mean a group working together *against* the enterprise.

My 'favourite' example of the latter, which holds many memories both good and bad, is that of Danny Connor, the Communist convenor of shop stewards in Ford's Dagenham plant in the late 1970s. Danny was the brilliant leader of the most effective team in the company, the shop stewards' committee – a team which had its own genuinely shared long-term goal of furthering the revolution; its mid-term goals of creating disruption and tension, and winning concessions and disputes; and its short-term goals of making everyday life as difficult as possible for the managers and supervisors, and to do as little real physical work themselves as possible. It was always much more fun sitting in an office arguing the toss with a manager than being on the production line building cars!

Danny Connor was appointed convenor about the same time I was appointed labour relations manager with the brief, 'Get back management control of the Body Plant!' We were in constant battle. He and the militant stewards opposed Ford in every area at every opportunity, and in the late 1970s we were often in a state of physical (riots, punch-ups, demonstrations, property damage and so on) as well as verbal conflict. But I always had a respect for his ability, and there can be no doubt that he led a real team which embraced the key words of the definition.

HORIZONTAL, VERTICAL AND DIAGONAL TEAMS

All of this reinforces the view that real teamworking has little to do with structures and everything to do with leadership and commitment.

In 1991 I was invited to address a 'Teamworking' conference in Hamburg, Germany and was the final speaker of four. The first three were 'structuralists' and I then presented the argument that teamworking was more about leadership and commitment than structures, and can exist at all levels, irrespective of the structure. I was received with open hostility from some of the audience. Two years later when invited back to speak on a similar theme, and in anticipation of a similar attitude, I spent considerable time preparing my thoughts visually, eventually working up a few horizontal, vertical and diagonal lines on a sheet of paper. My secretary, Pam Coates, commented that my scribbled lines looked something like the UK flag and pulled it out of her computer. I have subsequently used this to great effect in many presentations, always giving credit to Pam.

Figure 8.2   Real teamworking

This is not intended to be particularly patriotic – just a great illustration of a concept. Unfortunately, reproduced in black and white it is nowhere near as dramatic as in colour when we are able to concentrate on the red bars, but for the benefit of those who do not know, I will be referring to the light shaded bars within the white background.

The horizontal bar, which is the biggest and is unbroken, represents the many groups of people in the enterprise who work permanently together; perhaps the production teams and their supervisors, the school teachers and their heads of department, the sales forces and their area managers or the directors and the managing director. Such groups are the foundation of the enterprise – without them little else can be achieved. Every person in an enterprise is in such a group and there are scores, or hundreds, or thousands of them. It is the people in these groups who work together every day to determine and achieve the shared goals, and when they succeed they become a strong chain of interlinked teams. In the 'team' literature these permanent teams are usually neglected in favour of the short-term, multifunctional, multi-level task forces which need to be 'built', and in so doing the authors perform a considerable disservice to the business world.

The unbroken vertical bar, the second largest, represents the next most important teams – the permanent, continuous, multi-level, vertical teams – people who report to you, you, your boss and so on, up and down the hierarchy. Such teams meet regularly, often every day, to determine and share goals, assess progress and communicate, always intuitively reinforcing the values and sense of purpose. They are the important supportive link between the horizontal teams. Again, we are all in such a team, probably more than one.

It is not too difficult for people at three or four consecutive levels to become a real vertical team but can such teams reach all the way through the hierarchy? Is it as easy for someone at the operating level to say, 'I'm in the same team as the CEO' as it is for the CEO to say, 'We're one big team in this company'? The answer is obvious. It is not. The best you can hope for is that people will say something like:

> **I work with a great bunch of people.**
> **We'll sweat blood for each other.**
> **And I trust the people at the top.**

If you have that, you have the ingredients for success.

But trust of the top is very difficult to achieve. As we have already seen when discussing the heart of leadership certain people, including bosses, are not readily trusted, primarily because we believe we can never rely on them, they do not give us straight answers; perhaps we even suspect them of lying. Certainly we think that many of them are in it for their own ends and that manipulation if not corruption is endemic. The politician who is trusted is the one who is seen to be open and honest, who tells people both the good and the bad, who walks the talk, who is seen to be in it for the long term and is not simply in the personal nest-feathering, 'get out before found out' business. The same goes for business leaders.

On the flag, seemingly lying behind the horizontal and vertical bars are the diagonal shaded bars – smaller and discontinuous. And this is right, for enduring strength rests on the permanent horizontal and vertical groups. These discontinuous, diagonal bars represent the temporary, multi-level, multifunctional groups which in B. W. Tuckman's words (1965), 'form, storm, norm and perform' or, as Andrew Leigh puts it in *Life and Death in Teamwork* (1996), 'Starting, sorting, stabilising, striving, succeeding and stopping' (with a further 18 sub-divisions!). These are the groups that fascinate most researchers and which are said to come together to solve those intractable problems or deliver the new product or service. These are the groups which are said to need the team-building processes and which should be constructed from the ideal mix of personality types. These are the groups full of those 'wonderful people who achieve wonderful things', and which make great copy for populist business books and from which legends are made!

These are also the groups which can become isolated and distract us from the latent power of the permanent team. But when people are members of their permanent teams and, as the norm, are committed to working together to achieve shared goals, the foundations of real team-working are in place. Then can the temporary diagonal groups readily become real teams, for they build on solid foundations. The temporary teams do not have to be sent on team-building exercises, because from practical experience they are already team members.

In the energised enterprise an individual will always be in two teams – the horizontal and vertical permanent teams, and at the same time is likely to be a member of two or three diagonal teams. Membership may vary as needs change and in some enterprises the relative sizes and relationships of the bars may need to change – the 'pure' version of the flag analogy works best for what we might call 'natural' teams, groups of people who work physically together in the same location at the same time.

But in some enterprises and functions, particularly those concerned with high-tech development work and consultancy, life may seem to consist of little else but constantly changing, temporary teams, and in such enterprises the diagonal bars may need to be larger relative to the horizontal and vertical. At Danish-owned Tetra Pak Converting Technologies, for example, nearly all of the 100 or so staff spend virtually all of their time on projects. Consultants working for Oracle may have a long-term relationship with a particular client but also spend much of their time on frequently revolving assignments. This matters not, for the permanent team may then be the function, the business unit, the company or even the external group – the client; or perhaps it is the group of people whose paths regularly cross. If such groups can meet the definition they will be real teams; if not, they will not.

Taken to its extreme we are now seeing the development of what have come to be called virtual teams – groups of people who may have some characteristics of natural or project teams but who are separated by location, organisation and time. People in such teams use computer-based technology to share ideas, stimulate thinking and to keep in touch.

BP Exploration with people dispersed throughout the world, often in remote locations, likes 'to keep track of people who know the recipe' by using what it calls a virtual team tool kit, comprising video conferencing, software which enables users to work simultaneously on shared documents, shared electronic whiteboards, multimedia e-mail, Lotus Notes, Internet browsers and document scanners. But does such technology make a team? In itself, no. It may help a widely dispersed group communicate more effectively (*if* they choose to use its full capabilities), but when we understand that even people working side by side may not be 'working together to achieve shared goals' the problems in a widely dispersed group are much greater. This does not mean that so-called virtual teams cannot be real teams. But reaching this state requires much more than technology – and to achieve this the principles and 'rules' are not so very different, just variations on a theme.

But what of the character of the team? Meredith Belbin has spent his career researching and teaching in this area, and has identified nine roles and personality types† that go to making up effective teams. His work is widely known and used for team selection but it has always seemed to make something special of what should be the norm. I have long argued that we do not want an ideal mix of personality types – we want a lot of innovative people who constantly seek to challenge the *status quo* making life uncomfortable for the established order, but in a constructive way.

We don't want a nice cosy group in which every protrusion is smoothed away and everyone dovetails neatly together – we need the grit in the oyster which produces the pearl!

Working together to achieve shared goals does not mean seeking the lowest common denominator solution, on which everyone can agree but which satisfies no-one, and leaves the company with a barrow load of less than best solutions. Working together to achieve shared goals does not mean everyone's pet solution being incorporated into the final outcome. One of

---

†Plant, resource investigator, co-ordinator, shaper, monitor/evaluator, teamworker, implementer, completer and specialist. (Belbin, 1993)

---

the reasons why Japanese products are often over-complex is that no-one is prepared to say, however diplomatically, to another member of the team, 'Your idea is a load of rubbish – there's no way it can be included'. No-one is prepared to say, 'We have to make a decision NOW!' Consensus is great when you have got all the time in the world and are guaranteed profits 'for ever', but even the Japanese now recognise that the world is different. Unfortunately for them the habits of generations are difficult to unlearn.

Effective real teams are, therefore, not comfortable places – people challenge each other's ideas and solutions and may have big arguments which some win and others lose. They are about finding the *best* solution not the lowest common denominator, and good people will fight for their ideas. Some will be temporarily disappointed, but if they are really good they will recognise the better idea and will work equally vigorously to make that one a success.

Let me give an alternative listing of team characteristics. Ian Thomas, a safari guide and student of wildlife, has spent many years observing the behaviour of lions. His self-published book, *The Power of the Pride* (1992) is just sixty pages long, half of which comprise beautiful photographs of lions in action, but in these few pages he says more of value about effective teamworking than all the 300 page door-stoppers put together. He concludes:

The pride has evolved as a potent example of teamwork for maximum effect. Their combined co-operative effort working towards a common objective leads to a winning team situation where both the pride and the individual thrive. The lesson from lions to business is – teams are successful because:

Each individual member is powerful

The total focus is on clear-cut and realistic goals

Team members are alert to communication

Incentives motivate and reward success

Spirit consists of trust, confidence, respect, and pride

The structure is flat

Strict selection ensures there are no passengers

Training is intense

Image enhances function

**Synergy – the pride is more powerful than the sum
of the strengths of its individuals**

The unremitting application of these ten power points puts the pride in a win–win situation: *the pride and its members thrive.* **The business and the individuals thrive.**

What a brilliant analysis!

Most of us have only seen a pride of lions on our television screens, but who can doubt the relevance of Ian Thomas's observations to our human enterprises? Ask yourself if your teams match up to its demands. And remember, *a pride is made up of a permanent horizontal and a permanent vertical team – there are not too many temporary, multifunctional, multi-level task forces around*!

Some may argue that the sense of purpose of a pride of lions is different from a human enterprise – the pride is about survival. If we do not have real teamworking, then in today's environment we will not survive – at least not for long, and we certainly will not win–win.

To stretch the analogy, remember all those television programmes: there are long periods of harmony in a pride of lions, both when they are lying around in the sun and when working together to achieved the shared goal, but there is often considerable conflict between members. There are petty squabbles and major fights, and members who do not fit have to leave. Members of the pride do not have to like each other all the time, *they have to achieve*. There is no lowest common denominator solution in a pride of lions!

In 1997, for three hours five of us watched two cheetahs hunting impala on the foreshore of Lake Kariba, Zimbabwe – a mother was teaching her son. To observe this natural rite and to appreciate their relationship was a privilege I will never forget. Building on that experience and learning from Ian Thomas's approach I would add to his lessons for successful teams:

> - **Tremendous energy combines with great patience**
> - **Leadership is clear**
> - **The relationship is intense**
> - **Trust is total**
> - **An intuitive understanding exists between members**
> - **The rules of behaviour are understood**
> - **While not right first time, they learn from their failures**
> - **The goals are time-bounded**
> - **They keep going until the goals are achieved**

While Ian Thomas, being there first, grabbed most of the best lines, one very clear factor emerging from both the lions and cheetahs is that their teams have very positive leadership, and this might be thought to fly in the face of much contemporary thinking about self-managed work teams, semi-autonomous work groups, leaderless groups and so on. But I am very clear – *there is no such thing as a leaderless group.*

It is true that responsibility and authority can be devolved and groups can take over their own hiring decisions, methods of working, order scheduling, vacation rotas, customer contacts and so on, but if there is no appointed leader within the group, or the person to whom the group formally reports is remote, *a leader will emerge.* It happened in our group of friends when we were children and it happens throughout our lives, particularly at work. And when at work, if that leader does not have the best interests of the organisation at heart the results can be disastrous.

The theory is that given time and real responsibility and authority a genuine sense of commitment will emerge – and it may well do – but when you are seeking to develop real teamworking you need positive leadership committed to the success of the team, and a leader who has the skills to develop the team.

A celebrated real-team company is US turkey producer Bil Mar Foods, a major division of the Sara Lee Corporation. Says Jimmy Nelson, organisation development coordinator:

Bil Mar uses supervisor skills and talents to build commitment to teams, by them being active facilitators. I must admit that when [we] first started we did not believe or understand this principle. We even excluded supervisors from some team meetings because we felt team members would share more if the supervisor was not in the room. What we discovered was that they would share more, but solving problems was next to impossible without a supervisor's active involvement... [We must] use the talents and skills of all employees, especially supervisors, by training the latter to be team facilitators.

Our original team programme was started without supervisor or management involvement which was a critical error. Without their involvement, teams were destined to fail, and they did. (Nelson, 1997)

One of Bil Mar's problems was their initial belief that 'team members would share more if the supervisor was not in the room'. The energised enterprise, however, carefully selects and properly trains its supervisors to be both a member and leader of the team. They are responsible for selecting team members, and work with them, have their breaks with the team and so on; in such circumstances 'holding back' while the supervisor is there would be seen as a significant failure.

But Bil Mar learned from its mistakes. Jimmy Nelson has established a highly focused facilitator skills training programme designed to develop the supervisors into team champions. He reckons that if the facilitators are to take their teams to high performance they must be great teachers, great leaders, great actors, great managers and great planners and has built his programme around these qualities.

The supervisors/facilitators have to bring their experience to the role not rely on packaged 'one minute' off-the-shelf programmes; they must know where the team is going since they cannot lead if there is no desti-nation, they need goals – 'probably the single most important element a team can have'; they need to be able to dramatise ideas to keep the team's attention; they need to be able to provide direction; they need to be listeners; they need to be able to document achievements; they need to be able to devolve responsibility and hold people accountable; they need to be able to celebrate success. Jimmy Nelson is full of great ideas – I do not agree with all of them but in his main thrust he is spot on!

GUIDELINES FOR ESTABLISHING REAL TEAMS

We have used the lions and cheetah analogies but a human enterprise *is* different from a pride of lions. Every one of the characteristic put forward by Ian Thomas, and extended by me, has virtually 100 per cent correlation with a human enterprise, but in our complex world there are additional features that make for success, so let us have a look at some of them.

Setting the scene

Before anything happens the environment must be right. You cannot graft a rose on to a pear tree – at least most of us cannot. No doubt there is some master gardener somewhere...

◆ The strategy, values, sense of purpose and goals of the enterprise have to be well defined, conducive for teamworking and permeate the whole organisation. You cannot construct an edifice which has any chance of remaining stable without the foundations being properly in place. Seeking to establish real teamworking without changing anything else is a recipe for failure.

◆ Top executives have to create the environment by setting the example of effective teamworking at the top. They must be seen to participate in horizontal, vertical and diagonal teams, for if people perceive that go-getting individualism is the way to succeed no amount of weasel words will have an impact.

◆ Appoint managers and supervisors who have an empathy with team-working – whose technical skills and aptitude are a given and whose personal qualities fit this way of working. Look for those with a challenging mind, who are able to establish a rapport with others and who wish to contribute beyond the routine. Make sure that these attributes are reflected in *everyone* you hire.

◆ Ensure that they first have significant problem-solving and improvement responsibilities in their 'day job'. You can't expect anyone to contribute effectively to new ways in general if they have no such responsibility in specific.

Establishing the team

Most permanent teams will select themselves for they will comprise the people who already work together. But on many occasions you will need to pull out three or four people to perform a specific task; at other times you will want to set up a real multifunctional, multi-level diagonal team. This section is primarily concerned with the latter type but the lessons apply to all.

◆ For the permanent, horizontal teams begin by having the formal leader run the first projects. It is his or her task to equip the team. But do not feel that the supervisor has always to be there, for once people gain confidence they will want to walk on their own. *With experience come skill, with skill comes confidence and with confidence comes trust.* And you are then in the positive upward spiral – no-one is threatened.

For the diagonal teams, it is probably best if the first leaders are appointed from outside, but again as experience, skill, confidence and trust begin to feed off each other the teams will be able to find their own way.

◆ Select the right people for the task ensuring, as best you can, that there are no passengers. If you want to use a 'scientific' selection method, so be it, but for the most part your choice will be restricted to the small number of available people. You will find that a good mix of people of different ages and sexes will bring a valuable diversity of experience. In any case, as you progress along the path to becoming an energised enterprise your selection will increasingly have been undertaken at source. If you subsequently find that some individuals do not fit then that is a problem with the initial selection decision, and the person may well have to be tackled in another way.

◆ Involve people from all functions who will have a significant input. But get the balance right, otherwise you will overload the team with bored part-time contributors who, Murphy's Law being what it is, will fade away just before they are needed. You can always pull in individuals for advice on a specific problem or for temporary membership as the need arises.

◆ Establish clear, time-bound goals which must be within the capability and control of the team, and ensure that the members are accountable for achieving them. But should the goals be set from outside or from inside the group? Quite honestly, it will be horses for courses. When the team is established top-down to work on a particular task it may well be right for the goals to be determined for them. When the team emerges bottom-up to work on something which it wants to tackle then clearly, self-determined goals will be right. Between the two, a manager may set the broad direction and the team establishes the specific goals. No doubt there are many permutations but the important point is that the team must know what it is to achieve.

◆ However, recognise that not all goals will be tangible. A tremendous bonus from teamworking is the thrust it gives to the 'continuous development' of the participants (see pp. 199–207 of *The Ascendant Organisation*) enabling them to grow and develop as individuals throughout their working lives. But how do you measure the personal growth and development of the team members? How do you recognise improvements in morale? How do you assess improvements in relationships both between colleagues and with people from outside the company? How do you capture improvements that emerge which are not part of the initially determined goals?

Of course, you can talk of attitude surveys and the like (and they have their place) but we are discussing what the enterprise *feels like*. Often, this is the biggest benefit of all because it permeates everything you do.

So, seek to balance the tangible and intangible.

◆ Teach the process skills the team will require, but do so just in time and often not until the team itself actually recognises the need. Team members will need to learn how to define the task, breaking it down into its constituent elements; they need learn how to plan that it will be achieved in time by the proper organisation of resources, by allocating responsibilities and by establishing a schedule; they need to learn how to use analytical problem-solving tools and how to evaluate their trials and prototypes; they need to be able to assess the impact of their ideas on other people and processes before they implement their better way.

But do not send them on training courses months in advance because without the experience within which they can place their new knowledge much of its relevance will be lost – and then forgotten by the time they need it.

◆ Ensure the team has the authority to achieve its task. If they feel they have to call in specialists from other functions, from suppliers or talk with customers make sure they know they can do so without having to go through some vast approval process. Ensure the budget is there so that if they need to work overtime they can do so.

◆ Provide *all* the resources to do the job – and in particular the scarcest and most valuable resource – time. Money and facilities are the easy part – but time is always at a premium. Team members find it easy to understand that money is scarce and that there is a great demand on facilities, and that can be forgiven. But when time is not allowed, that goes to the very heart of the commitment. Management's failure to deliver 'time' says that the task is not important. Nothing is more demoralising, and it is not forgiven. Better that you had never started.

◆ Provide support. This takes many forms, including training but as, if not more, important is the support that comes from being there when needed, shielding the team from the impatience of others, and representing it when representation is needed. As sports teams know, it is easy for supporters to be there when things are going well; the really valued supporters are those who remain when the going gets tough.

Team dynamics

Real teams take on a life of their own but if they are to be successful a number of guidelines will help:

◆ Allow the teams to develop their own ways of working, their own 'how'. Often, the 'how' is more important than the 'what'. Do they want to define roles and responsibilities at the beginning or let members find their own level? Will they keep detailed records or will they be informal? Do they want to meet on a fixed schedule or as and when necessary? There are no universally correct answers. What matters is not that their methods initially are ideal (they will soon learn) but that they are shared, understood and owned.

Then leave the team alone to get on and do its job – unless they ask for help, and then be ready to provide it. But there is nothing worse than managers who keep poking their noses in wanting to know how things are going. It's annoying for the team, builds up bureaucratic 'noise' and resentment, and sends out the message that the team is not trusted. Unfortunately the 'nose pokers' are the very people who are not available when really needed.

◆ Providing an appreciation of the dynamics of a team will help. Knowing, to use Andrew Leigh's terminology, that they will start, sort, stabilise, strive, succeed, and stop will help them to appreciate that their inevitable frustrations are not unusual. However, if they attempt precisely to follow a model they will quickly find that the real world is not like that and will end up being even more frustrated. The watch-words must be to understand and use wisely, not to follow slavishly.

◆ Recognise the need for both 'top-down' and 'bottom-up' teams. Top down – 'Can the four of you get together and find a way by Friday week of transferring the offcuts to the pallets so that Michael does not strain his back every time'. Bottom-up – 'We reckon that if we were to re-write the form, applicants would not get so confused and we would get a better take-up rate'.

◆ Try to ensure that improvement activities benefit the members as well as the enterprise. 'What's in it for me?' remains very powerful.

◆ Encourage and ensure the involvement of all team members. Just because someone has specialist knowledge does not mean that he or she should be restricted to that specialism. Just because some are initially quiet does not mean that they cannot make a profound contribution. This is where the skills of the coach/leader come to the fore. Imagine what can happen to such people if they are excluded. The team will be amazed at what they have to offer beyond the obvious.

◆ Appreciate that there will be conflict. As stated earlier an effective real team is not always a comfortable place. There may be internal conflict and jockeying for position, particularly for leadership, but this is natural phase on the road to maturity. As real teamworking develops and people gain experience of working in many teams it will become easier, a way of working will emerge and many teams will be able to slot quickly into striving and succeeding.

◆ Recognise that while achieving a task, a team is an entity in which members can contribute and direct their intellectual and practical capabilities and energy towards both the success of the enterprise and their own personal growth and development. By encouraging people to exercise judgement they become genuinely part of the enterprise; and when supported, guided and recognised, teams are the most powerful tools imaginable for improving every aspect of the business.

The whole is greater than the sum of the parts and a large part of the 'whole' is personal development. Team members should be able to take back to their 'day job' experience and capabilities that will bring about permanent benefit.

◆ The team initially may set its own boundaries but will quickly find itself pushing against them. No problem – for in the energised enterprise you will have hundreds of teams all pushing the boundaries. Occasionally they may trip over the boundary rope, but remember, you only trip when you are moving forward! If you are standing still nothing happens, no waves are made and no progress achieved.

It's easy to say, but just recognise that they will have boundary problems and sort them out as they go along.

◆ Encourage the teams always to challenge the established way, especially if it is working well and people are comfortable with it. The Japanese say, 'Squeeze the dry towel dry.' There is always more to be gained. I have often asked teams to throw a pebble in the pond and see where the ripples spread to. The results can be surprising.

◆ Go for a few early successes, for nothing succeeds like success (and when complacency sets in, nothing *fails* like success!). When they have tackled small things, start becoming ambitious and go for some big goals. Get beyond the solution to today's problems and tackle fundamental improvements in the way of doing business.

◆ When the team has improved something, leave it for a while and then go back later and improve it some more.

◆ Recognise achievement in an appropriate way. Here I speak of non-financial recognition which can take many forms – from the 'hoopla and hats' loved by Americans and the, 'Let's go to the pub for a celebration pint,' favoured by the British, but experience tells us that while such events initially work well, their staying power is limited if they become mechanical.

Much more powerful in the long term is recognition by managers and, in particular, their peers that they have done a great job. This does not mean requiring that the team makes grand presentations to the managers – we do not want them spending more time preparing the presentation than they did doing the job. Anyway, when you have hundreds of permanent and temporary teams, managers will not be able to sit through them all.

But when top managers are walking around, make sure they pick up on achievements – genuine interest in an off-the-cuff demonstration in the workplace is worth a hundred formal presentations in which everyone goes through the motions. Saying 'thank you' is worth a thousand.

Then having had this face-to-face contact, follow up with a personal *handwritten* note expressing your appreciation of a job well done. To me this is the most powerful recognition of all – it shows that you were paying attention and it is something meaningful which people can take home to show their family. People keep these notes for years. They're not part of a routine 'Employee of the Month' award and they should never become 'ten a penny'. When in 1996 I met one of the personnel officers who worked for me in my Ford days in the late-1970s he said, 'You know, I've still got that note you gave to me after the underbody assembly strike. That did more for my morale than anything else anyone's ever done before or since.'

Often, the best reward for a successful team is to participate in another team with an even bigger task!

◆ At all times, communicate, communicate, communicate – within, between and beyond the teams. Or, in simple language, talk together. Everyone's opinion counts and everyone should feel safe and free to express it.

Communication must be meaningful and relevant and in appropriate language. When coming from the top it must not stop at the one-off big news items or be restricted to the vision statement. Most people like to know what is happening in their business, what it is doing and where it is going. While they pay greatest attention to issues that immediately affect them, no-one should ever be able to say, 'If only they had told us we could have done something about it.'

But the teams are not just the recipients – they must be open, and share their experiences and concerns with others.

Winding up

There are only a small number of guidelines here:

◆ When the team has completed its task, make sure it breaks up and the members move on to other challenges. There is nothing worse than a team that keeps a project going beyond its useful life. It ends up as some self-perpetuating committee.

◆ Ensure, however, that the achievements are recorded and the lessons transferred. I have always found when presenting or listening to the achievements of successful teams that the biggest difficulty is putting over what it was like *before* they began their initiative. One way is to take photographs or videos at the beginning and end, or retain the previous procedure or the record of customer complaints.

◆ Ensure that the lessons are transferred. This is something that everyone talks about but few actually do particularly well. When discussing innovation teams we saw the British Aerospace example, but few can go to such lengths. One of the great things about the ener-gised enterprise is that people can talk freely with their colleagues up, down and across the organisation. All you have to do is make it happen!

TEAM REWARDS

There is one major omission from the above listing – financial rewards, and I am afraid that here I have to disagree with the many consultants and some practitioners who advocate a team-based reward structure. My starting point has always been that:

◆ **It is management's job 365 days of the year to motivate the workforce – not the reward structure's.**

◆ **The reward structure must be an outcome of good man-agement, not a substitute for it.**

◆ **Over-reliance on the reward structure causes managers to abdicate their responsibility to motivate the workforce.**

Because in the energised enterprise real teamworking is the norm, debates about rewards for team performance are a waste of breath. When real teamworking is the norm individuals will at the same time be members of several different horizontal, vertical and diagonal teams. Some of the diagonal teams may be formal top-down project groups, others will be an informal group of colleagues who, without saying anything to anyone, get together in their free time to try something out.

In their permanent horizontal teams they will have both short- and long-term goals concerned with meeting their schedules and improving their performance. *This is what they are paid to achieve; they should not be separately rewarded for achieving what they are paid to achieve.* Attempts to construct team-based reward structures for these permanent teams lead to confusion and short-term thinking and can often militate against the very concept of teamworking. However sophisticated such a reward structure may seem, it is doomed to fail because it is based on the concept that teams are about structures and that they are special. They are not.

Anyway, an individual may be involved in a number of teams some of which may spectacularly succeed while others may achieve less than the desired results. It is not inconceivable for a person to make a poor contribution to the former and a good contribution to the latter. In such an environment how can a team-based reward structure be constructed? The answer is that it can not.

One of the most interesting studies of recent years was conducted by Motorola, the 145,000-strong electronics company that is regularly cited as one of the exemplar companies that begin the business fad cycle (Gedvilas, 1997). Motorola began to introduce teamworking in 1987 and at the same time refocused its reward structure to give greater emphasis to team performance. As the programme matured the HR managers somehow got the feeling that the rewards weren't what made the teams most effective and decided in 1994 that across five production sites around the world they would take the entire programme apart to find out what worked and what did not. The research team, led by Maggi Coil, Motorola's compensation director, interviewed senior managers, coaches and team leaders but most attention was given to the people actually living with and performing in teams.

The results bore out the suspicions. Team rewards were a necessary but not sufficient ingredient for team success. The most vital ingredients were employee involvement and empowerment and, said James Stoeckmann, compensation and benefits manager at the Phoenix plant:

From the interview we learned that management behaviour was critical in reinforcing team effectiveness.

Surprise, surprise!

The following findings stood out (Gedvilas, 1997):

◆ Employees were clear: money was not high on their list as an incentive.

◆ Better communication was needed to convey what is offered.

◆ Recognition was needed for the right things, not the firefighters.

◆ Treat people fairly and do not dwell on money.

◆ Be prepared for the management issue.

◆ Take the time to say thank you to employees.

◆ Integrate teaming into performance measures.

◆ Ensure that training is provided in team processes.

◆ Be cautious of 'teams for teams' sake'.

◆ Emphasise team processes over results

◆ Rewards should align to the team cycle.

There is very little in these results that does not correspond exactly with everything I have written, but there is one interesting addition. Said James Stoeckmann:

Individuals also expressed the desire to be recognised as individuals amid the organisation's team environment.

And, Maggi Coil added:

They cited real concerns with cash as a reward vehicle for teams because they felt it can so easily be dysfunctional. No matter how well a team reward system is designed, you still need to reward people individually.

This is spot on. People want individual financial recognition, even when they get all the pats on the back and 'Thank you' notes. Pats on the back do not buy bread!

The Motorola study showed that employees overwhelmingly wanted annual merit increases linked to individual, not team performance. This is from one of the best led and managed companies in the world, one which has been deeply committed to real teamworking for more than ten years now and which had the confidence and maturity to study if what it had been doing was right. There are some fundamental lessons to be learned.

Some 13 years earlier all of this thinking was in our minds when we were setting up Nissan. We were committed to 'management motivating the workforce 365 days year', but we also said that our reward structure should recognise those things we considered important, teamworking being not least among them. The reward structure had to be an outcome of good management not a substitute for it.

Nissan UK is an enterprise more committed to the concept of real teamworking than virtually any other company, anywhere, and although at the beginning it was not as rational or logical as now it seems to be, we had this gut feeling that we had to find a way of integrating real, multidirectional teamworking with rewarding individual contributions. For some ten years I received more questions about this than any other issue of detail. 'Isn't there a fundamental contradiction between teamworking and individual merit?' so it must be problem to many.

We decided to square the circle by including 'teamworking' as a vital element of our performance appraisal and management system. Using our standard methodology of defining a number of performance levels related to the element under consideration, a useful set of definitions (though not precisely those now used by Nissan) is:

> **Teamworking**
> Always participates fully and respects the needs of the team
> Works well as a team member
> Becomes involved when encouraged
> Not supportive of team working
> Prefers own company – a loner

This system is more fully discussed in *The Ascendant Organisation* (pp. 128–34) but, briefly, all those elements of individual performance we consider important (including quality, innovation, flexibility, motivation, performance against objectives and some dozen more) are assessed. An overall rating based on performance against all of the criteria is then given and development needs and plans determined. Individuals receive a merit increase related to their overall performance, which includes their contribution to teamworking. It has now worked well for some 15 years.

The central thrust of real teamworking is involving everyone in improvement – doing things better – innovating, so let us now look at innovation in more detail.

9

Everyone an Innovator

Have you ever held a conversation or listened to a presentation and found yourself in full agreement, only to realise half an hour later that you had been agreeing with someone who used the same words as you but meant something very different?

This happens all the time when discussing innovation. We all glibly use the word, but give it many different meanings. Interpretations range from 'continuous improvement' to 'invention'; from 'creating the new' to 'developing the old'; from internal changes to changes which impact only on external relationships. For some, you can only innovate with regard to a product or service; for others innovation covers any improvement in any aspect of our lives. For some, innovation comes from within, requiring a supportive culture and planned research; for others it requires technological change and external pressure and stimuli.

All of us are born creative in the sense of having free-flowing imagination. Who but a child could have described these natural phenomena so evocatively and accurately?

> 'Thunder is a big source of loudness.'
> 'Wind is like air, only pushier.'
> 'Evaporation gets blamed for a lot of things people forget to put the top on.'
> 'It's so hot in some places that the people there have to live in other places.'

Except for a very few, our upbringing drives out this imagination and creativity, and seeks to substitute logic, judgement and caution. Very few of us are genuine inventors, people who create something – a device or a method – that was not there before. But the right environment can stimulate everyone's latent imagination and creativity. Therefore I use 'innovation' to cover all thinking by all people which leads to new actions, new products and new services, whether they be incremental or radical, large or small. There is a continuum and to attempt fine distinctions is to move into angels on pinheads territory. Therefore:

> ## ALL OF US CAN BE INNOVATORS

This is a high expectation – but when you set low expectations, people have no difficulty in living down to them! According to George Bernard Shaw the reasonable man adapts himself to the world, the unreasonable man persists in trying to adapt the world to himself. All progress depends therefore on the unreasonable man. We can therefore all be unreasonable!

We used to distinguish between the incremental and the radical, between Japanese *kaizen* – 'continuous improvement' – and Western 'innovation' or radical improvement. For years, advocates of the Japanese approach, myself included, extolled the virtues of *kaizen*, arguing that success comes from recognising that the people doing a job know more about that job than anyone else and that the managerial task is to tap that knowledge, bringing out the hundreds of 0.01 per cent improvements that only the person doing the job can know about. 'No improvement is too small', we said. If you have continuous improvement you should never need to radically improve. We were right – the power of *kaizen* is enormous, but we were also wrong – *kaizen* alone is not enough. We now know that:

> ### Kaizen works when a company is already highly effective.

Kaizen worked in Japan in those companies which were already at a high level of effectiveness – it was not the way out of trouble for those companies which were at rock-bottom. It worked well in the export-led automotive and electronics industries. It was barely tried in domestically orientated companies.

Kaizen will never make the in-and-out Christmas shop into a Käthe Wohlfahrt. If you are at rock-bottom it will never give you the major lift-off you need. By the time you have *kaizened* yourself up a percentage point or two the competition will be out of sight. *Kaizen* will not create the new product. As Joseph Schumpeter so astutely observed, improvements in mail coaches did not lead to the railway, nor did improvements in ice storage lead to the refrigerator. *Kaizen* will improve the present, it will not create the future.

We were enthralled and blinded by Japanese success. Brilliant manu-facturers and engineers, with an artificially weak currency, cheap money, low profit requirements, a protected home market and the ability to sell everything they produced, they could afford to seek the hundreds of 0.01 per cent improvements. But when the going got tough, when the yen more than doubled in strength, when their financial bubble burst they found that *kaizen* alone was insufficient – they needed *kaikaku* – radical improvement.

The West, on the other hand, opted for radical change. We had little time for *kaizen*. We thought that periodic major improvements were enough, that 'new' was better than 'improved' – we were not interested in the hundreds of 0.01 per cent improvements. But as with *kaizen,* radical change alone was not enough. For we were then content to leave things alone, believing that the improvements would be sustained – they were not. The benefits were often lost as, in typical butterfly fashion, our atten-tion turned elsewhere.

Let us compare the approaches graphically (Figure 9.1).

The trick, of course, is to combine the radical with the incremental. It does not really matter where you begin. More does not always mean better, but the more of the 'hundreds of 0.01 per cent improvements' you achieve, the greater are your chances that you will hit on the 0.1 or 1.0 per cent, or maybe even the 10 per cent, radical improvements. They are the continuously fertilised soil in which the big ideas can flourish. Or a steady stream of significant changes can create the environment in which everyone is prompted to seek the hundreds of 0.01 per cents. Wherever you begin, the combined improvement curve shown at the bottom right is steeper than either Western radical change or Japanese *kaizen* can achieve by itself.

Incremental and radical innovation are not enemies – they mutually reinforce. The challenge is to achieve the steep curve.

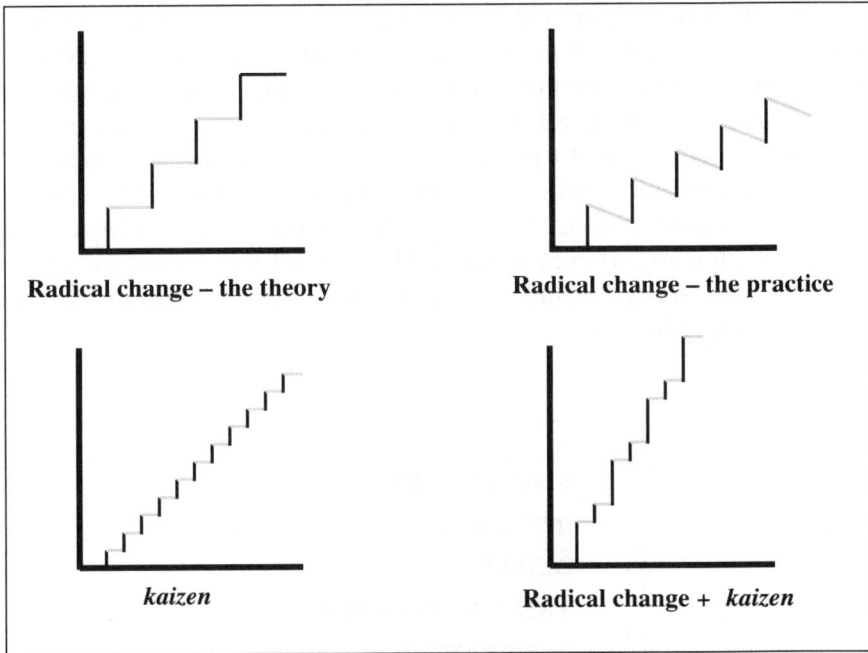

Radical change – the theory

Radical change – the practice

kaizen

Radical change + *kaizen*

Figure 9.1 Japanese *kaizen* and Western radical change

Innovation does not have to be wholly original, even when new or radical. Most likely it is a development of something which already exists, maybe we have taken an idea from someone and built on it, maybe we have 'borrowed' from elsewhere, sometimes it is sheer chance that a receptive mind happens to light on an idea, but provided it is new to us, it is an innovation. So, what is innovation?

> Innovation is the implementation of a new or revised product, service or process – and it can be applied in every area of the enterprise and at every level.

I emphasis *implementation*. It does not help very much to have a wonderful idea swimming around in our heads never to emerge, nor to have it gathering dust on a shelf at home. And of those ideas which do emerge, 99.9 per cent will not work first time; many will not even get past the first hurdle, and those that eventually are applied will be the result of accumulated knowledge, a fair sprinkling of intuition or instinct (maybe even guesswork), a lot of trial and error, considerable debate, sometimes inspiration, and much hard work... and more hard work... and yet more hard work! James Dyson, inventor of the cyclone cleaner, tried for ten years to get his invention to market and whenever he is asked to explain what it takes, always includes 'determination'. So the innovation sum looks something like this:

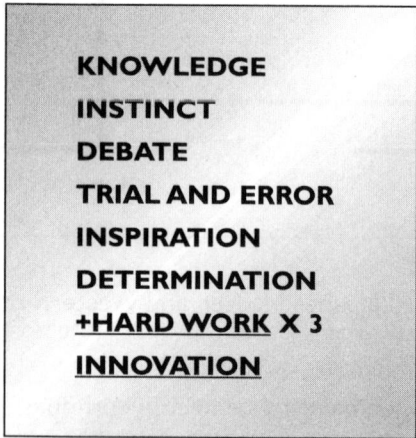

> **KNOWLEDGE**
>
> **INSTINCT**
>
> **DEBATE**
>
> **TRIAL AND ERROR**
>
> **INSPIRATION**
>
> **DETERMINATION**
>
> **+HARD WORK X 3**
>
> **INNOVATION**

But when it goes well you can add to the outcome:

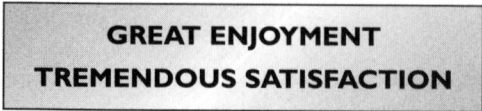

> **GREAT ENJOYMENT**
>
> **TREMENDOUS SATISFACTION**

It's a great feeling, and if you want to energise your enterprise, this is it! You cannot compel innovation but if people gain enjoyment and satisfaction, you will have difficulty stopping it!

Note also, the second part of the definition; 'and it can be applied in every area of the enterprise and at every level'. Really, that is not part of a definition but it is included to emphasise that, as with leadership, we are talking about innovation *throughout* the enterprise and *everyone* being an innovator as a normal part of their work. This is not about some jumped-up suggestions scheme, however 'modern', and however close to the origin the go/no-go decision is made. Nor is it about trying to provide a formula which guarantees success – no such formula exists. Innovations come about as a result of the loner who tries to buck the system and through the highly structured approach of Kodak, Siemens and 3M. It comes about as the result of the great leap forward and from the tiny step. In reality *it is about reaching the point where every single person in the enterprise is paid both to do and to think and where there are no negative assumptions about inability.*

When everyone is paid to do and think, no-one is paid more for doing what they are paid to do! Think about it. If you are a manager or senior executive; if you are an engineer or a customer service representative you are paid both to do and think – why should it be any different if you are an operator on the factory floor or a sales assistant in the department store? Tom Peters goes on about people such as the housekeeper, the doorman and the bellhop at the Ritz-Carlton Hotel in San Francisco who have on-the-spot personal authority to spend up to $2,000 to fix customers' problems (Peters, 1997). This is, no doubt, an extreme example (I wonder what would happen if one of these empowered individuals regularly spent $10,000 a week – there might be the odd constraint or two thrown in!) but it is a very powerful one. We may feel that we have to scale it down, but when people are treated as responsible adults they generally respond as responsible adults. Rarely do they abuse that responsibility.

It's also about commitment. It's about people being dedicated to innovation. While the world is full of stories about dedicated individuals, think about the power of an enterprise full of people who are dedicated to innovation – people who have open minds, who are always seeking the better way. Returning to the model of the ascendant organisation, who can doubt that commitment wins over control?

Think also of the opposite – how many excuses can the closed mind think of? An extraordinarily dynamic lady with a tremendous 'can do' spirit, Tracy De Beer of South African floor tile manufacturers, NCI, showed me one of those photocopied lists which people like putting up on notice boards. For Tracy it is a list of everything to avoid. I've changed it somewhat, but its spirit is true to the original:

25 REASONS FOR DOING NOTHING!

1. We've tried that one before.
2. This place is different.
3. It's too expensive.
4. That's beyond our responsibility/authority.
5. We're all too busy to think about things like that.
6. I'm not paid to think — that's the boss's job.
7. It's too radical a change.
8. We do not have the time/staff/money/resources/space...
9. It will make our existing equipment/processes/methods... obsolete.
10. Our company is too big/small/diversified/centralised...
11. The staff will never buy it.
12. We've never done anything like that before.
13. It's not our problem. Let someone else run with it.
14. What's wrong with our current method/product/service...? It still does the job.
15. I just do not like the idea.
16. You're right... but...
17. You're two years ahead of your time.
18. It's not in the budget. Can't it wait until next year.
19. It may be good in theory, but it will not work in practice.
20. Let's put it on hold for a few months — then we may get around to it.
21. Put it in writing and then we'll look at it.
22. Not that one again. Where did you dig it up?
23. Let's form a committee/study group/review body... to really dig into it.
24. I know someone who tried something like that, and look what happened to him.
25. It's impossible!

No doubt you can add many more. There is always a reason for doing nothing.

When we were starting up Nissan in the mid-1980s one of our very strongest pillars was, as previously stated, that people are paid both to do and think. We said,

It is the leader's job to motivate the workforce, not the payment structure's.

Another aphorism was an expression I coined for *The Ascendant Organisation* to reflect what actually happened, and to challenge the popular sentiment that 'knowledge workers' are a new, different species:

Every worker is a knowledge worker.

The result is that about 90 per cent of innovations come from the people doing the job. Of course there must be recognition, both formal and informal, and 'innovation' is an integral part of the appraisal process, but when you free people from the mental straitjacket which forces them to ask, 'If I put this idea forward how much will it be worth to me?' it is like opening the floodgates – you cannot stop the ideas flowing. Suggestions schemes are flawed mechanisms for encouraging innovation – they may have short-term success but rarely is their impact long lasting. They lead to bureaucracy and deceit, but worst of all they lead to the attitude that, 'I am not paid to think but if I do I should get something for it!'

One of the most deceptively simple questions I have ever been asked was, 'What should innovation be about?' It is one of those questions that after the event you feel that in responding you should have gone virtually into autopilot, but the deceptively simple are invariably the most difficult. The lady was not asking about specifics in her own insurance company, and I think my off-the-top-of-the-head response was about two-thirds right, but having given it further consideration I offer the following.

Successful innovation means providing a product, service or process in a way which is:

NEW – BETTER – CHEAPER – FASTER – EASIER – SAFER – MORE ENJOYABLE

It seems obvious, doesn't it?

New

Introduce a product, service or process that was not there before. It may be brand new, a major improvement or a new use for something that already exists.

Better

Improve the quality and perception of the product, service or process. Enhance its ease of use, performance, reliability, longevity, safety and so on. There are many different aspects of quality and performance and the innovative enterprise seeks to impact on them all.

Cheaper

Reduce costs, and provide the product, service or process at a lower price or increased unit profit.

Faster

Reduce the conception to delivery time or the speed of delivery of the product or service or the rate at which it is produced.

Easier

Make the product or service easier to use, produce or deliver so that the staff benefit from innovation. And, as a side effect, make their work more satisfying.

Safer

Make work safer and healthier, always being aware of the impact on people of the 'new, better, cheaper, faster' innovations. It's no good achieving one set of goals at the expense of the very people who make everything happen.

More enjoyable

Why not have that as a goal? It was not in the original list but someone at a seminar in Edinburgh was so convinced that we should be aiming to make work more enjoyable that he persuaded the rest of us that it should be added. When you think of it there are very good reasons why it should be included for it is both an input and an output. Being involved in innovation by itself makes work more enjoyable but if the outcome is also to make it more enjoyable we have a double whammy. So, let's go for it!

There is no set pattern or methodology. Some innovations happen as the result of a carefully structured programme with hundreds of people spending hundreds of thousands of hours in the search for a new product and patents – this is the way drug companies do it, and Siemens, one of the most innovative companies in the world, has some 40,000 patents registered in its name. Other highly innovative companies do not bother with patents. Herman Simon quotes Klaus Grohman of Grohman Engineering, supplier of machines and systems for the assembly of electronic products:

> **We don't apply for patents because we don't have the people to do it, and we hate the bureaucracy. Anyway, the speed of innovation in our industry is much too high in relation to the speed of the patenting process... In the time it would take to get them, we usually have made enormous progress in development. Patents are like a horse and buggy, and we fly a jet plane. (Simon, 1996: 130)**

At the other extreme a lone individual has a great idea which he or she is able to force through or can persuade someone to sponsor; others occur when someone fights *against* the system. Somewhere in the middle are the hundreds of permanent and temporary teams in which people at all levels are encouraged constantly to challenge the existing way There is no one way which guarantees a steady flow of innovations BUT

> **The task of the energising leader is to create the environment in which the knowledge, instinct, creativity and imagination of every single person is brought out, developed and used, so that it translates into innovations which benefit the enterprise, its suppliers, its customers and/or the individual.**

'Creating the environment' is much more than just making encouraging noises and writing 'We believe in innovation' on the laminated sheet attached to the wall in the reception area.

But note that we speak of benefiting suppliers and customers. Benefiting ourselves we can understand, but why suppliers and customers? In Nissan we reached the conclusion that we could be only as good as our suppliers, and when you think that today in manufacturing some 70 per cent of total costs comprises bought-out components and materials this is not a surprising conclusion. Therefore we set up supplier development teams, groups of experienced people whose task it is to work with suppliers to improve every aspect of their performance – quality, productivity, costs, delivery time, safety, morale and management.

Other companies concentrate on their customers. W. L. Gore Inc. the American company famous for its Gore-Tex weatherproof fabrics, spends considerable time working with its customers in the garment and footwear industries, seeking to understand their processes and then employing its high-level research and development resources to help them find solutions to their manufacturing problems. Gore-Tex is used as a brand name on the finished product and the better the quality of that product the more likely are end-users to seek out Gore-Tex as the fabric of choice.

Finding innovative solutions to customers' problems is now a vital ingredient making for competitive success.

The innovative leader is known and seen as a catalyst, constantly seeking to challenge the *status quo*. Richard Branson, Jack Welch, Percy Barnevik, Andy Grove and all those other famed business leaders are known not for their financial acumen (the financial results are the *result* of what they do), but for doing things differently. They change the existing order. They add something that is new.

There is a vast amount written about the learning company, but remember that old saying, commonly attributed to stick-in-the-mud old stagers:

'I've forgotten more than you'll ever learn!'

In my days as an economics undergraduate, one of the most readable of the economics classics (good teachers always have the ability to put over complex ideas in a way which is accessible to the non-expert) was John Maynard Keynes's *General Theory of Interest, Employment and Money*. Said the great man:

> **The greatest difficulty in the world is not for people to accept new ideas, but to make them forget about old ideas (Keynes, 1936).**

We all like the familiar, the comfortable. We all like the existing mouse-trap. We say nostalgically of a car or a pencil sharpener, 'They don't make 'em like that any more', or of people like Charlie Hitchcock, in the 1970s one of Ford's great character plant managers, 'All the real characters have gone.' We are wrong. Who can doubt that the vast majority of today's products are better than those of forty years ago? (Not always of course – but then some people are even becoming nostalgic about the architecture of the 1960s!) Some of us are today's characters, of whom in a few years time our successors will say, 'All the real characters have gone'. *We* are building the products of today, of which in a few years time our successors will say, 'They don't make 'em like that any more'. *We* are building on the history of our enterprise right now – adding our layer, our part of the culture, which will be the nostalgia of tomorrow. So I do not mean 'Forget the past'; I mean:

> **Do not get so comfortable with the present that it prevents you from creating a positive future.**

Wherever you go, take notes of what you see and hear. If you do not you will forget. If Richard Branson can do it, so can you! Battista Errerra, CEO of Ceramic Industries in South Africa visited the 1998 International Trade Fair in Valencia and I was with him for the first two days of his return. Battista was bubbling with ideas, not only for new products but also for process changes and possibly a strategic shift in the positioning of the company. He had brochures, notes, drawings and samples; he under-stood where the competition was going; he had great ideas on the way forward, and the following day on the shop floor waxed enthusiastically to a plant manager about a minor change to a drying process which he was convinced would significantly improve quality.

As CEO, Battista may have a few pips on his shoulder but he under-stands his products, processes and markets; he knows good ideas when he sees them and is not afraid to admit that he learns wherever he goes. He also has the ability to inspire others, and being with him for those two days demonstrated time and again the value of a CEO who really under-stands and cares for his business. It also demonstrated the corollary – that except when there is a need for a company rescue, the CEO who does not understand and care for his business is a waste of space and money!

But you do not have to be a CEO to learn and apply the lessons. *All of us* can learn all the time, wherever we go and whatever we do. I encourage client companies to allow staff at all levels to visit other organisations of all types, not just to have a nice day out but with a brief to make a note of everything they see and hear which can be applied back at the ranch. We then pull together the learning points and determine how we might apply them in 'our' company. The same goes for conferences, books, conversations, visits to other sections, things we hear on the radio or see on the television – all are experiences from which we can learn. The leader who 'does not have time' to read and visit and listen is missing out on rich sources of ideas.

But it does not just happen by itself. We have to put into place the processes by which the learning is shared – written reports, verbal briefings, demonstrations, follow-up activities and so on – and by so doing spread the learning and enable it to grow as it joins with the learning of others. When you read something that sparks an idea do you share it? How do you share it? Why not photocopy the article or paragraphs, pass it around, set up a discussion and see where it leads. Think of the alternative. When we do not share, not only is *our* own learning minimised because we do not have the opportunity of getting our colleagues' reactions and inputs, but *their* learning is zero.

Amazingly, at one stage Microsoft was sufficiently comfortable with the present and its own idea of the future that it almost lost sight of creating an alternative. Bill Gates for years argued that the Internet was a relatively useless toy, that all it did was enable inane chat around the world. Then, somewhere on the road to Damascus he realised its potential and was an overnight convert. Microsoft forgot about its old ideas. But not everyone does – until it is almost too late.

IBM was comfortable in its role as mainframe hardware supplier to the world and ceded the market advantage in software to Microsoft, PCs to Compaq, Packard Bell and the like, and laptops to Toshiba and others. The PC companies selling in the chain stores are in turn losing vast swathes of the market to the direct sellers such as Dell, Gateway and Dan Technology, who hold no stock of finished product but will build to your specification and despatch it to your for next-day delivery.

The Swiss watch industry was decimated by the quartz watch, even though it was a Swiss invention. The comfortable Swiss said, 'Watchmaking is a craft. The customer respects the experience and loves the feeling of centuries of Swiss precision. There can be no other way.' They believed their own mythology, until the Japanese showed that when offered an alternative the customer wants accuracy (and it does not have to be within a millisecond a year), good looks and a low price. For many of us a watch is now a fashion accessory – we have half a dozen.

In another direction, picture the typical bank – they all look pretty much the same, and so do the staff, mostly bored out of their minds, despite all their customer service programmes. But go to a branch of Die Erste Sparkasse Bank in the Styrian region of Austria. They are beautiful. The design combines the very best of traditional Austrian with the very best contemporary materials, lighting, lay out and so on. The ambience is just right – efficient and warm. The staff are genuinely cheerful, and alert; they are proud of their company, they all greet every customer both on arrival and departure. They feel that it is a great place in which to work.

There is a great company, Eurotherm Controls, that produces temperature controllers. They have 180,000 variants of their product in hardware terms and *millions* if you include the software permutations. They have tens of thousands of customers who order in lots varying from one to 100. For years Eurotherm attempted to develop the perfect planning system but totally failed – if it was not their MRP II system it was their customers who did not behave according to plan. They then realised they what they needed was not the perfect plan but *the perfect response* – a revolution in thinking and implementation which has made traditional planning and scheduling activities obsolete. Operations Director, Bill Davis describes it as 'demand-driven agile manufacturing'.

To get there, Eurotherm:

◆ Removed all walls and any other barriers that restricted their ability to configure their plant for maximum flexibility

◆ Established a uniform direction of flow of material and product, with distances between the processes minimised

◆ Created product-based assembly cells

◆ Built in dedicated test software as part of the assembly process

◆ Accepted that 30 per cent excess capacity over the average requirement was a 'must' to allow them to respond to peak demand

◆ Cross trained all operators so they can respond immediately to changes in demand

◆ Single-sourced materials and reduced the number of suppliers

◆ Minimised the number of set up changes and implemented 'quick changeover' on those which remained

◆ Eliminated non-value-adding activities

◆ Challenged and eliminated processes previously considered critical, for example heat soak and inspection

◆ Continuously innovated.

Their results are

> 100 per cent build to order
> > 90 per cent of orders uniquely customised
> 3.5 day average lead time with a 5 day promise
> 94 per cent of standard orders shipped on time
> 99 per cent of next-day orders shipped on time

Go back to their key words:

Forget the perfect plan – go for the perfect response

That is innovation.

To bring it closer to home, I am chairman of international consultants, Organisation Development International, and we have an extremely successful development programme for supervisors – we call it SuperVision – but Managing Director, Barry Venter and I agreed that we had to re-invent it if it was to remain best in the market. It wasn't broke, it didn't need fixing and a lot of people were very comfortable with it, but we said, 'If we do not reinvent our own product someone else will!'

We shared our views with the team and asked them to challenge every aspect of the current programme, and then take it to a new, higher level. We didn't know what the outcome would be, but as leaders of the project we constantly challenged their challenges. As we have seen when discussing teamworking, a team-based project is not a comfortable place – we were not going for a lowest common denominator solution – but we developed a tremendous enthusiasm for change. Team members came to own various sections of the programme and debated vigorously the merits and space requirements of their particular baby, but they worked together to achieve a shared goal.

Both through personal example and by the challenges given, Barry and I were undoubtedly subscribing to two of Akio Morita's celebrated aphorisms:

> **The only way to predict the future is to invent it.**
>
> **My chief job is to constantly stir or rekindle the curiosity of people that gets driven out by bureaucracy.**

Morita was right. Providing the impetus from the top to overcome the inertia of the bureaucracy is vital. Otherwise, as someone once said, 'Eventually, even the forces of inertia will rouse themselves to resist change.'

There are many structural roads to innovation. Kodak refers to it as an 'Ideas Mill', and describes its process for taking innovations from idea to implementation as being much like collecting, selecting, refining and baking grains. To develop the analogy, you have to grow before you collect, you have to prepare the ground before you grow; and after baking you have to take it to the market – but maybe I am being pedantic. The fundamental concept is right, wherever it starts and finishes. Kodak is talking about managing the innovation process and, in a company of its size and international scope, competing in a cut-throat sector in which technology races ahead in dog years, there is little alternative. On top of its Ideas Mill Kodak has a worldwide innovation network which is a bridge between ideas and commercialisation, making sure that new ideas, technology and products zip around its world at a rate of knots – always trying to keep ahead of the competition.

3M has long been famed for its drive to ensure that, currently, in any given year, 30 per cent of sales come from products new to the market within the last four years. No doubt the task will be tightened – perhaps to 35 per cent and three years – the pace is accelerating. But for 3M this is not about, 'Eurekas, miracles or accidental discoveries... It is based much more on a deliberate and rigorous commitment to technological development within a culture which is focused on customer needs and which encourages personal creativity.' UK Managing Director, John Mueller, described innovation as 'the heart-throb of the company'.

Development staff are encouraged to spend up to 15 per cent of their time working on their own projects that excite them. They do not have to ask for approval because 3M knows that this freedom not only attracts good people but actually delivers real results. The frequently told Art Fry 'Post-It' story is the classic example. They are encouraged to network, to get around seeing what is happening elsewhere, to attend exhibitions, to visit other companies. Everything you do can provide the catalyst which stimulates that new idea from which great things can grow.

But 3M goes much further. It sees itself as an $8 billion umbrella organisation designed to encourage innovation. It has some forty product divisions, each operated virtually as an independent enterprise, and each responsible for its own product development. As teams within the divisions successfully develop a new product or business line it is the responsibility of the divisional management to spin it off, with its own new management team who 'own' and have the drive to develop and grow a new self-sustaining enterprise. Out of the original Scotch Tape, first developed in 1930, came four separate divisions with hundreds of applications for business, home and surgical use. The surgical products led to a health care business and to the Medical, Surgical and Orthopaedic Products Division. Business products led to electrical-grade tapes which led to other divisions specialising in electrical connectors, terminals and insulation. That is long-term innovation!

Innovation, for 3M, depends not on large businesses concentrating on today but on small businesses run by the innovators, unshackled from today, concentrating on tomorrow. They have institutionalised 'forgetting' and call it DIVIDE AND GROW. The reward for success is not cash payments but recognition – with photographs and speeches and the like. That is what counts, for when you are paid to do and think there is surely no better reward than recognition from those you respect.

The 3M process inspires an updated example of the old nursery rhyme. Whatever your business –

> **The energising leader**
>
> **Provides the opportunities**
> **That give the experience**
> **That creates the catalyst**
> **That stimulates the thought**
> **That promotes the idea**
> **That results in the prototype**
> **That undergoes the trial**
> **That tests the theory**
> **That causes the change**
> **That results in the decision**
> **To build the product**
> **That goes to market**
> **And achieves success...**
>
> **And this is the house that Jack built**

Critically, the rhyme begins with the energising leader providing the opportunities that give the experience... Energising leaders recognise that it is experiences of all types that stimulate the thought processes. Energising leaders recognise that people at managerial levels have opportunities to get out and visit other companies, trade shows, attend conferences and so on. They know that such experiences are invaluable So, if they want 'everyone to be an innovator' why should such opportunities be denied to those at the operating level?

Towards the end of 1997 I was a judge at the final assessment of an internal, company-wide innovation programme held within the personnel functions of British Aerospace (BAe), a multidivisional company in which there is real decentralisation – so much so that there are major differences between the employment policies and practices of the different divisions. I've always been somewhat sceptical about such competitions, but this exercise worked superbly. Called 'Developing Us' it was led by Personnel Director, Terry Morgan (who, in a previous incarnation, was Managing Director of Land Rover), and the whole purpose was to recognise and share best practices. Over a period of several months every team in every division who had done anything that was at all innovative was asked to share it with their colleagues, and those considered to have the widest application were brought forward to the 'finals' in Birmingham.

In the true and original sense of the words, they literally created a marketplace (with stalls, displays and demonstrators) for innovation, except that in this market, everything was free!

In this marketplace were nearly thirty best practice innovations, each with a fully facilitised display. People from all over the company came along to view and take home anything they thought would be useful to them. The 'produce' ranged from the informality of 'The Doughnut Session' to the formal 'AVRO Stockport School Engineering Training Scheme (ASSET)'. The top six formally presented their wares to the judges and we gave the gold award to the Royal Ordnance Division's single-status programme, which was jointly presented by trade union and management representatives. It was a brilliant example of innovation; it was not brand new, many companies have gone down this road, but it was new for any division of BAe; they had borrowed from many different sources; they had worked long and hard and had suffered the pain and tribulations of negotiating with tough but constructive trade union representatives – and they emerged with a single status agreement which is the best I have ever seen.

But that is not the point. The point is that the whole event was inspiring. It was followed by a fantastic evening of dinner, drink and entertainment.

I spoke to many people, some of whom were also initially sceptical – but without exception everyone had picked up ideas and everyone was determined to push further ahead.

You might argue that the long-term benefits are unknown, that such ideas have a short shelf-life and that a really effective company should have no need of such junkets. All of this may be true, but BAe is still emerging from its old civil service mentality, particularly the Royal Ordnance Division, and Terry felt that it needed something radical to shake it up. They will do it again, and maybe a third time, and then the concept may take a different shape or it may run out of steam – who knows where it may lead? That's the great thing – as with discovering your values you do not know where the journey will take you – but you've got a pretty good idea that it will be exciting, that it will energise. It may even spread to other functions. The important point is not the form it takes, or the destination, but the environment it creates.

I love the story of Lego, the Danish manufacturer of the ubiquitous plastic bricks and miniature figures with annual sales around $1.2 billion. Company President, Kjeld Kirk Kristiansen, when convalescing from a serious illness in 1993–94, contemplated his company and concluded:

In the 1980s and early 90s we had in a way been too successful. We were being driven too much by the past and not concerned enough with the future, I realised we had to become less structured in what we do and react more quickly to external events.

There followed a series of predictable activities – devolving responsibility for product mix selection, packaging and future product determination, and so on. But Kristiansen also realised that Lego's competitors were not simply others in the model building business. They also included Sony, Nintendo, Sega and Microsoft, and all such companies competing for the pocket money and presents of the under-tens. The result was the establishment of alliances with software developers and the launch in early 1998 of the first Lego-branded, interactive, micro-chip models.

What are the lessons of the Lego story?

The President gave the lead in challenging existing thinking, and as a result an incredibly successful company broke into new territory. This is great, but should it have needed his serious illness for such innovative thinking to emerge? THINKING TIME IS A PRECIOUS COMMODITY, and throughout a company but especially at the top there is far too little of it. Ask yourself the question, 'Why is it that we just do not seem to have the time for really innovative thinking at the top?'

Is it that those who reach the top are not innovators, or is it that innovators who reach the top get bogged down in the minutiae of managerial and external responsibilities?

How many internal meetings (including meetings of the board) are scheduled for you in your diary and how many of these really add value? How many could you just chop? How many original ideas came from the board meetings? What would happen if you said, 'As from next month I will reduce the time I currently spend on routine internal meetings by 50 per cent, and so will everyone else! Fix it!' (That's central dictation for you – sometimes it really helps). 'And what's more, in six months' time it will go down to 25 per cent!' Think of the waves it will make, but I guarantee you that everything will still get done – probably quicker and easier than before. We all moan about the number of meetings we have to attend but have you ever thought that somewhere out there, there is a new twist to the Parkinson principles? *The number and length of meetings expands in proportion to the number of people who would rather attend meetings than get on with the job.* Why not check out who are the top ten meeting-attenders and ban them from attending any meeting for six months.

How many times do we just *have to* (want to, prefer to) go to that Chamber of Commerce meeting; meet that government minister; attend that lunch, give that speech and spend so much time telling people how well we have done in the past and how comfortable we are with the present that we forget that our priority is to create an effective future? Of course, we can justify it by talking about networking or being a good corporate neighbour, but HOW MANY WIDGETS DOES IT SELL?

If you really want to be an innovative leader, use the time you create to get where the action is.

- ◆ Talk with the people in your company to find out what really makes them tick.

- ◆ Talk with customers, both actual and particularly potential, finding out for yourself, not through some focus group, what they really like about your products or services or why they have not purchased them.

- ◆ Talk with suppliers, seeking to understand the problems *you* give *them* instead of always telling them the problems they give you.

- ◆ Meet the young development people, discovering their ideas which appeal to the 25-year-olds, but never even reach the

50-year-old, grey-suited executives comprising the Product Approval Committee, because someone, somewhere thought (undoubtedly correctly) that they would be rejected.

◆ Go round the stores observing how customers handle your products and ask them why they do or do not buy.

◆ Actually become a customer – see how you are treated; find out for yourself how easy or difficult it is to understand the forms you are asked to sign, or comprehend the instructions.

◆ Use your own product or service as a real customer does, not as an executive who gets given it on a plate.

◆ Meet with people from outside your company. Explore ideas with them, bounce things off each other. The concept of the ascendant organisation came about as the result of a late night conversation in a Düsseldorf bar with a German academic with a trade union background.

If you want to be an innovative leader, start here – but do not end here.

Michel Syrett and Jean Lammiman in their study, *Innovation at the Top: Where do Executives get their Ideas?* (1998) asked some 120 CEOs the location and circumstances of their best ideas. The responses included: 'On a Eurostar trip to Paris', 'While playing music', 'Watching television', 'Relaxing on the beach', and 'Reflecting in church'. They found that most were not thinking about a business problem when inspiration came – they were in situations in which their mind was able to 'dream and drift' in a random manner, making connections between the previously unconnected.

They tell the story of David Heslop, managing director of Mazda Cars who while driving and listening to music was reflecting on the link between the car and bicycles. His train of thought went something like this:

A bicycle is a bicycle – until you make it into a folding bicycle which can be fitted into a bag – and then it becomes a 'boot-bike' capable of being stored in the boot of a car while you are at work... So where can executives use a bike easily? Perhaps disused railway lines? ...Birmingham wants to put itself on the map. Why does it not promote itself as the bicycle city of the world, as part of the government's transport strategy? Why does not Mazda help it do so as part of its commitment to be more environmentally friendly?

To make such connections, executives – anyone – have to be exposed to knowledge and experiences beyond their normal working environment. In fact if there is no such exposure we would not be talking about 'the house that Jack built' but about 'Jack being a dull boy'.

The second lesson of the Lego story is that innovation is rarely totally new. Before Lego came along many small boys were given Meccano sets (and still are) for birthday presents, and it wasn't long before the sets became increasingly complex with them then demanding an engine to power the crane or lorry. Many parents succumbed and I always regretted that mine did not. In principle there is no difference between a wind-up engine for a Meccano set and a microchip-controlled Lego model!

Innovation does not have to be about the tangible things. Take the BAe example; it would be rather difficult for personnel people to come up with a better bullet, missile or wing of the Airbus. The gold award went to a single status package; but included in the marketplace were a brilliantly conceived international relocation package which enabled 240 key people and their families to *emigrate* from Britain to France; an interesting new slant on broadband pay structures from the American office and a great variation on the theme of distance-learning programmes. They were not product related; they were not brand new, but they were all new to BAe; they added a new dimension to the familiar, they provided for an international exchange (how often do we bemoan the fact that we should have some way of sharing best practice?), *and they all enabled the personnel people to provide a better service to their colleagues and customers.*

What then are the lessons for the innovative leader in all of this? Here are twenty-one:

---

21 LESSONS FOR THE INNOVATIVE LEADER

1. Above all, create the environment which encourages innovation and then lead by example.

2. Constantly challenge the *status quo*.

3. Seek innovations both large and small, both radical and incremental.

4. Expect all people at all levels both to do and to think.

5. Genuinely devolve real responsibility.

6. Get where the action is. Find out for yourself, not through carefully filtered reports.

---

7. Do not be so satisfied with the past and so comfortable with the present that you forget to create an effective future.

8. Make time for your own creative thinking and ensure that everyone else does the same.

9. Recognise that the best time to do something is *now*.

10. Always achieve the right balance between self-control and commitment, not seeking to control everything that goes on.

11. Create an organisation that is flexible and fits the people, rather than forcing people into predetermined boxes.

12. Be prepared to take risks, and not want every 'i' to be dotted and every 't' to be crossed.

13. Hire good people, give them headroom to spend time working on ideas that stimulate them, provide resources and do not sit on them all the time.

14. Encourage people to get on and 'do their own thing'.

15. Ensure that good work is recognised and rewarded in the right way and know that, for many, recognition is the real reward.

16. Encourage people to find ideas from every possible source and establish processes by which those ideas can be shared.

17. 'Get on with it. Find a way of trying it out', not wait for months or years for everything to be 'proved'. We're not talking about compromising safety here, but often the quick and dirty test can tell you enough about an idea to let you decide if it is 'go' or 'no-go' to the next stage.

18. Allow some contrariness, but seek to channel it constructively.

19. Have a positive attitude to mistakes along the way and do not be afraid of using the word 'fail'. No-one ever got it right first time. In the right environment it's all part of the learning process and we should never forget that *100 per cent of ideas that do not emerge, do not work.* The best piece of advice given to me EVER was, 'If you try, you might; if you don't, you won't'.

20. Ensure you are exposed to diverse experiences.

21. Create innovation teams.

And remember, we are always talking about leadership and innovation at every level of the enterprise. So let us look at the final lesson in more detail.

10

Innovation Teams

The last of the twenty-one lessons for the innovative leader was 'Create innovation teams'. We have discussed teamworking and innovation and I come up with the almost inescapable conclusion that:

INNOVATION + TEAMWORKING = INNOVATION TEAMS

Innovation teams are the most powerful means imaginable for enabling all people throughout the enterprise to direct their intellectual and practical energies towards innovation. In so doing they not only improve every aspect of the enterprise, its products, services and processes, but also ensure their own personal growth.

So powerful can innovation teams be, that it is almost surprising that most of what follows is not much more than good old-fashioned common-sense, and could apply to all types of teams.

Innovation teams (for obvious reasons I will not use the abbreviation, IT) are based on the simple fact that 99.99 per cent of the time

SEVERAL OF US TOGETHER CAN ACHIEVE MORE THAN EACH OF US ALONE

At their most basic, innovation teams are groups of people who work together to innovate. They can be about continuous improvement and about major step-change innovation. They succeed in all areas of the business, from the front line to the boardroom – although, inevitably, in the boardroom they will have some much grander sounding name!

Of course, there will always be the loners beavering away in the proverbial garret, who come up with their personal 'Eureka!' moments, but even for them innovation is the culmination of numerous experiences and interactions. Bouncing ideas off others, brainstorming, using problem-solving techniques and suchlike all help ideas develop and grow and are all group activities that may assist the loner.

Remember Quality Circles – one of the first 'miracle cures' we sought to copy from Japan. In most Western companies they had a shelf-life of two to three years, and real penetration, even in the companies that purported to be successful with them, did not extend very far. They were innovation teams of a particular type. The problem was that we believed the Japanese when they said that they were almost wholly about improving quality, and more seriously, we accepted their own self-deception that they were voluntary. We then attempted to persuade Westerners, brought-up with a 'never volunteer' mentality, that volunteering was a good thing. In Japan, quality circles are not 'almost wholly about improving quality', and they are certainly not voluntary – unless brave individuals accept that when they voluntarily choose not to participate, they also voluntarily choose to be frozen out and voluntarily give up all chances of promotion – that is if they do not voluntarily choose to leave!

So let us be clear. *Innovation teams are not voluntary.* If you, as my boss, ask me to participate, then at that time that is what I am paid to do. I do not have a choice. Well I do, but the choice is not dissimilar to that of the Japanese... plus, my leaving might not be 'voluntary'!

But, equally, they are not compulsory. If they comprise nothing more than top-down tasks imposed by managers concerned solely with their own objectives, the lack of enthusiasm will be visible, the voices of protest audible, and the chances of success zero. As my Japanese colleague, Iwao Kobayashi, puts it in *20 Keys to Workplace Improvement* (1995):

> If **improvement** teams [his term, my emphasis] are merely sub-units of the existing organisational structure, such as workplace groups led by their immediate supervisors, team members will feel like pawns asked to do extra work to meet someone else's goals. It is [then] pointless for team leaders to pressure members to come up with ideas.

Isn't our failure to appreciate Kobayashi's wisdom (even though it hadn't been translated at the time) one of the fundamental reasons for our previous lack of success?

The aim must be to get to the stage where the question of 'voluntary' or 'compulsory' is a non-issue – innovation teams are just our way of life, and until we reach that point we can be certain that their penetration and tenure will be slight. The conceptual leap begins when we recognise that innovation teams must have a much broader remit than just 'quality'; that they must cover every aspect of the enterprise's business and behaviour, that they must be bottom-up (working on areas that really interest the members and are chosen by them), as well as top-down, and that they must be both performance and people orientated.

When discussing teamworking I distinguished between permanent and temporary teams. Permanent teams comprise those people who work together virtually all of the time, and temporary teams those who come together to perform a task, do it and then disband. The permanent teams are the foundation on which the temporary teams are built. Both types of team are about innovation in our definition of the term but for the temporary team their whole role in life is, rather obviously,

TO INNOVATE

But I say the obvious, if only to re-emphasise that they are action based. Their aim is TO DO THINGS, they are not talking shops.

Innovation teams can comprise people wholly from one section, or they can be multifunctional and multi-level. They should be able to call in specialist internal advice without having to go through some vast bureaucratic procedure. They should be able to bring in and visit suppliers, both internal and external, to gain an understanding of mutual problems. They should be able to attend trade shows to learn and to seek ideas. They should be able to acquire materials and resources without having to go through the 'approved supplier'. They should be able to work 'innovation overtime'. They should be able to talk to internal and external customers to understand how anything they may do will impact on those on the receiving end, and how they might improve their service to their customers. They should be able to conduct 'back-of-an-envelope' calculations and 'cheap and dirty' trials.

For all of this there needs to be a budget which should be allocated to the formal leader of the permanent team who will use it at his or her discretion. And this means allocating an innovation budget to the first level of leadership – not to someone three levels up! With these requirements for success, can you wonder that most Western attempts at quality circles failed to live up to the initial aspirations?

Note carefully: all of this goes much further than Japanese practice, which is why, with the right approach, and when we really try, Westerners can achieve so much more than the Japanese.

When, after a few years experience of both approaches, Nissan's British supervisors went to Japan to work on the pilot build of the new Primera, their challenging, analytical and practical approach knocked the spots off their Japanese colleagues. They had become used to an enterprise in the UK in which everything was challenged all the time, they were used to *making* the rules of the game over and over again – unlike their Japanese counterparts who were always seeking consensus for change within the rules. They frightened the Japanese with their audacity and ability.

Imagine what it says to the front liners when they can go directly to suppliers and customers. Compare it with the usual practice, when only the purchasing department can speak to suppliers and only the sales department to customers. Imagine what it says when they can visit trade shows and bypass the formal 'expenditure authority procedure'.

If we have to use the word – that's real empowerment and the more people have of it, the more they want! Great, isn't it? That's the way to energise people. By encouraging people to exercise judgement and responsibility they become genuinely part of the enterprise; and not forgetting the teachings of Abraham Maslow, does it not also move them up his 'needs hierarchy' to the highest levels of 'self-esteem' and 'self-actualisation'? This, of course, is not their prime aim – but what a fantastic spin-off!

An innovation team should have a leader; often but not always it will be the formal leader or the most senior member. The best leader for particular project may be the person with the most, or with the least detailed knowledge; the person whose baby it is, or whose baby it is not; the one who can bring an objective outside view, or who is the most personally committed. All at various times may be a more suitable leader than the formal leader or the most senior member. There is no hard and fast rule. Remember, *everyone can be a leader* and when innovation teams really take off there will be so many different projects going on all at the same time that to insist on the formal leader always being involved, and then always heading up, will be a non-starter. And what glorious leadership development opportunities they offer.

Innovation teams can be top down: 'Will the four of you get together and find a way by Friday week of revising these instructions so that the customer can actually understand them', and bottom up: 'We reckon that if we were to build some sort of removable tray we could catch all the swarf that's falling under the machine and just pull it out. It will save us a rotten job, make our life easier and speed things up'. Effective leaders ensure that many innovation projects benefit the individual as well as the enterprise. They well understand the words of Victor Vroom, previously quoted in the prologue, who expressed the commonsense thinking of the front-line employee, and which bring instantaneous recognition whenever I use them:

> The amount of effort people put into a task depends on whether they believe the effort will produce a better performance, whether that performance will pay off in terms of outcomes and the extent to which those outcomes are attractive.

In simple terms, we must always recognise the WIFM factor – 'What is in it for me?'

So important are innovation teams that I'm going to give some guidelines – the vast majority of which apply whether they are top-down or bottom-up teams. We have already discussed the guidelines for team-working in general and inevitably there is some overlap.

Fourteen guidelines for successful innovation teams

1. They must be action focused, they are not talking shops. Their objective is to do, not to talk – or at least not for too long. Obviously there has to be discussion... but you know what I mean. They can begin either with a broad objective and then refine it, or with a very tightly specified task. It does not really matter. In either case it will most likely change as the group gets going. But before they are very long into their work, the 'action focus' must be clear.

2. There should (nearly) always be time constraints. But be sensible. If the timing is too tight the group will realise that they have no chance of success, and almost give up before they begin. If it is too loose they will go on for ever. 'Tough but just achievable' is a reasonable guideline. Nissan often now uses 'two hour' and 'two day' improvement activities but that is after more than a decade of building up a wealth of experience. Some still take two months. But whatever your experi-

ence, put some time pressure on them, or have them create their own deadlines – most people work best when there is a deadline.

3. Allow sufficient time for the project to be completed during normal working hours. Do not require and expect members to give up their own time – that's when people start to think management is out to get something for nothing. But when you do not 'require and expect' then, almost certainly, as members get caught up in the excitement of their project, they will put in all hours necessary to get it done on time.

4. However, allow for the long-term project – the group that has a bee in its collective bonnet which it cannot precisely specify but knows 'there is something there'. This does not mean total licence, but the good leader knows who can be trusted, and when and how to allow slack or rein in; balancing the right levels of control and commitment.

5. Allow also for the individual who is beavering away at an idea. Despite the power of the innovation team there will still be the loner who, probably in his or her own time, may come up with a brilliant concept. But remember, innovation is about application, and sooner or later the loner will need the support of the team.

6. Make sure that everyone can contribute. Do not worry too much about creating a team comprised of Meredith Belbin's nine personality types (in any case, most innovation teams will have far fewer than nine members). As Ian Thomas showed us, 'No passengers' is a good rule. But balance this by recognising that the only way people can really learn about innovation teams is to participate in innovation teams.

7. Aim for a good mixture of top-down and bottom-up projects, always seeking a balance between performance and people, and if possible combine the benefits. But do not be afraid of making waves. Allow good people the headroom to pursue 'break-the-mould' ideas. Not all the time, of course but enough to create some excitement around the place.

8. MEASURE, MEASURE, MEASURE – but be careful about it. For although we are constantly told that 'what gets measured gets done' we know deep down that 'what gets measured gets manipulated'. People (all of us – you and me, as well as 'them') if given half a chance, will always set goals we know we can achieve, so it often needs some top-down goal setting. An enterprise is not a democracy!

In Nissan in 1994 we developed a top-down, measurable goal – NX'96 – that, overall, productivity should be improved by ten per cent per annum compound for three years. That's pretty tough for an enterprise that was already the most efficient car plant in Europe. We knew that ninety per cent of this would come from the hundreds of 0.01 per cent improvements and left it to the managers, supervisors and their teams to determine how it should be achieved. They developed their own specific goals for new, better, cheaper, faster, easier and safer. Progress measures were installed and the goals were achieved. The drive came from the top, and with such macro-targets it has to, but the 'how' came from people at all levels. The target was achieved. Now, its successor, NEXT 21, is under way.

9. Ensure you have a 'control' process. It may be a complex project management system for formal large-scale projects or nothing more than the beautifully simple 'Improvement Statement' slip used by Bonas Machine Company for improvements that can be introduced almost immediately. The only instruction is:

Briefly describe the changes you are going to make, stating the before and after situation... Advise your team leader and implement the change. If your team leader bars the change he/she will explain why. Add this to your statement and pass it up through management.

The presumption is that the change will take place.

10. Make sure your performance management system includes 'innovation' as one of the criteria on which people are assessed; otherwise it will be left to chance and not be considered important.

11. Always provide support and encouragement. This may require a sponsor or champion, someone who may need to say no more than the occasional, 'How's your project going?', 'It looks as though it's coming on well' and so on. However, sometimes they may need help to release a logjam, to provide more time or to help sell and promote the innovation. Sometimes they may need a little constructive pressure; on others occasions the sponsor may need to protect the team from outside pressure. It is vital that you do not ignore what is going on and that they know the sponsor is there for them when needed.

12. Always communicate and recognise success and give encouragement to failure. Often the best recognition for a successful innovation team is to keep it together and ask them to have a go at a bigger project. And people like others to know that they have achieved something, so give publicity. It does not have to be a big public awards ceremony,

although if that is your style then do it well – there's nothing worse than a half-hearted fireworks display! Whatever your style, success breeds success – but people have to know about it first.

13. Recognise that an innovation team needs training to be an innovation team. There are process skills to learn. For example:

- How to define the task, breaking it down into manageable constituent parts; then building up and developing from the new foundation. As the English Literature academics so aptly put it, 'Deconstruct and then reconstruct'. But always be constructive.
- How to manage projects, so that they can be achieved on time by the proper organisation of the group and its resources, by agreeing specific responsibilities and by establishing a schedule and keeping to it.
- How to think analytically and the use of problem-solving techniques: learning about 'the seven tools', brainstorming, the plan–do–check–action cycle and so on.
- How to communicate effectively and openly, recognising that, for many, discussion and argument about ideas and concepts is new territory. Never must a team member feel unable to express views or make a contribution because of a feeling of inadequacy or a belief that he or she will be put down.
- How to evaluate ideas and proposals and their potential costs and benefits, in particular to appreciate that an expensive hammer to crack a walnut is no solution.
- How subsequent trials and prototypes might be introduced alongside the current methods and how to assess the results. They must never forget that today must continue while tomorrow is planned.
- How to assess its impact on other people, processes and practices, *before* they press the commitment button – no 'auto-destructs' required!
- How to make contact with others both inside and outside the enterprise, and how to obtain the information that is available. People in senior positions are used to visiting others, questioning them, probing for more detail and so on. If you are a front liner and, for business purposes, have never been outside the four walls of your office or factory, it can be a daunting task.

14. Create innovation centres (see below).

None of this is easy and making the mental leap is probably the biggest hurdle of all. Translating the words into deeds is a big job but if the leaders genuinely believe in innovation at all levels it is a job which cannot be shirked.

INNOVATION CENTRES

The professional innovators – researchers, product developers, engineers – have their laboratories, workshops, test areas, marketing trials, product placement exercises and so on. Why should innovation teams be any different? They also need somewhere to work, somewhere to try out their ideas, to experiment away from today.

Most startlingly, in manufacturing, this means the provision of facilitised physical areas. As the gospel of Continuous Improvement spreads I increasingly see areas set aside and called something like Continuous Improvement Area, but for me the best name is:

INNOVATION CENTRES

We have to get away from the idea that all we need is continuous improvement – we want the whole range of innovation. But whatever we call them they are places in which individuals first learn *near the job* about the safe use of the equipment and tools and then try out new ideas; construct improved storage and conveyor systems, modify existing facilities and create new ones, create new products and improve the existing ones: in fact anything which will create something which is new and/or improves quality, cost, throughput, ease of working and safety.

Near the job is vital. We're not talking about some lavishly equipped off-site centre or a corner of the maintenance workshop two buildings away. It should never be an effort or require a special journey to get there. People should be able to pop in for ten minutes or, when they are there, easily get back to their normal place of work. A large manufacturing site can have several innovation centres; a small site may need only one. In an office environment a defined space may not be as important but it *is* possible to set aside rooms or an area that people can use for ongoing projects – which does not have to be cleared away every time. 'Project rooms' close to the place of work are just as valuable as facilitised centres on the shop floor.

It is easy to counter that it is what happens there that counts not where it is, but experience tells that ease of access determines whether people go there at all.

In these centres or workshops people make their own back-of-the-envelope calculations; develop the alternative processes, build their own 'cheap and dirty' prototypes quickly and try them out; make their own mistakes in a safe environment. When it does not work first time they modify it and when that does not do the job they try something else, perhaps getting some expert assistance. Moving from the workshop they conduct their own on-line trials, again going through the learning process The important word throughout is OWN. How often do you find that people reject an idea or solution thought up by someone else, but when it is their own they will move heaven and earth to make it work – and make it work properly – and make it work properly today! I cannot emphasise strongly enough:

OWNERSHIP IS EVERYTHING!

Despite this proven success you cannot imagine (maybe you can) the resistance you can receive when promoting this concept. In one leather processing company some managers got very angry and all the usual objections came flowing out.

'How dare we put people into such a dangerous situation. We will be liable when they injure themselves.'

'We've got specialists who can do the job faster and better.'

'Just where do you think we can put them? We've not got enough space as it is.'

'We can't release people from their normal work – we haven't got the time!'

This went on for several minutes and on this occasion, and as it was not the main business of the day, it was obvious that we were at the 'unripe time' and moved rapidly on.

But these concerns are valid and have to be answered. You must train people properly but you will find that part of the waste of human potential is their unused abilities. You do not go straight into rocket science and electronics but once you begin you will be amazed how quickly you progress. Thorn Lighting has superbly facilitised centres and they provide training in the safe use of the equipment before they will let anyone loose to do their own thing.

You may have more highly skilled people, but ask yourself how often they are used for such work. Are they not so up to their ears in attending to breakdowns and scheduled maintenance that they have no time for such work, and even if they did would it not be about twentieth on their priority list? In any case they will not OWN it and if they do not own it they will not care enough to go through all the trials and tribulations of bringing the baby through from conception to successful delivery, in full working order.

On the question of space, the answer is simple. Every company has enough space. The issue is not the amount of space but *how it is used*. Spend a day in any company, look at the excessive inventory and ill-conceived lay outs, and with just a little effort you will find the space!

The question of available time is sufficiently important that I will shortly devote a small section to it.

In the service sector or in indirect areas of manufacturing enterprises, innovation may not always be as immediately physical, but when you begin you will be surprised how much it is – people are always doing something and are always in each other's way – and how much the same principles apply. Innovation gets in the way of today in an insurance company, super-market, railway station or classroom just as much as it does on the manu-facturing shop floor, and resistance can be just as, if not more, entrenched.

Reread the guidelines. Every single one applies in every sector. The innovation centre may be more mental than physical, it may not be one place (nor is it in manufacturing) but it is still there.

In practice, innovation centres should begin at a fairly modest level, but as people gain experience and confidence; as their capabilities and results increase; as they demand the involvement of experts, other functions, customers and suppliers, they will quickly move into a higher gear. Before long they will want to move on to building low-cost automation devices or dedicated specialist equipment to improve performance. In the service sector, people can set up their surveys and audits, conduct their own trials, test the market response and so on. There is no end to ingenuity and inven-tiveness once it is released.

Sadly, many managers do not believe that 'their' employees have these abilities, but *they do*. The inability lies not with the people but in the managers' inability to recognise the unutilised potential. Of course there is short-term expenditure but it is expenditure which is an investment not a cost – and such expenditure and such resources might even be the test of the leader's willingness genuinely to devolve responsibility and live the words. Then, people may come genuinely to believe.

A question often raised at my seminars is, 'Don't the teams run out of things to do? After all, there must be a limit?' The answer is:

There is no limit, there is no end to innovation.

In the summer of 1997 I revisited a section of the Nissan assembly plant that I had not seen for some 18 months and was astounded at the most recent innovations. In particular the use of 'shuttles' – platforms on which the operator is carried alongside the car, with all the necessary tools and components located in the easiest possible locations and with the minimum of handling. Previously the operator had to shuffle alongside the vehicle while fetching, carrying and manipulating the tools and components. The 'shuttles' are far cheaper and much more effective than a moving 'travelator', all the tools and components are to hand and positioned to minimise effort. They have turned an area that was somewhat frenetic into one in which real innovation has brought about considerable success for the benefit of everyone. 'Shuttle' has replaced 'shuffle'!

Some of the shuttles are very sophisticated and required specialist assistance but the concepts and the drive came from the manufacturing innovation teams. (For the curious, they are called 'shuttles' because at the start of a workstation they hook on to the vehicle's carrier and at the end they are released and 'shuttle' back to the starting point.)

The practical outcomes meet the goals of innovation:

NEW – BETTER – CHEAPER – FASTER – EASIER – SAFER – MORE ENJOYABLE

The whole concept and application is new. And as a result quality is higher, cost is lower, delivery is faster, the work is significantly easier, and it is a lot safer and more enjoyable. The by-products – improved morale and greater motivation – are also there.

It will continue to get better... for ever! There is no end.

FINDING THE TIME!

A great problem for any enterprise starting down this road manifests itself in the scream of anguish, 'We know you are right, but we just do not have the time! Everyone is up to their ears in it! We can't meet today's orders, and if we take people off the job we'll be in even greater trouble!' How many times have you heard – or uttered – such a cry?

Of course, it isn't true – there is in every company masses of wasted time, masses of time which is spent on work which does not add value. *Available time is different from effective time* and the task is to convert available time into effective time. But to do this you have to use some of the available time – and, 'We're up to our ears in it – we have no available time!' The circle could go on for ever. How can you break into it? You could follow the example of Calsonic Exhaust Systems where boldly displayed on the walls is the Improvement Activity Timetable. At the beginning of the year they determine their priority improvement activities, determine who will participate, and then schedule their build so that when the time comes they have built the required numbers, and people can be released.

But this is a company which has already seen the light. When you next are on the receiving end of the 'We do not have time' cry, try this – it works best on a white board because you can erase as you build up the stages, but a flip chart or slide will do.

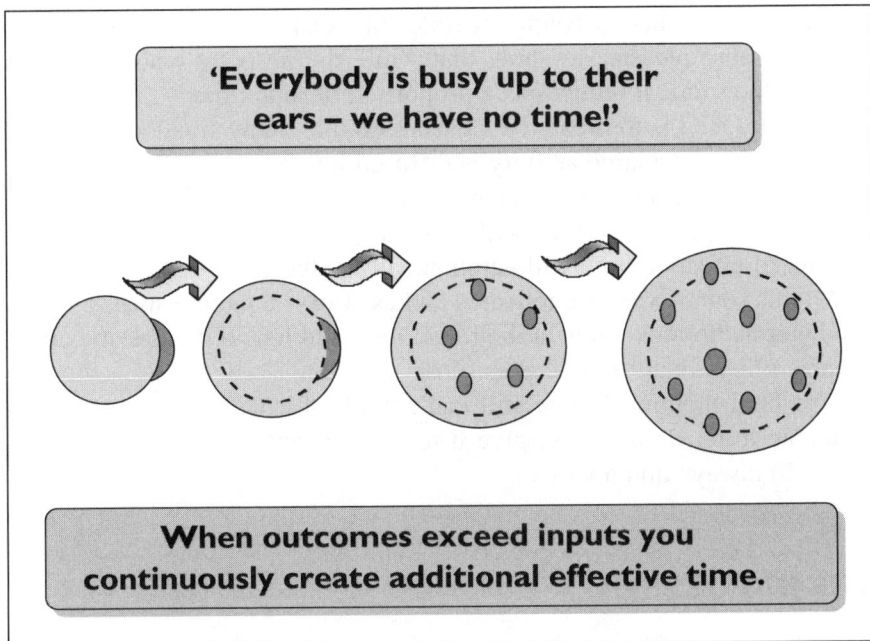

Figure 10.1 Finding the time

Draw a circle and call it 'available time'. The circle represents 100 per cent of available time and in this company the belief is that all the available time is being used – there is no time to spare. Any additional activity has therefore to be additional to the available time, so add a crescent shape on to the outside of the circumference of the circle and shade it in. This represents the additional activity – maybe it has to be undertaken outside normal working hours or by somehow creating the space during normal working hours.

The big mental leap comes when you can convince the manager of the difference between AVAILABLE TIME and EFFECTIVE TIME.

To do this, explain that the output from the additional activity must always exceed the input, so draw another circle with its circumference on the apex of the crescent, then if you have a white-board rub out the first circle. The area of the circle is now larger, and it is larger because your additional activity has enabled you to convert some of the available time into effective time. Not only do the outcomes exceed the inputs but the activity which began as additional work is now inside the circle. Because you now have more effective time the next activity can be completed within the 'available' time.

Repeat the process a couple of times but keep the area of the crescent the same absolute size to show that while the absolute amount of time remains the same, it reduces as a proportion of total time.

The final step is to break the crescent up into many small shapes, indicating that the one large activity is diffused into many small activities. At each step the total effective time increases. And it MUST increase because if it does not, then not only will your input exceed the outcome but the amount of effective time will automatically reduce.

All this sounds very complicated and as always a picture speaks a thousand words. So look again at the illustration and reread the previous paragraphs. I hope that it now makes sense.

One final thought. If you still can't think of a way to make the time available to tackle an issue, give it to some people who work for you – they will always find a way.

THE BIG QUESTION

When I work with companies that are seeking to enhance their leadership performance on innovation my benchmarking statements are:

We are comfortable with our products, services and processes and do not actively encourage either radical or incremental innovation.	Innovation is necessary for future success. We make sure we keep up with the best and use specialist skills and resources to ensure our future competitiveness.	Both radical and incremental innovation, and inventiveness are vital for our competitive success. Everyone in all areas of the business is continually encouraged, and resources are provided, to develop, try out and implement new ideas.

The vital words are contained in the right-hand box where innovation is clearly a long-term strategy, not a short-term palliative: 'Everyone in all areas of the business is continually encouraged, and resources are provided, to develop, try out and implement new ideas'.

In the energised enterprise everyone is an innovator. Everyone works together in innovation teams. Everyone is paid to do and think. Innovation is the way of life.

Using the same scoring system given in Chapter 4, where are you in the spectrum?

Organising the Energised Enterprise

It is people who bring the energised enterprise to life and make it happen, and it is important therefore that we look not only at the big picture but also at some of the detail.

This will not be a text on the mangement of people but some of 'the usual suspects' do have to be put on parade. (If they are not, we will not be able to pick out the guilty!) We will consider how people are organised and how they are treated, for if they perceive that little thought is given to them or if they are treated badly no amount of energising leadership will have any long-term effect.

We will begin with the organisation of work.

THE ORGANISATION OF WORK

The last couple of decades has seen thousands of reports and forecasts about the changing nature of work, usually forecasting the 'death of work as we know it'. Many of the names given to these 'new' practices are contained in the listing of business fads, sacred cows and transitory techniques, but let us remind ourselves of some of them:

Temporary working	Homeworking
Zero hours contracts	Networked company
Fixed-term contracts	Delayered/downsized
Core and periphery	Spin-out/spin-off
Outsourcing	Hot-desking/hoteling
De-jobbed organisation	Portfolio careers
Virtual organisations	Self-employment

There are many more.

Many are technology driven allowing greater flexibility and freedom over when, where and how we work. Predictions about changes to our working arrangements appear with great regularity, but alongside those who forecast 'the death of work as we know it' are others who reach a different conclusion. Using government statistics, Business Strategies said in 1996:

As many as 79.2 per cent of all employees will still be in full-time, permanent jobs in 2005, compared with 82.1 percent today and 83.9 per cent 10 years ago.

Whatever the truth, whichever of the forecasts is most accurate, *it does not matter for the energised enterprise*. Whether or not you are de-jobbed, hot-desked, outsourced or virtual you can be either energised or traditional. Relationships and attitudes do not depend on the nature of work or the way it is structured. Just as we found with teamworking, you can have a great real team comprising people who rarely meet each other, and a terrible team comprised of people who work cheek by jowl.

Technology also facilitates physical changes, although the objectives are often more to do with cost savings than with attempts to move to an energised enterprise. At the Ministry of Defence's Procurement Executive new open-plan office near Bristol, which brings some 15 locations together (primarily an efficiency and cost-based decision), the whole building is designed on the theme of so-called 'linked villages' with a central atrium. Space is allocated according to need rather than rank – or so they say – maybe it is just that the more senior you are the greater your need! At the previous locations, status was measured by the size of your carpet, but at the new facility senior civil servants work alongside junior colleagues. But it will take a lot more than building design to break down the Civil Service's hierarchical distinctions – although physical structures do help, as we found out at Nissan.

In Nissan we found that allocating a individual physical meeting area for every team, with the supervisor's desk being in that area, greatly helped sustain the teamworking ethic. And genuine open-plan offices (without, I emphasise, the dreaded 'cubicles' – which are undoubtedly worse than traditional offices) in which directors, managers and staff sat together enhanced communication a thousandfold. Although, even here we found that the directors (including me) always managed to secure the corner position for themselves. But there are no doors and we actively encouraged anyone who wanted to have a word with the directors just to wander up. Companies which operate a so-called 'open door' policy should try switching to a 'no door' policy. The usual excuses about confidentiality just do not hold water. 'No doors' benefits everyone; no-one abuses it – if they see you are tied up then common sense prevails, but even then we worked on the basis that if someone believes it is important to want to talk to you immediately then it is important that they feel able to do so. If you can develop such a feeling throughout your enterprise you will be fitting another piece into the energising jigsaw – irrespective of what you call your organisation structure.

The fundamental point is that physical conditions and modern technology are not enough. Without new thinking, new facilities are a waste of space – old habits and structures will creep back, that is if they have ever gone away. As I emphasise at virtually every presentation:

> ## IT IS NOT A GREENFIELD SITE THAT COUNTS BUT A GREENFIELD MIND!

However, while Business Strategies' forecast concludes that there will be no early end to full-time, permanent employment, there is no doubt that shifts are taking place. They predict that the number of employees with temporary contracts will increase from 1.5 million to 2.5 million in 2005; the number of self-employed will rise from 3.3 million to 3.6 million and the number of part-timers from 6 million to 6.7 million.

Research by David Guest and Kate Mackenzie Davey for the Careers Research Forum (a group of 31 leading private and public sector companies) into changes at the managerial levels found that:

Whatever is intended, certain characteristics of this new organisation and their consequent implications for career management can be identified. The organisation structure will be flatter, removing the hierarchy on which the traditional career largely depended. Flexibility will be achieved through new kinds of formal and psychological contract, and there will be new challenges in managing core, sub-contracted and temporary workers and the balance between them. (Guest and Mackenzie Davey, 1996)

Their consistent finding is that managers are working harder. A broadening of roles, a reduction in the number of support staff, regular reorganisations and increasing demands have both intensified and extended their work. In the early days of working with the Japanese we compared working practices, observing that the British worked more intensively and the Japanese more extensively. We said, disparaging the Japanese, 'It's not the hours you put into your work that counts – its the work you put into the hours!' Today, for many, it is both intensive and extensive. One senior manager in Guest and Mackenzie Davey's research said:

> **What we actually practice is Taylorism, chaining people to their desks and just turning the wick up under them to get more out of them. It's hypocritical and we'll lose good people because of it.**

If this is the type of comment being made by managers it is not surprising to find it echoed by more junior staff. Not many 'greenfield minds' here!

The UK's Roffey Park Institute examined how far employees have adjusted their career development to flatter structures by returning in 1997 to a group of 200 employees originally interviewed in 1994. They found that the perceived benefits of flatter career structures, which included greater responsibility and teamworking, were greatly outweighed by perceived disadvantages such as lack of career development, increased workloads, stress and inappropriate reward schemes.

Of course, the picture was not uniformly bleak. Two-thirds reported that their jobs were now more satisfying and challenging, and just over half thought that the changes had benefited their organisation. However, 'Most of our respondents appear to retain "traditional" views of career development, namely that career development is mainly progression through the organisation hierarchy.' Even those who approved of flatter structures often did so 'as a means of ensuring that they were well placed for potential promotions, however few' (Holbeche, 1997).

There is, however, another side of the coin – there always is! As we did in Nissan, many companies are finding that once they get to the point at which supply and demand are about in balance, it pays to give a guarantee of 'no compulsory redundancies', subject to the vagaries of the market place. Even Ford, at its Jaguar subsidiary, has said, 'There will be no compulsory redundancies as a result of efficiency improvements provided such efforts continue'. In Nissan we were the first British car company to include the ability to hire temporary workers as part of our agreement with the trade union. This gave us the flexibility which provided security for the permanent staff.

The difficulty for non-core workers is that such security for the core is usually at their expense. The Co-operative Bank negotiated its first employment security deal in 1983 and is convinced that this and subsequent similar deals helped its transformation from being a basket case loss maker in the early 1980s into a profitable and innovative financial institution in the 1990s, with clearly defined and distinctive values.

But as with most such agreements, in the difficult times the non-core staff will be the first to go. Says the Co-operative Bank, in the event of staff surpluses 'the employment of temporary contract and agency contract staff shall be reviewed and subject only to overriding contingencies... such staff shall be released.' Staff on temporary contracts number about ten per cent of its workforce, and that is a pretty good cushion for the core staff. But the temporary staff will be constantly aware that cushions are there for support – and to be sat upon!

Such structural changes can therefore work against the creation of the energised enterprise, and the question becomes, in oversimplified terms: 'How do you motivate people when perceived promotion opportunities are not there to the extent they once were?'

Many of the answers are contained throughout this book and, in terms of structures and organisation, it is no longer sensible to recruit people with the promise of progressive, long-term careers with your company. Some may stay for a long time, others may move between companies of a similar type, others may change their type of work, take career breaks, retire early, move into a different sector, take a series of short-term contracts, become self-employed and so on. All of this has been with us for centuries; it is the rate of it which is accelerating.

But as far as the customer is concerned, none of this makes much difference.

If you wish to compete effectively, *all* staff must all be able to perform to the required standards. You cannot say, 'They're only temps – we do not expect the same standards from them!' The customer is not interested in *who* provides the service – only that it is provided at the required quality at the right time and so on. You cannot offer a sub-standard product or charge a lower price because it was partly assembled by a contract worker.

When it really comes down to it you motivate non-core staff in exactly the same way as core staff. As people, they are no different. They must be trained to the same standard, although their variety of work may be narrower; they should not be regarded as cheap labour although they may begin at the bottom of the pay scale; they will be able to contribute to continuous improvement, indeed their fresh eyes may highlight things that the permanent staff miss. They value recognition in exactly the same way as core staff. The better they are treated, the better they respond. The company which wishes to be world class does not get there by treating some of its staff as second class.

However you organise your staff, whether they all work in one place or all work from home; whether they are full-time permanent or part-time contracted, whether you are a virtual company or a very real one, the same standards and the same treatment must apply to all. The energised enterprise simply cannot afford staff whose attitudes are determined by treatment which tells them that management's view is, 'You're only here for a short time so we do not really have to bother too much with you. If you're no good we can always get rid of you and find someone else.'

The phrase I have always used is,

You do not get a first-class response from people who are treated as second-class citizens.

And this applies to permanent as well as temporary staff. I have argued this fully in both *The Road to Nissan* and *The Ascendant Organisation* and believe that the case is now proven, even though implementation is uneven. When we seek to energise our enterprise there is absolutely no case for different groups of people having different benefits packages, different dining rooms, different car parking spaces, different holidays, pension plans, sickness benefits and so on; and while this does not mean that everyone should be paid the same it does mean, among other things, that the payment structure should be transparent. If top management has some exotic benefits package denied to the minions you cannot expect those who perceive they are treated less well to show the same level of commitment. A rule of thumb is that if top management gives to itself financial benefits they would rather keep quiet about, there must be something wrong.

However, I would not argue that anything less than total harmonisation means that you cannot make significant steps towards energising your enterprise; neither will total harmonisation guarantee success, for as with all reward and benefit systems their impact is but short lived. What we are talking about here is perceived fairness and taking away causes of dissatis-faction. Taking away dissatisfaction does not cause satisfaction but it elim-inates an obstacle and however carefully the reward and benefit structure is created that is all it can do. Real energy comes not from how people are paid but from how they are treated. Karl Albrecht put it best when he said:

> The way employees feel is ultimately the way your customers feel... Many organisations turn their employees into quality terrorists by the way they treat them. (Albrecht, 1988, p. 145)

THE ORGANISATION STRUCTURE

There are even more types of organisation structure than there are employ-ment practices – the list of business fads includes more than sixty. Some are proven and practical, others are little more than metaphors designed to give a trendy title to a book or attract a headline. Some extreme examples are more admired than copied – how many companies have followed ABB's path of 5,000 profit centres with an average of 50 employees? Not very many. Said Percy Barnevik at the Institute of Personnel and Devel-opment's 1997 conference:

> I believe strongly that people working in small groups are more entrepreneurial, get closer to customers, have a better overview and avoid bureaucracy.

But with Barnevik moving on there are already changes afoot, especially to his beloved matrix structure. (Would someone please explain how you avoid bureaucracy with a matrix structure?) For every recipe which is supposed to make for success today there will be another one for tomorrow – in the business fads you will find many, already discarded, old friends as well as many, soon-to-be-discarded, new ones. Will 'boundary-less' and 'horizontal' be with us in ten years time, or will they go the way of 'bureaucracy' and 'donuts'?

We saw in the Prologue when discussing re-engineering that its kernel of value is the battering it gave to the traditional functional silos and the resulting recognition that we need to achieve the optimum balance between processes and functions. But there is no single structure appropriate for all circumstances. Every business will make its own decisions on the fundamental issues of centralisation versus decentralisation, functions versus processes and so on.

However, there is more to getting your structure right than that.

Most organisation structures originate from the desire to make life comfortable for the people who originate organisation structures! However, the energised enterprise does not opt for the comfortable life and, in seeking always to add value for its customers, must have a structure that reflects this.

Cutting through all the hype that is written about 'the new way that will bring success' there are a number of principles that can be applied with benefit by every business. Again, I base the following on work with top managers, but this time include only two statements for each element. The closer you are to the right-hand statement the more likely you are to be energised. The closer you are to the left, the more traditional you are! Ask yourself how you measure up.

TRADITIONAL ORGANISATIONS	ENERGISED ENTERPRISES
Organisation logic Our organisation has 'just grown'. There is no apparent logic behind it. No-one really understands it and it seems constantly to change.	The logic behind our enterprise is well thought out, clear, simple and understood by everyone.
Organisation flexibility Our organisation structure is inflexible, mechanistic and bureaucratic.	Our enterprise's structure is flexible within a consistent framework. It can change to meet changing demands but possesses a basic stability. (See also 'Appointments' below.)
Centralisation/decentralisation Our organisation is highly centralised and is managed on the basis that 'big is beautiful'. Top managers are based at a large, powerful HQ.	Responsibility and authority are devolved by establishing autonomous business units and/or project teams. Top managers are based in the business units. HQ is small.
Organisation layers Our organisation is multi-layered with separate HQ, regions, divisions, business units and so on There are considerable overlaps and complex reporting relationships.	Our enterprise has the necessary minimum number of layers. Responsibility is clearly defined and devolved, and reporting is confined to a small number of key performance indicators.

Processes/functions
We have a high degree of functional spec-ialisation. The concept of business process is neither understood nor thought to be needed.

We have defined our business processes and have achieved the right balance between processes and functions.

Controls
We are top-down control orientated. There is a widespread belief, backed by practice, that results can be improved through stronger and more controls. No-one has discretion to do their job differently or to innovate.

Most of the control on the way the job is done is determined or strongly influenced by the person doing the job. People are encour-aged to innovate and the necessary resources are provided.

Cooperation
Departments and functions do not work together to achieve shared goals. There are frequent conflicts, territorial disputes and political power play.

Cooperation and real teamworking are the norm. Everyone works actively and unself-ishly together to achieve shared goals. Over-laps are worked out in a mature way between the people concerned,

Indirect (or staff) departments
Indirect functions regard themselves as being 'in charge'. They have little experience of, or regard for, the real business.

Indirect functions understand the real busi-ness, and are totally committed to providing a high quality service to the direct activities in a cost effective and speedy manner.

Value adding activities
We have not distinguished between value adding, necessary supporting and non-value adding activities.

We have eliminated most non-value adding activities. Necessary supporting activities have been identified and are at the optimum level.

Core and non-core activities
We have made no attempt to distinguish between core and non-core activities.

We have distinguished between core and non-core activities, and based on long-term strategic thinking have made clear decisions on what to retain, what to outsource and what to dispose of.

Job titles/job descriptions
We have 'hundreds' of job titles and job descriptions which have grown over the years. No attempt has been made to simplify or rationalise them.

We have the necessary minimum of job titles. We have achieved maximum flexibility by eliminating all job descriptions.

Appointments
It is important to appoint people who fit our structure. We are not interested in appointing those who do not fit the mould, however 'good' they might be.

We appoint good people and let the responsi-bilities develop around them. If necessary the organisation chart will eventually catch up.

This listing is not neutral – the energised enterprise will be much closer to the right-hand column than to the left. In particular I want to emphasise the final point:

The energised enterprise appoints good people and lets the responsibilities develop around them. If necessary the organisation chart will eventually catch up.

The spirit of that statement (reinforced by 'organisational flexibility' above) permeates every other element of the organisational principles. It is about flexibility and freedom within a consistent framework as opposed to shackling people to preconceived structures and methods. In Nissan, during our recruitment activities, we often came across superb people who did not fit the specific job we were seeking to fill. 'That's great.' I said. 'If they're that good and they are in line with our broad business needs and culture, then let's appoint them – we are fluid enough to accept and adjust to whatever they bring.' Every such appointment was a success and somewhere along the line the formal structure was amended – but by that time several other changes would also have taken place.

Most organisations, however, will not be at the extremes, and many will legitimately stop short of the right-hand column. That does not matter if it is a conscious decision; but it does matter if there is no decision at all, if your organisation has just grown its poor practices like Topsy. If that is your situation you are likely to be *apathetic*.

As you read the right-hand column, no doubt your head was nodding in broad agreement with most of the statements. But if there was one which caused your eyebrows to raise it may well have been, 'We have achieved maximum flexibility by eliminating all job descriptions'. I have been going on about this for more than twenty years and think that it is now getting through. As I said in *The Ascendant Organisation*:

If you aim for total flexibility, a flat organisation, teamworking, devolved responsibility and continuous improvement, with change being the only constant, then any process which analyses what people do at one point in time, writes it up in immense detail, assigns a grade and a specific job title, allows grading grievances and so on, ends up by restricting rather than expanding what people do. (Wickens, 1998)

Of course there are arguments in favour of job evaluation – an objective measure of comparative worth, a defence against trade union comparability claims and so on, but in so many organisations the tail is wagging the dog. The tail of maintaining the purity of internal and external relativities is wagging the dog of flexibility, teamworking, continuous improvement and rapid response to changing circumstances. Jobs and responsibilities are constantly changing; as people grow and their work changes with them. We must not get ourselves into situations in which people say, 'I can't do that, it's not in my job description.' Or we subsequently have to spend hours of non-value adding time updating the job description and reassessing the points value.

We had nothing of this ilk in Nissan and used to say to new starters something like, 'As an engineer you will do everything an engineer is required to do.' That's all you need. Of course, there were the caveats about training, safety, the definition and measurement of goals and so on; and to achieve predictable high quality a clear definition of the standard operation is critical; but once you have broken out of the job evaluation mindset, the freedom it gives, both to the enterprise and the individual, is incredible. You do everything you can and need to do without having one eye elsewhere. Of course people bump up against each other, but so what? In the energised enterprise they are big people – they have the freedom to sort out such problems for themselves; they do not have to run to the boss crying about turf protection.

Ask yourself, if you have job evaluation, job descriptions and the assorted paraphernalia, 'How much value do they add to our products or services?' The answer is a big ZERO. But you still have to pay for them – they form part of your costs, and therefore have to be included when you are calculating your prices. So, get rid of them! You may not be able to do so tomorrow for it first requires the mindset change, but at least begin your personal greenfield tomorrow!

And this mindset change is critical. We will discuss the change process in more detail in the next chapter but I must emphasise at this point that *structural changes must be an outcome of the change process, not an input into it.* If you change your structures too soon (and I am talking here of all structures, for example your organisation structure, your reward structure and so on) you will make some horrible mistakes which may be difficult to undo. You will not be ready, you will not know what is needed. On the other hand if you wait until you get the mindset change, the new structures will become almost self-evident, they will be spot on and will reinforce your achievements. They will be natural and accepted.

Of course, this does not mean do nothing until everything is complete. I have been through enough change programmes to know that 'everything is never complete', and to realise that 'something on account' can at a vital time make all the difference. But do not work at the extreme end of the spectrum which says: 'Change the structures and behaviour will change.' It will not – or at least not for long!

Finally, on this subject, no doubt you have seen at various conferences those 'interesting' organisation charts which show the chief executive at the bottom and the operating staff at the top. There are many permutations and they always generate a few laughs, but until August 1998 I had not found a company which used such charts outside of the conference hall. Bonas Machine Company, a world leader in the design and manufacture of computerised weaving looms, actually has its organisation chart displayed in every meeting area in its factory. It is given below and is intended to show that the manufacturing cells are the centre of it business and everyone else is there to support them. A nice touch!

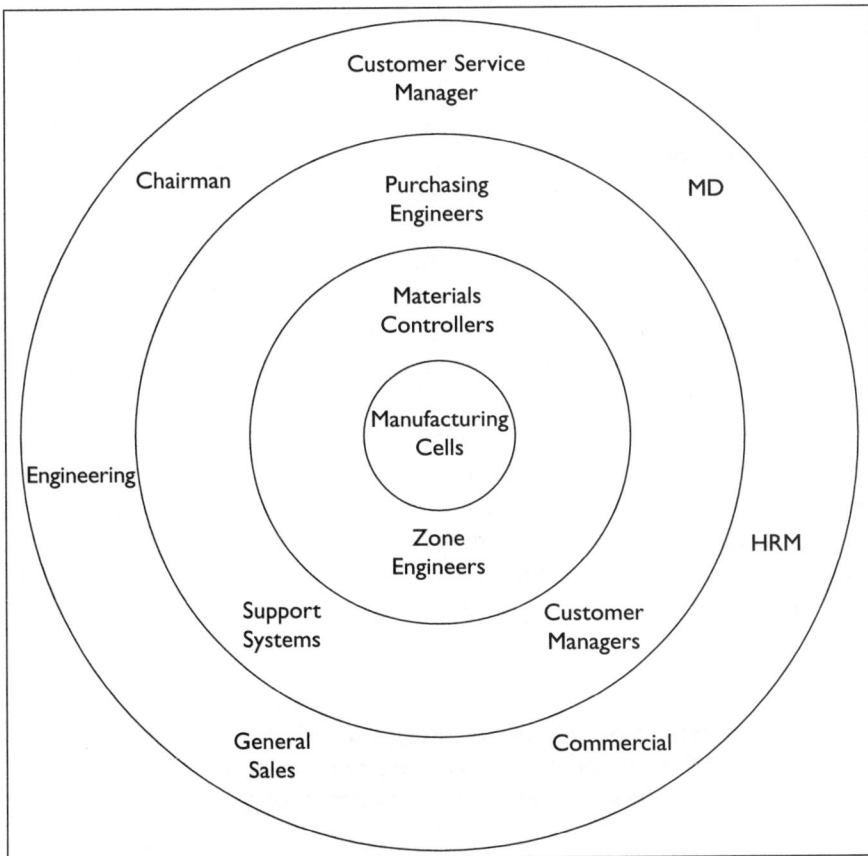

Figure 11.1   Bonas Machine Company organisation

12
Energised Change

'Energised Change' is a strange title. Should we not be discussing how to change to become an energised enterprise? I think not, for this whole book is about becoming an energised enterprise. But there is a further element, for whatever your aims there is an energised change process, which will not only help you succeed in your aims but will also in the process help create an energised enterprise. The medium becomes the message. Hopefully, all will become clear.

In Chapter 1, The Ascendant Organisation, we reprised the need to combine a high level of self-control of the processes and a high level of commitment of the people to lead to the ascendant organisation. Since then we have explored the commitment axis in considerable detail, looking at leadership, values, innovation, real teamworking and so on. Particularly when discussing values and goals, we shared a change process in which people at all levels were involved at the very beginning, not just as recipients of 'the great new idea from on high' but directly participating in assessing 'where we are now' and helping determine 'where we wish to be in three years time'. They helped determine the 'end' and the 'means' instead of just being recipients of a *fait accompli*.

> **Involving people in the change process at the very beginning and throughout, before the new way is set in stone, is central to energised change.**

One of the great problems, as we saw in the Prologue, is that chief executives and top managers have numerous opportunities to go to conferences, visit other companies, attend trade shows and so on. Their business world is not confined to their office or factory. They return with the BIG IDEA and want it to happen tomorrow. They want to go from where they are now to where they want to be in one giant step – from being inept or comfortable to becoming world class within three months – if they allow that long!

The difficulty with this approach is that people at the operating end of the business rarely have such opportunities – their working life is confined to their four walls; they do not share the broad business experience of the chief executive; they see things from where they stand – and their stand is in the valley or foothills compared to the chief executive's mountain top.

Those readers who spend time in the mountains know that when you are in the valley you cannot see the top of the furthest mountain – you see the top of the first mountain but not beyond that. Only as you climb that first mountain (to be pedantic, the first is probably a hill) does the next one become visible. As you continue your journey you will then see the next mountain and so on, until eventually you will reach the highest. For our purpose the whole of this mountain range is called 'Education' – wherever you are in it, you are in 'Education'.

Many change initiatives fail because the chief executive fails to communicate an understanding of what is at the top of the highest mountain to those in the valley. Often, it is doubtful if the chief executive understands it anyway and therefore is not really at the top of the highest mountain. Where then is the incentive to begin? The trouble is that the gap between the chief executive's notion of the mountain top and the view of those toiling away in the valley is too great – it cannot be bridged in one giant step and the big idea falls into the abyss.

Figure 12.1   'The abyss'

The vital point is to recognise that there are many hills and mountains on the journey, and that we have to scale each one in turn before we progress to the next. As we progress we become fitter and better experienced – our ability continually grows. Eventually we may successfully climb the highest peak And I mean *climb* – there are no easy, get-there-in-one-day helicopter trips here, however enticing the sales patter may seem. Our progress can be illustrated in Figure 12.2.

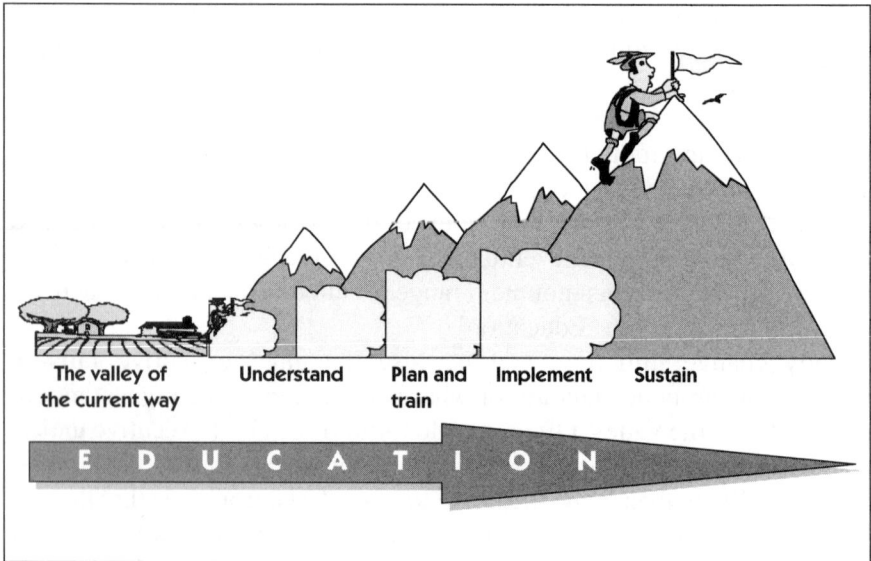

Figure 12.2 The four levels of change

In the valley we may be comfortable with the current way or we may be totally inept. In either case there is little appreciation that there can be a better way and no-one is too concerned about finding out if there is one. Our approach can range from, 'We are paid to do a job and we do as little as we can get away with' to, 'Our business is comfortable, our jobs and pensions are secure, we receive our annual salary increase and bonuses and do not have to try very hard'. In other words, we are alienated or apathetic.

Often the top team, although ostensibly sitting at the peak will, in reality, be in their own *mental valley*. There *must* be a better way. There is, and it means climbing each succeeding mountain.

Mountain One – Understanding

Remember Albert Hickman's observation in Chapter 4, 'For us the break-through came when we realised that the more you educate people the more they are receptive to change', and the first step to education is under-standing – so the first mountain is 'understanding'. Although the first, it is almost the toughest, for as we know when we have not exercised for many years we must first get ourselves mentally prepared and then take those very demanding first steps.

> **Understanding must begin with those who are at the organisational top but are in their own mental valley.**

There is usually a catalyst – someone reads a book or article, visits another company, is persuaded by a consultant, perhaps attends a conference; maybe is stunned by unsatisfactory performance figures – any one of which may create dissatisfaction with the current state and spark an idea. Perhaps it is the lightning flash which begins the energising process.

But that initial exposure does not create understanding. So often the big idea fails because the initiator wants it to happen straight away, with little analysis of the current state and what the new way may contribute, nor of the problems it may create – almost certainly he or she will have sidelined possible negative outcomes.

Do not just accept it at face value. Assess the possible impact on your staff, suppliers and customers – and on your competitors. Read other books and, particularly, critical articles which may suggest that the idea has reached eight o'clock or later on the business fad cycle. Visit compa-nies which have gone down your proposed route. Go away for a day or two and thrash through the issues seeking a shared understanding among the top team, both of where you are now and what you wish to achieve. As we saw when discussing goal alignment you will find that even at the top there are many different perceptions of today, let alone tomorrow.

Do not, at this stage, be too precise. You will not be able to define or prove everything, and indeed, you should not attempt to do so. You may not have a monopoly of wisdom, but at the top there will be things in which you passionately believe. Ivor Vaughan, an old friend, calls it a 'stand'. For him it was 'simplification' – his vast experience and accumulated wisdom convinced him that for Rearsby Automotive 'simplification before automation' was the key. It was not guesswork but he could not *prove* it. Said Ivor:

> I declare... there is no evidence that it will work; if you wait for evidence it is not a stand. Our stand in Rearsby was simplification.

But beware – Ivor Vaughan had led the management buyout. He was the chairman and charismatic leader – there are not too many like him – *but he had the wisdom to know that he had no monopoly of wisdom* and he listened to people throughout the company and gave them their head to do sensational things.

The task for the top team (remembering that in the energised enterprise, leadership is present at all levels and the 'top' does not necessarily mean the *very* top) is then to create the broad strategy and the approximate route, determining where you are now and where you wish to be in, say, three years time. They may also begin identifying the 'rocks' they see before them – the impediments to change – and how they will tackle them, but at this stage it is likely that they will do little more than seek an overview. The more detailed assessment will come at the next stage. However, the great thing is that you can spread understanding, educate people, define and share your goals and begin tackling the rocks all at the same time.

When discussing values and goal alignment we used a process in which people at all levels of the organisation were involved in 'determining where we are now' and 'where we want to be'. That process can be applied to almost all situations. It requires groups of people at different levels separately to analyse 'where we are now' and then, together, to determine 'where we want to be'.

There is though a major difficulty – for if your working world has been constrained by those proverbial four walls and you have not been to conferences, read books or visited other businesses – and the vast majority of people at the operating level have not – *you do not know what you do not know*; so how can someone at the operating level know what it is possible to achieve? It is for this reason that I have previously used descriptions of 'best practice', values words and so on – all designed to indicate what might be desirable and possible to achieve.

My Japanese colleague, Iwao Kobayashi, whose wisdom and authority I gratefully acknowledge, has taken it much further. His programme, 20 Keys to Workplace Improvement, presents a fully integrated model detailing twenty interrelated areas an organisation has to address if it is truly to become world class. It is not my intention to go through all twenty keys – they are listed in the Appendix to this chapter – but he reasoned that for each Key there has to be some way of showing people what 'better' and 'best' really are. Short of taking everyone to see companies that are at the various levels, he discovered that the best way is to present such information visually, so he drew pictures depicting five levels for every key – deceptively simple but extraordinarily detailed and powerful cartoons. Look, for example, at his cartoons covering Key One, 'Cleaning and Organising to Make Work Easy':

LEVEL 2
Sort things out and throw useless things away. Floor cleaning-up is completed.
Easy to hang and take
GOALS
Let's throw useless things away, rather than keep them.
Fire Extinguisher
Ashtray
Sparkling clean
Rubbish
Do not place things directly on the floor. Throw away things that have no clearly foreseeable use.
Assess vertical surfaces.
But still we can see oil stains
Paint is peeling off.
Don't place things in the aisle.

LEVEL 3

Cleaning of equipment has been completed. You can see where the aisles are. There is nothing placed along the wall.

I paint my own work area

Clearly assign the areas you work on. Competition starts between groups.

First Assembly
Aisle
Second Assembly

Decide on inspection dates and let groups compete with one another.

Our desks and shelves are still in a mess.

Assess shelves.

Place tools and parts in the workplace that needs them. Number each section of the shelves. Indicate both the number and the title of each section.

Remove the cause of any dirt. Clearly indicate the quantities. Employees are committed to keeping the place clean.

Check every month and make a habit of keeping the place in a good condition. Regular rubbish should automatically be disposed of.

I am not going to explain the detail of each level – it is there to see and read, but the magical moments come when you go through these cartoons in detail with people at different levels in a company and gradually there comes a realisation that there *is* a better way and an appreciation of what they have to do to get there.

We work on different days with people from top management, middle management and the operating levels and lead them through all five levels for all twenty keys. We first ask each person individually to score their company against each Key (on the 1 to 5 rating) as to where they believe it is now and where they realistically think they can get to within three years. We then ask them to form into groups of four to six and ask each group to reach a consensus on the current and desired positions. The final stage of the day is to weld each group's views into an agreed position so that we end up with the agreed assessments of people at each level. These assessments can vary widely. We ensure that the critical decision makers, 'influencers' and 'normal' people are involved. If there are difficult trade unionists or sceptical middle managers, we seek to bring them in from the beginning.

The exercise is tough. They are not fun days but everyone ends up with an understanding of what 'better' and 'best' really mean and it always results in a far better understanding of the business.

Next, we compare the different assessments from the different groups, highlighting areas of agreement and disagreement and *then have everyone who has participated come together* to receive and share the results. The task is to reach agreement between all participants at all levels on where they are now and where they want to be.

And this is where the fun starts, especially when top managers find that their perception is totally contradicted by operational staff. One of the Keys is Small Group Activities. In one company the top management group said, 'We've been at it for eight years, we've had plenty of success' and assessed themselves as being at Level 4. The operating staff said:

If that's what they think they're completely out of touch. They blow hot and cold. We have a few attempts and then we find something else has to take priority. There is never any money available to do what we want, so we have pretty much given up. Can we rate ourselves lower than Level 1?

In the joint session my comment was, 'In this Key you are where the operating staff say you are, not where top management likes to think you are.'

We agreed on Level 1, but everyone then committed to reaching Level 4 within three years.

I do not want to bore you with the intricate details of such a process but the important point is that we end up with a shared assessment of where the company is now and an agreed view on where we want to get to within three years. This is critical, for if it works well you have a critical mass of people from all levels agreeing 'Where we are now' and 'Where we want to be'. This is so powerful you can almost feel it!

We then agree our priorities and how we will get from where we are now to where we want to be. We set bottom-line targets. We talk about equipping the company continuously to improve itself for it's no good having some consultant come in and achieve wonderful things in six months and then go away. It will not take too long to slip back to square one – or worse. We talk about energising the enterprise! But we do not set anything in stone at this time – it is far too early for, as we will see, increasing knowledge and understanding brings about a different perspective.

This really is involving people and gaining their commitment. Everyone who participates OWNS the target. It is not something handed down from on high. Everyone participates in *how* the shared goals will be achieved and everyone becomes an ambassador to take the message to those not directly involved. Of course they will need help, but when operating staff have been involved from the very beginning the biggest step of all has been taken.

They begin to be energised and the impact is wonderful. We saw examples when discussing teamworking. Management must take the first step and initiate actions that demonstrate trust. It may start one-way, but when people find that they can talk about both the good and the bad in a non-threatening manner, that is when you can develop a genuine high-quality, two-way trusting relationship and can define and achieve goals far beyond anything you previously thought possible.

Can you imagine climbing a mountain with someone you do not trust? It is no different in the world of work. The more you involve people the more they will give. When you do not involve them you should not be too surprised when they live down to your expectations.

We have only reached the top of the first mountain!

Mountain Two – Planning and Training

As with most mountain ranges there are very few mountains that are clearly and individually defined from top to bottom, they all overlap – by climbing the first you will already have made considerable progress to conquering the second. By reaching 'Understanding' you will have already made considerable progress towards 'Planning and Training'.

Compared with the other mountains, the second does not take very long to climb but it is a vital link and, again, if you are to energise your enterprise it must involve people at all levels. Planning takes 'What we wish to achieve' and turns it into 'How we will achieve it'. Training equips us for the task.

It is well to remember that this may be the first time that people at the operating level have been involved in anything as esoteric as planning and they may therefore have to be familiarised with the concepts – but shorn of the gobbledegook it is not difficult. It first means defining your specific goals. If appropriate use the goal alignment process discussed in Chapter 4, although for many this will be too big a step at this early stage. But at least recognise that those at the top do not have a monopoly of wisdom and, especially as you get into more and more detail, those at the operating level will know best what it is possible to achieve.

Whatever the actual structure of the groups handling the planning process, its members must:

◆ have a record of achievement with resulting personal credibility

◆ be innovators

◆ be effective communicators.

As a result they are likely to be trusted. They may also include some doubters. There are advantages and disadvantages – the doubters may well become early converts, or their questioning may disruptively challenge the values of the majority. On balance a small number should be included for if the concept is so weak or the majority so uncommitted as to be unable to withstand criticism it is better to find out sooner rather than later.

The planning group(s) must be able to contribute effectively to the thought processes and refine the goals and ideas coming from Mountain One. They can help prepare the organisation by further questioning and weakening commitment to the existing order. They can help determine and give positive direction to the implementation programme. They can also give further consideration to defining the 'rocks' and how they might be tackled. What might these rocks be? Perhaps:

Obstructive top managers
Militant trade unionists
Demoralised first-line managers
Poorly educated workforce
Investors interested only in short-term results
Customers wanting quick solutions
Poor quality suppliers
Lack of funds
...and so on

You need to begin consider these impediments to progress and how you will tackle them. Will you climb over them, work your way around them, chip away at them or seek to blast them out of existence? If you do not consider how you will tackle the rocks before you reach them you will have many surprises when they do appear and may well decide that the comfort of the valley is much more attractive – and turn back. But, continuing the metaphor, you will only be able to determine the *details* of your approach once you reach the obstructing rocks, and even then you will watch carefully and modify your steps as you go along.

The members of such groups may well become the prime drivers of the new way. Real, long lasting change does not just happen – it has to be made to happen and as we have constantly seen real changes in peoples' thinking come about as the result of real changes in actions. But many have to be trained in the new ways. There will be new techniques, processes and practices. If you want to become a world-class manufacturer, everyone has to learn about cleaning and organising, quick changeover from one product to the next, how to define and eliminate waste and so on. If you wish to achieve high levels of customer service you have to learn how to respond rapidly to changing customer demands, how to anticipate customers' needs, how to measure customer satisfaction and so on.

But even before you do this your managers and supervisors must become familiar with the new way. You cannot leave the training to outsiders and professional trainers. Energising your enterprise requires them to understand the new way, to become credible coaches and problem solvers. These are the nuts and bolts of the change process and they have to be worked at. Training is also often forgotten – indeed I have seen it omitted altogether. No wonder so many change initiatives do not achieve the sought-after results!

But also from the training may come a need to vary the plan, the goals and the route. As people become more familiar with the new they come to recognise that the original thinking was perhaps a little uninformed and modifications need to be made. It is for this reason that it is unwise to set the original version in stone too early.

It is wise to remember that at this stage the group(s) should not seek to make significant changes to the formal structure and systems of the organisation. You have to continue managing today as well as creating tomorrow, and if you attempt to force through structural change not only will you confuse but also you likely to make unfortunate mistakes which will require subsequent correction. You will in fact find that as your behaviour changes the necessary changes to your structures and systems will become blindingly obvious. Except in the most extreme situations:

> **Changes in structures must be an outcome of the change process, not inputs into it.**

A classic example is the payment system. By working in real teams, constantly innovating with total flexibility of working practices it will become quickly obvious to everyone that a reward structure based on narrowly defined jobs and additional payments related to volume achieved is no loner appropriate. But changing too soon will be much more difficult and will not relate to the new way of behaving. If it is not right it will have to be changed again.

Mountain Three – Implementation

Implementation can take many forms – from pilots and prototypes to big bang.

Pilots may be necessary when you are unsure and want to try something out but, going back to Elton Mayo and his pioneering studies of organisational behaviour, we need to remember that any group which is singled out for a special exercise is likely to respond positively. A successful pilot is not necessarily a good predictor of widespread success. But where you have enthusiastic groups ready to go, and feel that experimentation is the best way for you, then do not hesitate. But always learn from the pilot and have those involved spread the message – there is no greater ambassador than someone who has done it, provided the ambassador facilitates and encourages rather than simply saying, 'This is what worked for us, so it must work for you.'

As with all things, you learn, accept, modify and reject, and gradually you find the consistent framework within which you can apply flexibility. It does not matter too much if people do a little wheel reinvention, for it then becomes *their* wheel; but if they do not learn from others' experiences they will fail to tap into a valuable source of knowledge.

There may be some occasions when the big bang approach is the right way – when, for example it is a case of 'change or die'. But such an approach can only be imposed from the top and there is no guarantee of a hearts and minds conversion. As we saw in the Prologue, the big mistake of the re-engineering movement was to seek to impose from the top.

As you gain experience, it becomes easier. Not every part of your enterprise will progress at the same pace but again this does not matter. Often you will find that some sections or business units are going off doing their own thing. Provided it is not taken to the extreme of high commitment and no control, which leads to anarchy, this is no bad thing. Provided they keep their collective eye on the shared values and goals, and have a shared sense of purpose, people at the periphery can achieve wonderful things which can set an example for the whole enterprise. Use such successful practices as exemplars of what can be achieved – show other managers and staff, inviting them to learn.

One vital point in the change process – do not automatically assume that automation is the answer, especially when you are working with the processes. Of course it might be, but so many companies have made the mistake of saying something like, 'Our manual processes are poor so let's automate them and get rid of the people.' All that happens is that you end up with poor automated processes. The answer is to make the manual processes work well, eliminating waste, improving changeover times, reducing waiting time, minimising the physical length of the process, combining processes and so on. Once you have done that you may find that you do not need to automate or, if you do, you will be automating something that is simple rather than something that is complex. In simple terms, get things right before you start spending the big bucks!

Mountain Four – Sustain the Gain

Conquering Mountains One to Three is the easy part. Understanding, planning and implementation are exciting but once you have got there the pressures to move on to something else are enormous, and when the going gets tough it is easy to slip back into the old ways. This does no mean that there can be no further change – you must continuously develop, for if in three years time you are precisely where three years ago you said you wanted to be, then you will be out of date. Hopefully your values and sense of purpose not only will have been retained but will have been reinforced but your day to day practices will have been adjusted to take account of changing circumstances and within your framework of values, other initiatives will come along. Within the energised enterprise this will always be the case.

But there has to be consistency and over the years a number of guidelines directed at top management emerge:

◆ Maintain your long-term commitment to all aspects of the change process and by your behaviour ensure that everyone recognises this.

◆ Ensure that your leadership of change is maintained, that you provide support, and that people are developed in accordance with the new way.

◆ Regularly review progress against the overall strategy, ensuring that behaviour accords with the values, and goals. Recognise achievement when appropriate, cajole when necessary and act when required.

◆ As the needs become evident, facilitate changes to the structure and systems, including the organisation structure, reward system, working arrangements, development programmes and so on.

◆ When hiring new staff ensure your selection criteria reflect the new way. When promoting internally ensure that those who are committed to and succeed in the new way are those who rise through.

◆ Continuously communicate the new way to all stakeholders: shareholders, customers, suppliers, staff, trade unions – and ensure that their interests are properly reflected and balanced.

◆ **Understand the competition and continuously improve your product, services and processes to ensure that 'today' remains profitable while you are working towards tomorrow.**

◆ **Never cease to learn. Do not be impatient, for real change takes years to bed in.**

◆ **Take the tough decisions at the right time to tackle the rocks and pray that you build up sufficient goodwill in the good times to see you through the tough times.**

Machiavelli in his overused quotation called the change process difficult, doubtful of success and dangerous. Maybe he was right – but he need not be. Just climb the succeeding mountains with a good guide, do not try to get from the valley to the top of the highest mountain in one go, recognise that the journey will be a long one and be patient!

That's all there is to it! Before I conclude, a final word...

APPENDIX 12.1: 20 keys to workplace improvement

Iwao Kobayashi's 20 Keys to Workplace Improvement

Key 1   Cleaning and organising to make work easy

Key 2   Goal alignment

Key 3   Small group activities

Key 4   Reducing work in process

Key 5   Quick changeover

Key 6   Methods improvement

Key 7   Zero monitoring

Key 8   Coupled manufacturing

Key 9   Maintaining machines and equipment

Key 10   Commitment to effective working

Key 11   Quality assurance

Key 12   Developing your suppliers

Key 13   Eliminating waste

Key 14   Empowering staff to make improvements

Key 15   Skill versatility and cross training

Key 16   Production scheduling

Key 17   Efficiency control

Key 18   Using information systems

Key 19   Conserving energy and materials

Key 20   Using technology for strategic advantage

13

A Final Word – Energising Leadership to the Energised Enterprise

Our journey to the energised enterprise has taken us along a fairly simple route (although with a few detours and, no doubt, some signposts missed). I think that a plan of our route might look something like this:

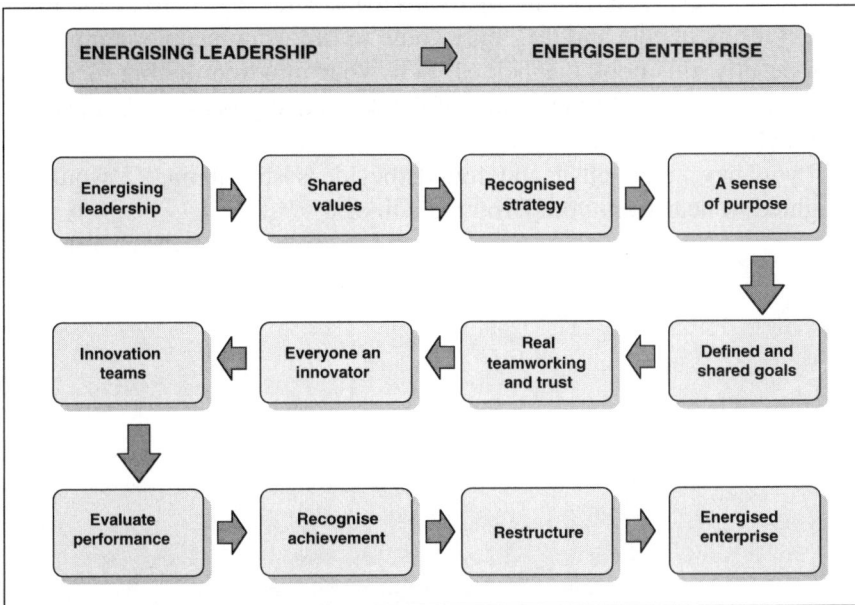

Figure 13.1   The route to the energised enterprise

But as we all know, simply looking at a map, while extremely helpful, does not actually get us there. Hopefully it gives us the confidence to begin the journey and points to some of the pleasures and potential pitfalls along the way. Sometimes you would prefer to start from somewhere else. But you are where you are, not where you would prefer to be.

We cannot stretch this analogy too far, for no doubt you will have made progress in some of, if not all, the areas we have discussed. To me it is important that we understand the full picture and appreciate their interaction. As we saw in the Prologue the world is full of instant, single-focus solutions, but to make real progress we need to recognise that there is no such thing as an instant, single, magic remedy. To make real progress we have to work on many fronts without getting ourselves bogged down with a multiplicity of conflicting initiatives. The great thing about working towards energising your enterprise is that it provides the overall framework within which you can, to return to the words used in the Introduction, do bold, difficult and courageous things.

The very first point of the Introduction was that the only things that really count are the quality of leadership and the quality of people. Everything else flows from that. Pick any of the business fads – they are all led and developed by people. An organisation is a legal entity, a collection of facilities, processes, practices, procedures, products, services and so on. But a legal entity or a pile of money achieves nothing by itself. Processes and facilities achieve nothing by themselves. They are there as the result of activity by people and they only come to life when people interact.

Hopefully, this book has helped focus your mind on the big picture as well as helping you through some of the detail and processes. Believe me, it works!

If you have enjoyed it and found the ideas stimulating, I would be delighted to hear from you. Drop me a line.

PETER WICKENS

References

Note: This listing contains some references that have not been specifically quoted but which may have been used in the preparation of this book.

Albrecht, K. (1988) *At America's Service.* Dow Jones-Irwin, New York.

Belbin, M. (1993) *Team Roles at Work.* Butterworth-Heinemann, London.

Bennis, W. (1992) *On Becoming a Leader.* Century Business, London.

Blanchard, K. and M. O'Connor (1997) *Managing by Values.* Berrett-Koehler, San Francisco.

Business Strategies (1996) *Labour Market Flexibility and Financial Services.* Business Strategies.

Byham, W. C. and J. Cox (1991) *Zapp.* Century Business, London.

Caulkin, S (1993). The Lust for Leadership, *Management Today* (November).

Clark, J. (1995) *Managing Innovation and Change.* Sage, London.

Collins, J. C. and J. I. Porras (1994) *Built to Last.* Century, London.

Covey, S. R. (1992) *The Seven Habits of Highly Effective People.* Simon & Schuster, London.

Creelman, J. (1997) Leading at the Line, *Teams* (May).

CSC Index Survey (1994) Re-engineering: Critical Factors for Success, *Information Week* (September).

Davenport, T. H. (1993) *Process Innovation Reengineering Work Through Information Technology.* Harvard Business School Press, Cambridge, MA.

Davenport, T.H. (1995) Why Reengineering Failed: The Fad That Forgot People, *Fast Company* (December).

de Geus, A. (1997) *The Living Company.* Nicholas Brearley, London.

DePree, M. (1989) *Leadership is an Art.* Doubleday, New York.

DePree, M (1992) *Leadership Jazz.* Dell, New York.

Farkas, C. M. and S. Wetlaufer (1996) The Ways Chief Executive Officers Lead, *Harvard Business Review* (May–June).

Financial Services Research Centre (1995) *Quality Initiatives in the Financial Services.* FSRC.

Ford, H. (1991) *Ford on Management.* Blackwell, Oxford.

Gedvilas, C (1997) The Electronic Teams, *Teams* (May).

Grey, C. and N. Mitev (1995) Re-engineering Organisations: A Critical Appraisal, *Personnel Review* **24**(1).

Guest, D and K. Mackenzie Davey (1996) Don't Write Off the Traditional Career, *People Management* (February).

Hall, G., J. Rosenthal and J. Wade (1993) How to Make Re-engineering *Really* Work, *Harvard Business Review* (November–December).

Hamel, G and C. K. Prahalad (1994) *Competing for the Future*. Harvard Business School Press, Boston.

Hamermesh, R. G. (1996) *Fad Free Management*. Knowledge Exchange, Santa Monica, CA.

Hammer, M. (1990) Reengineering Work: Don't Automate, Obliterate, *Harvard Business Review* (July–August).

Hammer, M. (1996) *Beyond Reengineering*. HarperCollins, London.

Hammer, M. and J. Champy (1993) *Reengineering the Corporation*. Harper Business, New York.

Hammer, M. and S. A. Stanton (1995) *The Reengineering Revolution*. HarperCollins, London.

Hersey, P. and K. Blanchard (1982) *Management of Organisational Behaviour*. Prentice-Hall, New York.

Holbeche, L (1997) *Career Development in Flatter Structures*. Butterworth-Heinemann, London.

Jackson, J. (1997) *Dynamic Organisations*. Macmillan, London.

Keynes, J. M. (1936) *The General Theory of Employment, Interest and Money*. Macmillan, London.

Kobayashi. I. (1995) *20 Keys to Workplace Improvement* (rev. edn). Productivity Press, Portland, OR.

Leigh, A. (1996) Life and Death in Teamwork, *Teams* (May).

Mayo, E. (1949) The Social Problems of an Industrial Civilisation in D. S. Pugh, *Organisation Theory* (3rd edn). Penguin, London.

McKechnies Limited (1997) *Achieving Investors in People: Action Projects*. Gower, Aldershot.

Merck (1993) *Values and Vision: A Merck Century*. Merck, Rahway, NJ.

Mintzberg, H. (1994) The Fall and Rise of Strategic Planning, *Harvard Business Review* (Jan–Feb).

Morita, A (1987) *Made in Japan*. Fontana, London.

Nelson, J. A. (1997) Super Teams Process Turkeys, *Teams* 2(4).

Nohria, N. and J. D. Berkeley (1994) Whatever Happened to the Take-Charge Manager? *Harvard Business Review* (Jan–Feb)

Oram, M. and R. S. Wellins (1995) *Re-engineering's Missing Ingredient*. Institute of Personnel and Development, London.

OTR (1993) *Business Process Re-engineering – Real or Hype*. OTR Group, Brussels.

Ouchi, W. (1981) *Theory Z*. Addison Wesley, Reading, MA..

Parkinson, C. N. (1986) *Parkinson's Law*. Penguin, London.

Pascale, R. T. (1990) *Managing on the Edge*. Viking, London.

Peters, T. (1997) *The Circle of Innovation*. Hodder & Stoughton, London.

Rajan, A. and P. van Eupen (1997) *Leading People*. Create, Tunbridge Wells.

Royal Society of Arts (1995) *Tomorrow's Company*. Royal Society of Arts, London.

Re-engineering Report, *Information Week* (June 1994).

Schonberger, R. J. (1987) *Japanese Manufacturing Techniques*. Free Press, New York.

Senge, P. (1990) *The Fifth Discipline*. Century Business, London.

Senge, P. (1994) *The Fifth Discipline Fieldbook*. Nicholas Brearley, London.

Sewell, C. and P. B. Brown (1990) *Customers for Life*. Doubleday Currency, New York.

Sewell, R. (1994) *Fly with the Geese*. Sewells International, Darrington.

Shapiro, E. C. (1995) *Fad Surfing in the Boardroom*. Addison-Wesley, Reading, MA.

Simon, H. (1996) *Hidden Champions*. Harvard Business School Press, Boston.

Smith, A. (1776; Repr. 1980) *The Wealth of Nations*. Methuen, London.

Smith, L. (1994) Stamina: Who Has It. Why You Need It. How You Get It. *Fortune* 28 (November).

Steele, M. and A. Brown (1990) *Leadership*. Cranfield Press, Cranfield.

Syrett, M. and J. Lammiman (1998) *Innovation at the Top: Where Do Executives Get Their Ideas?* Roffey Park Management Institute.

Thomas, I. (1992) *The Power of the Pride*. Ian Thomas, Benmore, RSA.

Thurow, l. (1993) *Head to Head*. Nicholas Brearley, London.

Tichy, N. M. and S. Sherman (1993) *Control Your Destiny or Someone Else Will*. Currency Doubleday, New York.

Tuckman, B. W. (1965) Development Sequence in Small Groups, *Psychological Bulletin* **63**.

Vroom, V. H. (1964) *Work and Motivation*. John Wiley, New York.

Walsh, J. (1998) Comeuppance for the CEO who Devalued his People, *People Management* (9 July).

Watson T. J. Jr (1963) *A Business and its Beliefs*. Columbia University, New York.

Wickens, P. D. (1987) *The Road to Nissan*. Macmillan, London.

Wickens, P. D. (1993) *Lean Production and Beyond*. University of Sunderland, Sunderland.

Wickens, P. D. (1998) *The Ascendant Organisation* (rev. and updated edn). Macmillan, London.

Wilmott, H. (1994) Business Process Re-engineering and Human Resource Management, *Personnel Review* **23**(3).

Womack, J. P. and D .T. Jones (1996) *Lean Thinking*. Simon and Schuster, New York.

Womack, J. P., D. T. Jones and D. Roos (1990) *The Machine that Changed the World*. Rawson Associates, New York.

Index

A

ABB 7, 27, 28, 184
Albrecht, Karl 184
Allen, Bob 111
Apple Computers 7
Armstrong, Geoff xi
AT&T 10, 111
Atlee, Clement 28

B

Bain and Co 4
Baring Brothers 24
Barnevik, Percy 27, 28, 47, 120, 150, 184
Belbin, Meredith 125, 168
BICC Group 65
Bil Mar Foods 128–9
Birchenhough, Mark 118
Black and Decker 77
Blair, Tony 53
Body Shop 27
Boeing 65
Bonas Machine Company 169, 189
BP 28, 125
Branson, Richard 27, 87, 120, 150, 151
British Aerospace 157–8, 161
British Airways 47
British Gas 46
BT 89
Business fads 1–21
Business fads cycle xii, 1–17

C

Calsonic International Europe 32, 55, 175
   goals 66–7
   sense of purpose 112–13
Ceramic Industries 55, 151
Champy, James 8–17
Chrysler 27, 28
Churchill, Winston 27, 28
Ciba-Geigy 10, 88
CNN 27
Coates, Pam 122
Coil, Maggie 137–8
Common terms and conditions 183
Communications 78–80
Compaq 152
Connor, Danny 121
Consulting firms, number of 4–5
Continental Can Company xi, 55
   supervisors 57
Continuous improvement *see Kaizen*
Co-operative Bank 182
Culture 83–4

D

Dan Technology 152
Davenport, Tom 13
De Beer, Tracy 145
Dell 152
De Pree, Max 27, 52
Devolved responsibility 33–5
Diana, Princess 80

Disney 95
Dolleschal, Rheinhard 23
Downsizing 50
Dräger 63
Dunlap, Al 50–1
Dürr 55
Dyson, James 144

E
Empathy 60–2
Empowerment 33–5
Energised change 190–207
    failure of change programmes
       191–2
    four mountains 191–207
    implementation 204–5
    planning and training 201–4
    sustain the gain 205–7
    understanding 193–201
Ergonomics 61–2
Errera, Battista 55, 151
Erste Sparkasse Bank, Die 153
Eurotherm Controls 153–4

F
Fad surfing 3–4
Ford, Henry 110–11
Ford Motor Company xi, 7, 8, 95,
    116–17, 121, 151
Fry, Art 155

G
Gardner, John 40
Gates, Bill 27, 152
Gateway 152
General Electric 27, 41, 63
General Motors 7, 65
Gerry and the Pacemakers 113
Ghandi, Mahatma 27
Gibson, Sir Ian 55, 59, 90
Girolami, Paul 47
Glaxo 47
Goal alignment 63–74
Goals 63–7
    Big, Hairy, Audacious Goals 64–5
Gore, W.L. Inc. 150
Grohman, Klaus 149

Grove, Andy 27, 150
GTE 10

H
Hallmark Cards 11
Hamel, Gary 12, 48
Hammer, Michael 8–17
Handy, Charles 13
Hayden, Bill 116–17
Herman Miller 27
Heslop, David 160
Hewlett-Packard 7, 88, 95
Hickman, Albert 55, 75–8, 79, 193
Hitchcock, Charlie 151
Hitler, Adolf 27, 28
Honda 7, 27
Honda, Soichiro 27, 28
Hoshin kanri 74
House of Käthe Wolfahrt 42–3, 142

I
Iaccocca, Lee 27, 28, 120
IBM 7, 47, 51, 77, 85–6, 152
ICL 77, 118
Inge, General Sir Peter 38–9
Innovation 140–62
    British Aerospace 157–8, 161
    Ceramic Industries 151
    creating the environment 149
    defined 143, 147–9
    Dell 152
    Erste Sparkasse Bank, Die 153
    Eurotherm Controls 153–4
    everyone an innovator 141
    failure to innovate 152
    Gateway 152
    Grohman Engineering 149
    IBM 152
    Kaizen and radical change compared
       141–3
    Kodak 155
    leaders 150, 159–62, 176–7
    Lego 158
    Microsoft 152
    Nissan 147, 150
    note taking 151
    Organisation Development
       International 154

reasons for doing nothing   145–6
sum   144
3M   155–6
time availability   158–61, 167–8,
    174–6
Innovation centres 171–4
Innovation rhyme   157
Innovation teams   163–77
    Bonas Machine Company   169
    defined   163–5
    guidelines   167–71
    Nissan 166, 168–9, 174
    Thorn Lighting   172–3
    top down and bottom up   166–7
    training   170
Institute of Personnel and Development
    xi, 184
Intel   27

J
Jackson, David   41
Job evaluation   187–8
John Lewis Partnership   95
Johnson and Johnson   86–7

K
Kaizen   141–3
Kawamoto, Nobuhiko   28
Kelleher, Herb   27, 47
Kennedy, John F.   64, 120
Key performance indicators   70–4
Keynes, John Maynard   150
King, Lord   47
King, Martin Luther   27
Kitchen Range Foods   2
Kobayashi, Iwao   xi,   164–5, 195–201
Kodak   155
Koresh, David   27
Kristiansen, Kjeld Kirk   158

L
Leaders
    charismatic   27–9
    innovative   150, 159–62, 176–7
    non-charismatic   28–9
    as strategists   41–51

Leadership
    appropriate style   29
    creating the environment   32–8
    description of   31–8
    earning trust   57–63
    energising   26–40
    heart of   52–82
    fundamentals   53–5
    inspiring people   74–82
    qualities of   38–40
    respect for your ability   55–7
    sharing goals   63–74
    throughout the enterprise   30–40,
        166
Lebus, Simon   2, 3
Leeson, Nick   24
Lego   158
Leigh, Andrew   124, 133
Lindahl, Göran   28
Listening effectively   81–2
Lloyds Bank   28

M
Management by objectives   67–9
Mandela, Nelson   27
Marriott Hotels   95, 114–15
Mars   95
Marshall, Sir Colin   47
Maslow, Abraham   166
Massachusetts Institute of Technology
    8
Maxwell, Robert   27, 28
Mayo, Elton   119, 204
Mazda Cars   8, 160
Merck and Company   110
Microsoft   27, 45, 152, 158
Ministry of Defence   179
Mintzberg, Henry   46
Mirror Group   28
Mission   83–4
Montgomery, David   28
Morgan, Terry   157–8
Morita, Akio   27, 86, 154–5
Motorola   7, 137–8
Mueller, John   155
Murdoch, Rupert   28
Mutual Benefit Life   8

N

NCI 145
Nelson, Jimmy 128–9
News Corporation 28
Nintendo 158
Nissan xi, 28, 77
    continuity at the top 37
    earning trust 60–3
    innovation 147, 168–9, 174
    job evaluation 188
    office layout 179
    philosophy 47, 49, 96
    pressure equation 61–2
    real teamworking 139
    sense of purpose 112
    supervisors 57, 166
    supplier development 150
    trade union 92
    values 90–5
Nordstrom 95
NSK-AKS 113

O

Oracle 124
O'Reilly, Tony ix
Organisation Development International
    154
Organisation of work 178–83
    Bonas Machine Company 189
    Co-operative Bank 182
    Ministry of Defence 179
    Nissan 179
    structural changes 178–82
Organisation principles 185–9
OTR Group 11

P

Packard Bell 152
Panskus, Gero 55
Panskus Team, The 55
Pascale, Richard xii, 2
Peters, Tom 36, 120, 145
Philip Morris 65
Positive instinct 47
Prahalad, C. K. 12, 48
Proctor and Gamble 7, 95

Q/R

Quality circles 164
Rank Xerox 10
Ravazzotti, Gianni 55
Real teamworking x, 117–39
    BP Exploration 125
    Belbin's personality types 125
    Bil Mar Foods 128–9
    defined 120, 122–3
    guidelines for establishing 129–36
    horizontal, diagonal and vertical
        teams 121–4
    between hunting cheetahs 127–8
    ICL 118
    life cycle of teams 124
    Motorola 137–8
    Nissan 139
    old style 116–19
    Oracle 124
    in a pride of lions 126–8
    rewards 136–9
    team types 117
    Tetra Pak 124
    virtual teams 125
Rearsby Automotive 193–4
Re-engineering 1–17
Reilly, Mike 32–3, 55
Ritz-Carlton Hotel 145
Roach, Stephen 50
Roddick, Anita 27, 28
Rogers, Lynn 103–7
Roosevelt, Theodore 27
Royal Military Academy, Sandhurst, The
    63

S

Sacred cows 4
Samaritans 81–2
Schleif, Bob 55
Schmidt, Reinhard 55
Schonberger, Richard 77
Schumpeter, Joseph 142
Scott Paper 50–1
Sega 158
Sense of purpose 108–15
    AT&T 111–12
    Calsonic 112
    defined 108

Marriott Hotels   114–15
Merck and Company   110
Nissan   112
NSK-AKS   113
Simon, Hermann   55
Simon, Lord   28
Slim, Field Marshal Sir William   38–9
Smith, Adam   9, 22
Sony   27, 86, 158
Southwest Airlines   27, 47
Stanton, Steven   9
Stoekmann, James   138
Strategy   41–51
    British performance   50
    emerging goals   43–4
    long-term   45–6
    Microsoft   45
    Mintzberg, Henry   46
    positive instinct   46–8
Sunbeam   50–1
Sunrise Medical   88, 110

T
Teamworking   *see* Real teamworking
Tetra Pak   124
Thatcher, Margaret   27
Thomas, Ian   126–8, 168
Thorn Lighting   55, 75–8, 172–3
3M   7, 63, 155–6
Time availability   79, 158–61, 167–8,
    174–6
Toshiba   51, 152
Toynbee, Arnold   7
Toyota   7
Truman, Harry   28
Tsuchiya, Toshiaki   28, 55, 62, 80
Tuckman, B. W.   124
Turner, Ted   27
20 Keys to Workplace Improvement
    195–201, 208

U
Unilever   7, 95
University of Sunderland   55

V
Vagelos, P. Roy   110
Vallance, Sir Iain   89

Values   81–96
    BT   89–90
    Ciba-Geigy   88–9
    defined   85
    fitting in with   94–5
    Ford   95
    Hewlett-Packard   88, 95
    IBM   85–6
    John Lewis Partnership   95
    Johnson and Johnson   86–7
    Marriott Hotels   95
    Mars   95
    Nissan   90–5
    Nordstrom   95
    Proctor and Gamble   95
    Sunrise Medical   88
    Unilever   95
    values words   99–100
    Virgin Group   87
Values, Discovering your   97–107
    Barnsley Alcohol and Drug Advisory
        Service   102–7
    discovery process   100–7
    Tesco   98
Valuing people   36
Vaughan, Ivor   193–4
Venter, Barry   154
Virgin Group   27, 28
Vision   83–4
Vroom, Victor   6, 167

W
Wal-Mart   7, 65
Walton, Sam   65
Watson Jnr, Thomas J.   85
Welch, Jack   27, 41, 63–4, 150
Williams, Al   47
Winner, Michael   116
Wright, Anne   55, 56–7

X
Xerox   7

Z
Zander, Benjamin   36